KIRULE ISLANDS

Attu　Kiska　Dutch Harbor

ALEUTIAN ISLANDS

SUBPAC OPERATING AREA

PACIFIC

• MIDWAY

HAWAIIAN ISLANDS

Pearl Harbor

MARIANAS

OCEAN

MARSHALL ISLANDS

'RUK·

KWAJALEIN

CAROLINES

GILBERT ISLANDS

TARAWA

SOLOMAN ISLANDS

Bouganville

Guadalcanal

SUBSOWESPAC OPERATING AREA

CORAL SEA

Brisbane

500 mi

35. ω

SUBS
AGAINST
THE
RISING
SUN

Jack Matthews
12 Ann Logan Circle
Raymond, NH 03077-1232

by

Keith M. Milton

Yucca Tree Press

First Printing   November 2000

Milton, Keith M.

SUBS AGAINST THE RISING SUN

       1. World War, 1939-1945 - United States - Naval Operations - Submarine, Pacific Theater.   2. Submarine Combat.   3. Submarines (Ships), United States - Pacific Theater.   4. Submarine Warfare.
       I. Keith M. Milton.   II. Title

Library of Congress Catalog Card Number: 00-104711
ISBN: 1-881325-45-8

Printed in Canada

Cover design: Stephen M. Matson
Photo: Crewmen standing watch aboard *U.S.S. Sandlance* (SS 381) in May 1945 during a Pacific war patrol. Courtesy: National Archives, USN Neg # 468152

Dedicated to Robert B. Westjohn, Sr.
Radioman, *U.S.S. Finback* (S.S. 230),
my brother-in-law and good friend.

I would like to express my appreciation and gratitude to the personnel of the Naval History Section, Washington Navy Yard, and the Navy Archives of the National Archives and Records Adminisration, College Park, Maryland, for their patience in locating records and photographs. Truly this book could not have become a reality without their help.

Table of Contents

INTRODUCTION

It is generally assumed that dropping the atomic bombs brought Japan to the surrender table in World War II. That was the immediate cause, of course, but current information about the state of affairs in wartime Japan leads experts to believe she would have been forced to surrender within three to six months whether or not the bombs had been dropped—and whether or not the island had been invaded.

> [The] policy of standardized design and ever more advanced equipment, coupled with the thorough training and high morale of the submarine crews, was so effective that U.S. submarines with two percent of the Navy's personnel were able to destroy sixty percent of all Japanese merchant and naval vessels sunk during the war, shipping on which Japan depended for survival and the loss of which forced her to begin peace overtures for fear of acutal national starvation months before the first atomic bomb leveled Hiroshima.[1]

Indeed, with no oil for her navy, no gasoline for her army and air force, and no food for her people, including her armed forces, she would have had little choice.

An island nation that entered the war with over six million tons of merchant shipping and an excellent navy larger than the U.S. Pacific Fleet, ended with less than a million tons of shipping for her supply routes and a decimated navy to protect those lines. She could no longer import raw materiel for her war industries, and she had never been able to feed her entire population only on the produce provided by her islands. Fish composed almost a third of the Japanese diet and her fishing fleet had been almost destroyed. Japan was literally being strangled by a ring of United States submarines.

The United States had long felt that un-restricted submarine warfare was not only unfair, but morally repugnant. However, this attitude changed quickly with the surprise attack on Pearl Harbor and general orders went out to commence, "unrestricted submarine warfare against Japan."

If the early United States Navy submarines had been equipped with reliable torpedoes, the war might have been shorter. But, like all other navies, proper testing of torpedoes was extremely expensive and, therefore, had not been undertaken. It was a year and a half before United States submarines had dependable, operational torpedoes. Then it was a matter of time until the vastly superior production capacity of the United States overwhelmed her enemies.

---

[1] Commander Edward P. Stafford, USN, *The Far and the Deep*, New York: G.P. Putnam's Sons, p. 254. Other authors who support this theory: *I saw Tokyo Burning,* by Robert Guillain. *Japan at War in World War II*, Time-Life Books. *Japan's War,* by Edwin P. Hoyt.

The "Fleet Submarines" being produced for the U.S. Navy were originally designed to operate in conjunction with the fleet to protect the larger ships in much the same way that destroyers and frigates did during fleet actions. They were, therefore, designed for high speed, greater range, and long endurance. In practice, those attributes proved to be exactly what was needed to operate against a distant enemy either alone or in packs of two to five boats. With just two percent of all the Navy's personnel, U.S. submarines accounted for just over half of all Japanese shipping destroyed during World War II. Their casualty rates were much higher, however, and six submariners died for every one non-submariner who lost his life in naval service.[2]

Two-hundred-forty-nine submarines conducted 1,584 Pacific war patrols, during which fifty-two boats were lost. U.S. submarines came from eleven classes, which ran the gamut from the small **"S"** boats built post-World War I in the late teens and early twenties, to the **"Tench"** class which were being built at the war's end.

The Torpedo Scandal

The United States entered World War II with two basic torpedoes. Similar in appearance and size, they were the Mark Ten and the Mark Fourteen. Mark Ten had been in general use for just over ten years and was the standard arm of the S-Class boats. It used a contact exploder—it detonated on contact with the side of a ship and blew a hole in the ship. Mark Fourteen was, in essence, a Mark Ten with a magnetic exploder added. This device used the influence of a steel vessel's magnetic field to set off the explosive charge. Modern warships had sufficient side armor that rendered a torpedo useless. These new ships were most vulnerable from underneath, so these new weapons were set to run under the ship where the ship's magnetic field set it off and the explosion blew a hole in the bottom of the ship.

The torpedo is a very complicated instrument. Driven by steam generated by forcing a spray of water through an alcohol torch, its direction was controlled by gyroscopes. A delicate hydrostat controlled the depth at which it ran. Internal timers could be programmed to change course or depth, and a small propeller in the nose armed its firing devices. Needless to say, if one system failed, the entire torpedo was useless. It was also very expensive. This high cost held testing under actual conditions to a bare minimum. Testing with recoverable mock-ups was considered sufficient.

When war came and the torpedoes were put into service, they proved to be very temperamental. It might leave the tube and propoise along the surface, giving the target time to evade. It might run correctly, dive on cue under the vessel and fail to explode. Some were seen to strike the vessel cleanly and yet fail to detonate, or to run a circular course and threaten the sub that fired it.

In the early days, the Bureau of Ordnance dismissed the submariner's complaints; failures were due to inexperience, poor maintenance and bad marksmanship. As the complaints continued to pour in, they learned even the reliable Mark Ten was running four to six feet deeper than set, and the Mark Fourteen as much as ten or twelve feet too keep. Corrections were made but the complaints continued. Submarine commanders began to doubt their ability to make a proper set-up, and morale suffered. Most baffling were the premature fires. From the periscope they looked like perfect hits, but actually were fifty to sixty feet from the target. Some prematured immediately upon arming and not

---

[2] 3,131 enlisted men and 374 officers.

only gave away the sub's presence but its position. The Bureau suggested increasing the arming distance and running depth when using the magnetic device to decrease the chances of premature explosions. On July 24, 1943, Admiral Chester W. Nimitz, Commander in Chief Pacific Fleet ordered the magnetic exploders de-activated. This was not a complete cure as some of the problems continued to occur. The contact exploder was also defective, especially with good solid hits. Glancing-type blows usually activated the warhead, but direct hits sometimes misfired. Testing at Pearl Harbor finally revealed a problem in the firing mechanism, and corrections were made. This was September 1943—the war was almost two years old!

By late 1943 the Mark Eighteen electric torpedo began coming off U.S. assembly lines. It had a slower speed and boat skippers grudgingly accepted it because it left no tell-tale wake. It proved to be much more reliable with its simple contact exploder and accurate depth controller. It was also easier and cheaper to produce. During the last six months of the war, over half of the torpedoes used were electrics.

When steamboat inventor Robert Fulton named the new invention *torpedo*—for the cramp fish, t*orpedo electricus*, which kills its prey by electrocution—he had no idea how accurate he was.

Naming the boats

Submarines were originally numbered only, with the class letter preceding the number. The early **"R-Class"** and **"O-Class"** boats carried numbers as did the **"S-Class"** boats. When the **SALMON** Class came out they were also numbered with the first letter of the class used for the name. Officials then realized they already had an "S-1" and "S-2," etc., and confusion reigned. To resolve this duplication, they named all subsequent boats after marine creatures. The S.S. number indicates the boat's chronological position with relation to other boats. The various shipbuilding companies were assigned a block of SS numbers and as each boat is begun it was assigned an SS number and a name. If a company was slower than others, their completed boats would have lower numbers commissioned at a later date.

Battle Stars

The number of Battle Stars presented to a boat are indicated by a " ★ " for each Battle Star awarded. These are located immediately above the boat's list of patrols.

S-Boats

Six S-Boats were built for the Russian Czar following World War I. Because of the Russian Revolution, these boats were held in stored and knock-down condition until the results of the Revolution were clear. They were eventually purchased by the U.S. Navy, but none took part in World War II and most were scrapped before 1941. They were designated H-4 through H-9 and became SS 147 through SS 152. This explains the jump in SS numbers as S-42 became SS 153 instead of SS 147 as would be the case in a normal progression.

UNITED STATES SUBMARINES IN THE PACIFIC

Each of the 249 United States submarines that made a Pacific war patrol is listed here, along with a photograph and her combat and victory record. The Joint Army-Navy Assessment Committee (JANAC) provided the information included. After the war JANAC scanned enemy records to match submarine claims with Japanese admitted losses to confirm victory claims. This procedure began in 1946 and, as with most data, are subject to change with the discovery of new records. It was a monumental task and a tribute to the JANAC that very few adjustments have been made. There is still controversy over some of the figures and claims, and this controversy will probably never be resolved.

SUBS AGAINST THE RISING SUN is intended as a source book on U.S. submarines which operated in the Pacific during World War II. The information provided is based upon sources considered to be the most accurate. The photographs and identification were obtained from the Naval Archives of the National Archives and Records Administration at College Park, Maryland, and the History Section, Washington Navy Yard. Some general information about these World War II submarines will help the reader understand how they operated—their strengths and their limitations.

Reading the data

A "0" in the Patrol Column indicates participation in the Battle of Midway. The Navy did not consider the Battle of Midway as a war patrol. When a boat did not return from a patrol a "00" is placed in the duration column. In many instances the Navy knows only the date of last transmission, not the actual date of the loss. It considers any patrol not completed as having had no duration. When a boat was ordered to change base, a "to" before the area tells the new base.

The miniature Japanese flags displayed on the conning towers of world War II submarines, or flown from the periscope shears were "Brag Rags" and indicated a vessel destroyed. The meatball (red globe on a white field) was for merchant ships, and the rising sun (red globe with radiating rays) was for warships.

When a Naval vessel is de-commissioned it is removed from active service and placed in the reserve fleet, but it is still in the Navy lists. Once stricken from the lists, it is eventually disposed of by being sold for scrap, used for a target, or sent to another country.

As mentioned earlier, claims made by boats were confirmed or not by JANAC. For example, *S-34* claimed what *may* have been the first sinking, but since JANAC could not confirm this from available records, *S-34* was not allowed to claim it as a confirmed sinking.

Photographs

White circles and markings on photographs indicate changes or additions made during a refit.

Two boats, *SEALION* and *DORADO* did not make any Pacific wartime patrols, but are included here because of their special circumstances.

U. S. S. SEALION
S. S. 195

On December 10, 1941, the Japanese attacked Cavite Naval Base just outside Manila. Leisurely and deliberately, the high-level bombers cruised over the base at 20,000 feet, well above the 15,000-foot range of Cavite's anti-aircraft batteries. A few fighters came up to challenge them, but they were well handled by the Zeros who were protecting the bombers. The bombers took their time and did a thorough job. Boats which were refueling or provisioning hurriedly cast off and took evasive action in the harbor or submerged as soon as they had depth enough. *SEALION* and *SEADRAGON* were underoing overhaul and, therefore, immobilized.

SEALION was hit almost simultaneously by two bombs and settled by the stern. *SEADRAGON* was badly damaged by fragments from the bombs that hit *SEALION*, but her hull integrity was maintained. She was repaired and returned to duty against the Japanese. Since the machine and repair shops at the base had also been destroyed, the closest repair facility capable of repairing *SEALION* was Pearl Harbor, well out of reach. She was deemed a total loss. Her radios, instruments, and sonar gear were removed and she was towed into deep water and scuttled to prevent her capture. Thus she became the first U.S. submarine casualty of World War II.

SEALION is shown at the Electric Boat Company dock in Groton, Connecticut on July 5, 1938 during a fitting out.

U. S. S. DORADO
S. S. 248

This *GATO*-Class boat, built at Electric Boat Company in Groton, Connecticut, was launched on May 23, 1943, and commissioned two days later. After a shakedown cruise and working up a crew, she was provisioned, armed, and dispatched to Panama for her canal transit and subsequent journey to Hawaii.

All U.S. submarines were alloted a safety lane while cruising the Atlantic coast, Gulf of Mexico, and Carribean Sea. This was a space fifteen miles on either side of her projected course, and was known to all U.S. anti-submarine forces in the area.

On October 12, 1943, The Commandant, NOB, Guantanamo, Cuba, assigned a bomber to give coverage to an Allied convoy traversing the area near *DORADO*'s safety lane. That same evening the bomber sighted an unidentified submarine and dropped three depth charges. About two hours later the bomber encountered another submarine which was challenged and failed to answer. Not only that, the submarine opened fire on the bomber and was duly depth charged. The first boat was assumed to be *DORADO* but nothing has ever been proven. The Court of Inquiry found she went down due to unknown causes—an enemy submarine, an accident, friendly fire, no one knows for sure. Perhaps it was faulty instructions to the bomber regarding *DORADO*'s safety lane.

DORADO - down the ways at Electric Boat Company, Groton, Connecticut on May 23, 1943.

U.S.S. SEALION
S.S. 195

U.S.S. DORADO
S.S. 248

S-Class

S-Class boats were designed during World War I, and were meant to replace the older *"R"* and *"O" Class* boats that were active during that war. They were about 850 tons and 220 feet long. They had a range of 5000 miles and carried twelve 21-inch torpedoes for the four bow tubes. They carried one 4-inch deck gun and one .50 cal machine gun. The crew complement was 42. A total of forty-eight were built at four different yards between 1918 and 1932. Bethlehem Steel at Quincy, Massachusetts built most of the *S Class* boats that served in the Pacific. Bethlehem Steel at San Francisco, California built *S-30* through *S-41* boats. Six of the "Sugar Boats," as they came to be called, were dispatched to Dutch Harbor, Alaska in early spring 1942 and spent much of 1942 and 1943 harrassing the Japanese fishing fleet in an attempt to cut this important food source. When more fleet boats became available, they were withdrawn and used for training.

U. S. S. S-18
S. S. 123

S-18 was built by Bethlehem Steel and commissioned on April 3, 1924.

★

S-18'S WARTIME PATROLS

NO.	CAPTAIN	DATE	DUR.	BASE	AREA	CLAIMED	CONFRMED
1	WJ MILLICAN	4201	10	ATLANTIC	ATLANTIC	0	0
2	WJ MILLICAN	4202	20	ALASKA	ALASKA	0	0
3	JH NEWSOME	4202	12	ALASKA	ALASKA	0	0
4	JH NEWSOME	4205	51	ALASKA	ALASKA	0	0
5	JH NEWSOME	4207	18	ALASKA	ALASKA	0	0
6	GH BROWNE	4210	29	ALASKA	ALASKA	0	0
7	GH BROWNE	4211	28	ALASKA	ALASKA	0	0
8	GH BROWNE	4301	23	ALASKA	ALASKA	0	0

S-18 did not claim any victories, nor was she credited with any.

S-18 and several of her sisters spent most of 1942 patroling the Aleutians and the further approaches to that chain.Miserable weather, fog, cold, and rough seas were their lot. She is shown at rest in Pearl Harbor, circa 1927.

S-18 was decommissioned on October 20, 1945, stricken from the lists and sold for scrap.

_____

As far as can be determined, not a single United States merchant vessel was sunk in error by U.S. submarines during World War II.

U. S. S. S-23
S. S. 128

S-23 was built by Bethlehem Steel and commissioned on October 30, 1923.

★

S-23'S WARTIME PATROLS

NO.	CAPTAIN	DATE	DUR.	BASE	AREA	CLAIMED	CONFIRMED
1	JR PIERCE	4202	10	ALASKA	ALASKA	0	0
2	JR PIERCE	4205	43	ALASKA	ALASKA	0	0
3	HE DURYEA	4207	34	ALASKA	ALASKA	0	0
5	HE RUBLE	4212	20	ALASKA	ALASKA	0	0
6	HE RUBLE	4301	28	ALASKA	ALASKA	0	0
7	HE RUBLE	4303	28	ALASKA	ALASKA	0	0

S-23 claimed no sinkings, nor was she credited with any

Her missing fourth patrol is the subject of much mystery. Since five months elapsed between Patrols #3 and 5, it was probably her trip to San Diego for refit. The aerial photo shows *S-23* under way in 1927.

S-23 was decommissioned on November 2, 1945, stricken from the lists and sold for scrap.

───────────

The I-17, a Japanese submarine made the only attack against an American mainland target when she shelled the oil fields at Santa Barbara, California, on July 18, 1942.

U.S.S. S-27
S.S. 132

S-27 was built by Bethlehem Steel and commissioned on January 22, 1924.

S-27'S WARTIME PATROLS

NO.	CAPTAIN	DATE	DUR.	BASE	AREA	CLAIMED	CONFIRMED
1	HL JUKES	4205	00	ALASKA	ALASKA	0	0

S-27, while on patrol in a dense fog near Amchatka Island, was driven aground on a reef and could not be removed. The crew abandoned the boat and made their way in rubber boats to a small island where they were picked up six days later by a PBY.

S-27 is shown in a prewar photo. The date and location are undetermined.

U.S. submarine torpedoes contained only sixty percent of the explosive power of Japanese torpedoes. The Japanese built their torpedoes for use against warships and the United States built theirs for use against merchant ships.

U. S. S. S-28
S. S. 133

S-28 was built by Bethlehem Steel and commissioned on October 30, 1923.

★

S-28'S WARTIME PATROLS

NO.	CAPTAIN	DATE	DUR.	BASE	AREA	CLAIMED	CONFIRMED
1	JD CROWLEY	4205	40	ALASKA	ALASKA	0	0
2	JD CROWLEY	4207	34	ALASKA	ALASKA	0	0
3	JD CROWLEY	4209	24	ALASKA	ALASKA	0	0
4	JD CROWLEY	4212	27	ALASKA	ALASKA	0	0
5	JD CROWLEY	4302	22	ALASKA	ALASKA	0	0
6	VA SISLER	4307	35	ALASKA	ALASKA	0	0
7	VA SISLER	4308	40	ALASKA	ALASKA	1/4000	1/1368

S-28'S VICTORY

DATE	VESSEL	SIZE	TYPE	CAPTAIN	LOCATION
430919	KATSURA MARU	01368	GUNBOAT	VA SISLER	KIRULES

S-28, after patroling the Alaskan waters, was assigned to training duties. It was while performing this type of duty that a diving accident off Pearl Harbor caused the loss of *S-28*. The exact cause has never been determined, but she went to the bottom with all hands in 1500 fathoms.

This *S-28* photo was taken off the Naval Air Station at Seattle, June 18, 1943.

U.S.S. S-30
S.S. 135

S-30 was built at Bethlehem Steel and commissioned on October 20, 1929.

★ ★

S-30'S WARTIME PATROLS

NO.	CAPTAIN	DATE	DUR.	BASE	AREA	CLAIMED	CONFIRMED
1	FW LAING	4204	12	ATLANTIC	ATLANTIC	0	0
2	FW LAING	4205	13	ATLANTIC	ATLANTIC	0	0
3	FW LAING	4205	12	ATLANTIC	ATLANTIC	0	0
4	FW LAING	4208	32	ALASKA	ALASKA	0	0
5	FW LAING	4209	20	ALASKA	ALASKA	0	0
6	WA STEVENSON	4304	28	ALASKA	ALASKA	0	0
7	WA STEVENSON	4305	29	ALASKA	ALASKA	0	1/5228
8	WA STEVENSON	4307	34	ALASKA	ALASKA	0	0
9	WA STEVENSON	4307	28	ALASKA	ALASKA	0	0

S-30'S VICTORY

DATE	VESSEL	SIZE	TYPE	CAPTAIN	LOCATION
430611	JINBU MARU	05228	FREIGHTER	WA STEVENSON	KIRULES

S-30 spent her first three patrols in Atlantic waters before she was transferred to the Pacific. She participated in the Alaska patrols to harrass Japanese fishing fleets.

S-30 was decommissioned on October 9, 1945, stricken from the lists and sold for scrap the following year.

U.S.S. S-31
S.S. 136

S-31 was built by Bethlehem Steel and commissioned on March 8, 1923.

★

S-31'S WARTIME PATROLS

NO.	CAPTAIN	DATE	DUR.	BASE	AREA	CLAIMED	CONFIRMED
1	TF WILLIAMSON	4112	12	ATLANTIC	ATLANTIC	0	0
2	TF WILLIAMSON	4112	12	ATLANTIC	ATLANTIC	0	0
3	TF WILLIAMSON	4207	34	ALASKA	ALASKA	0	0
4	RF SELLARS	4208	33	ALASKA	ALASKA	0	0
5	RF SELLARS	4210	28	ALASKA	ALASKA	1/3000	1/2864
6	RF SELLARS	4303	28	PEARL	to BRISBANE	0	0
7	RF SELLARS	4307	21	BRISBANE	BISMARCKS	0	0
8	RF SELLARS	4308	27	BRISBANE	BISMARCKS	0	0

S-31'S VICTORY

DATE	VESSEL	SIZE	TYPE	CAPTAIN	LOCATION
421026	KEIZAN MARU	2864	FREIGHTER	RF SELLARS	PARAMUSHIRO

S-31 was in Atlantic waters for her first two patrols, but was moved to Alaska when it became evident that she would be most useful there. Her last few patrols were out of Brisbane in the spring and summer of 1943. She was then relieved and sent Stateside for training duties. This aerial shot of *S-31* was taken on March 12, 1943, while she was underway at sea.

S-31 was decommissioned on October 19, 1945, stricken from the lists and sold for scrap the following year.

U.S.S. S-32
S.S. 137

S-32 was built by Bethlehem Steel and commissioned on February 22, 1932.

★ ★ ★ ★ ★

S-32'S WARTIME PATROLS

NO.	CAPTAIN	DATE	DUR.	BASE	AREA	CLAIMED	CONFIRMED
1	MG SCHMIDT	4201	12	ATLANTIC	ATLANTIC	0	0
2	MG SCHMIDT	4201	12	ATLANTIC	ATLANTIC	0	0
3	MG SCHMIDT	4207	34	ALASKA	ALASKA	0	0
4	MG SCHMIDT	4208	19	ALASKA	ALASKA	0	0
5	MG SCHMIDT	4210	19	ALASKA	ALASKA	0	0
6	MG SCHMIDT	4302	23	ALASKA	ALASKA	3/4300	0
7	MG SCHMIDT	4303	22	ALASKA	ALASKA	1/9000	0
8	FJ HARLFINGER	4305	19	ALASKA	ALASKA	0	0

S-32 claimed four victories but they could not be confirmed.

S-32 served in the Atlantic for two short patrols and then was transferred to Alaska. In the spring of 1943, she was moved Stateside where she finished out the war in a training role. In the photo, the crew of the *S-32* receive awards at Dutch Harbor Alaska on April 22, 1943.

S-32 was decommissioned on October 19, 1945, stricken from the lists and sold for scrap that same year.

U. S. S. S-33
S. S. 138

S-33 was built by Bethlehem Steel and commissioned on February 22, 1923.

★
S-33'S WARTIME PATROLS

NO.	CAPTAIN	DATE	DUR.	BASE	AREA	CLAIMED	CONFIRMED
1	WP SCHOENI	4202	12	ATLANTIC	ATLANTIC	0	0
2	WP SCHOENI	4207	36	ALASKA	ALASKA	0	0
3	WP SCHOENI	4208	33	ALASKA	ALASKA	0	0
4	WP SCHOENI	4210	27	ALASKA	ALASKA	0	0
5	WP SCHOENI	4211	16	ALASKA	ALASKA	0	0
6	CB STEVENS	4304	28	ALASKA	ALASKA	0	0
7	CB STEVENS	4306	27	ALASKA	ALASKA	0	0
8	CB STEVENS	4307	23	ALASKA	ALASKA	0	0

S-33 claimed no victories, nor were any credited to her.

S-33 was in Atlantic service when war broke out. After only one patrol, she was hurried to the Alaskan Theater. In the summer of 1943 she was moved Stateside where she served in a training role until the end of the war. The photo of S-33 was taken in the Philippines on December 22, 1926.

S-33 was decommissioned on October 23, 1945, stricken from the lists and sold for scrap the following year.

U. S. S. S-34
S. S. 139

S-34 was built by Bethlehem Steel and commissioned on April 23, 1923.

★
S-34'S WARTIME PATROLS

NO.	CAPTAIN	DATE	DUR.	BASE	AREA	CLAIMED	CONFIRMED
1	TL WOGAN	4204	28	ALASKA	ALASKA	0	0
2	TL WOGAN	4205	29	ALASKA	ALASKA	0	0
3	RA KEATING, Jr	4209	25	ALASKA	ALASKA	0	0
4	RA KEATING, Jr	4210	29	ALASKA	ALASKA	0	0
5	RA KEATING, Jr	4212	24	ALASKA	ALASKA	0	0
6	RA KEATING, Jr	4304	28	ALASKA	ALASKA	0	0

S-34 claimed no sinkings, nor was she credited with any. The photograph was taken December 18, 1930 at Subic, Bay, Philippines.

S-34 was decommissioned on October 23, 1945, stricken from the lists and sold for scrap.

U. S. S. S-35
S. S. 140

S-35 was built by Bethlehem Steel and commissioned on May 7, 1923.

★

S-35'S WARTIME PATROLS

NO.	CAPTAIN	DATE	DUR.	BASE	AREA	CLAIMED	CONFIRMED
1	JE STEVENS	4204	19	ALASKA	ALASKA	0	0
2	JE STEVENS	4205	35	ALASKA	ALASKA	0	0
3	JE STEVENS	4207	29	ALASKA	ALASKA	0	0
4	HS MONROE	4210	30	ALSAKA	ALASKA	0	0
5	HS MONROE	4212	18	ALASKA	ALASKA	0	0
6	HS MONROE	4306	38	ALASKA	ALASKA	1/8200	1/5430
7	HS MONROE	4307	23	ALASKA	ALASKA	0	0
8	RB BYRNES	4310	20	ALASKA	ALASKA	0	0

S-35'S VICTORY

DATE	VESSEL	SIZE	TYPE	CAPTAIN	LOCATION
430702	BANSHU MARU #7	05430	FREIGHTER	HS MONROE	S CHIGNIK

S-35 was caught in an Arctic storm during Christmas Week, 1942, which nearly did her in. A giant Tsunami-type wave engulfed her conning tower, severely injuring her captain who was standing watch and sending several tons of ocean brine into the control room. The water shorted out electrical systems and started several fires. Twice, all hands were forced topside when the fires were out of control. The blaze was finally contained and *S-35* managed to return to Dutch Harbor, Alaska. S-35 is shown here in San Diego Harbor on April 4, 1946.

S-35 was decommissioned on March 3, 1945, and sunk as a target on April 4, 1946.

U.S.S. S-36
S.S. 141

S-36 was built by Bethlehem Steel and commissioned on April 4, 1923.

★

S-36'S WARTIME PATROLS

NO.	CAPTAIN	DATE	DUR.	BASE	AREA	CLAIMED	CONFIRMED
1	JR McKNIGHT	4112	18	MANILA	W LUZON	0	0
2	JR McKNIGHT	4112	00	MANILA	CELEBES	1/11500	0

S-36 claimed one victory, but it was not confirmed.

S-36 was on patrol, with *S-39*, when war broke out. On her second patrol, she had just completed an attack on a small freighter in Calapan Harbor at Mindoro, and was preceeding to Sarabaja, Java. In early morning of January 20, 1942, she ran hard aground in Makassar Strait. Despite repeated efforts, she could not be moved. A Dutch launch picked up her crew the following afternoon and *S-36* was scuttled and abandoned.

S-36 is shown at the Potrero Works of Bethlehem Steel on March 29, 1923, shortly before her commissioning.

United States Submarines spent a total of 70,838 days on war patrols during World War II.

U. S. S. S-37
S. S. 142

S-37 was built by Bethlehem Steel and commissioned on April 4, 1923.

★ ★ ★ ★ ★

S-37'S WARTIME PATROLS

NO.	CAPTAIN	DATE	DUR.	BASE	AREA	CLAIMED	CONFIRMED
1	JC DEMPSEY	4112	10	MANILA	S LUZON	0	0
2	JC DEMPSEY	4112	35	MANILA	CELEBES	0	0
3	JC DEMPSEY	4202	18	JAVA	BARRIER	0	1/1900
4	JR REYNOLDS	4202	21	JAVA	BARRIER	0	0
5	JR REYNOLDS	4206	29	BRISBANE	SOLOMONS	0	1/276
6	TS BASKETT	4208	27	BRISBANE	SOLOMONS	0	0
7	TS BASKETT	4210	28	BRISBANE	SOLOMONS	0	0
8	RA KEATING, Jr	4306	39	ALASKA	ALASKA	0	0

S-37'S VICTORIES

DATE	VESSEL	SIZE	TYPE	CAPTAIN	LOCATION
420208	NATSUSHIO	1900	DESTROYER	JC DEMPSEY	MAKASSAR
420708	TENZAN MARU	0276	PASS-CARGO	JR REYNOLDS	BISMARCKS

S-37 was in Division 201 of the Asiatic Squadron when war broke out and went on patrol at once. She was the first U.S. submarine to sink an enemy destroyer in World War II.

S-37 was decommissioned on February 6, 1945, and sunk as a target the following spring.

LCDR H.G. Munson shown alongside the conning tower of S-38 in Brisbane on September 1, 1942.

U. S. S. S-38
S. S. 143

S-38 was built by Bethlehem Steel and commissioned on September 14, 1923.

★ ★ ★

S-38'S WARTIME PATROLS

NO.	CAPTAIN	DATE	DUR.	BASE	AREA	CLAIMED	CONFIRMED
1	WG CHAPPELL	4112	18	MANILA	S LUZON	2/10000	1/5445
2	WG CHAPPELL	4112	20	MANILA	CELEBES	0	0
3	HG MUNSON	4201	22	JAVA	BARRIER	0	0
4	HG MUNSON	4202	19	JAVA	BARRIER	0	0
5	HG MUNSON	4204	25	BRISBANE	SOLOMONS	0	0
6	HG MUNSON	4206	13	BRISBANE	SOLOMONS	1/8000	1/5628
7	HG MUNSON	4207	25	BRISBANE	SOLOMONS	0	0
8	HG MUNSON	4209	30	BRISBANE	to PEARL	0	0
9	CD RHYMES	4306	30	PEARL	to BRISBANE	0	0

S-38'S VICTORIES

DATE	VESSEL	SIZE	TYPE	CAPTAIN	LOCATION
411222	HAYO MARU	05445	FREIGHTER	WG CHAPPELL	LUZON
420808	MEIYO MARU	05628	TRANSPORT	HG MUNSON	BISMARCKS

S-38 was in Submarine Division 201 of the Asiatic Fleet stationed at Manila when war broke out. She immediately commenced war patrols. On December 12, she may have had the first sinking of the war when she hit a transport, but it could not be confirmed. *S-38* was nearly destroyed during a foray into Lingayen Gulf on the night of December 21 when she fired four torpedoes at four sitting-duck transports. The torpedoes were faulty and missed, but the working over she got after she was discovered nearly did her in. The performance was repeated on Christmas Eve, and her hairbreadth escape would have made Hollywood writers envious. *S-38* made the first shore bombardment by a U.S. sub against an enemy base on February 27, 1942, under command of H.G. Munson, as she tore up installations on Bawean Island.

S-38 was decommissioned on December 12, 1944, when an accident made her a total loss, and she was sunk as a target on February 20, 1945.

U.S.S. S-39
S.S. 144

S-39 was built by Bethlehem Steel and commissioned on September 14, 1923.

★★
S-39'S WARTIME PATROLS

NO.	CAPTAIN	DATE	DUR.	BASE	AREA	CLAIMED	CONFIRMED
1	JW COE	4112	18	MANILA	E LUZON	1/1500	0
2	JW COE	4112	23	MANILA	CELEBES	0	0
3	JW COE	4202	32	JAVA	BARRIER	1/5000	1/6500
4	FE BROWN	4205	27	BRISBANE	SOLOMONS	0	0
5	FE BROWN	4207	00	BRISBANE	SOLOMONS	0	0

S-39'S VICTORY

DATE	VESSEL	SIZE	TYPE	CAPTAIN	LOCATION
420304	ERIMO	06500	TANKER	JW COE	JAVA SEA

S-39 was in Submarine Division 201 of the Asiatic Fleet stationed at Manila when war broke out. She immediately commenced war patrols. On December 13, she may have acquired the first sinking of the war when she hit a transport, but it could not be confirmed. *S-39* was assigned a rescue mission to pick up Admiral Spoorer and his staff of Royal Navy Aides along with several downed Australian airmen from tiny Chebia Island where they had been stranded. After two futile nights of attempts, the crew learned the Admiral and the others had been captured. On her fifth patrol she ran aground east of Rossel Island in the Louisade Archipeligo. Despite gallant efforts by her ship's company, and *HMAS KATOOMBA*, which had been sent to help, she could not be moved and was pounded to pieces in the surf.

This photo of *S-39* was taken off Olongapo, Philippines, in 1935.

U.S.S. S-40
S.S. 145

S-40 was built by Bethlehem Steel and commissioned on November 20, 1923.

★
S-40'S WARTIME PATROLS

NO.	CAPTAIN	DATE	DUR.	BASE	AREA	CLAIMED	CONFIRMED
1	N LUCKER, Jr	4112	9	MANILA	S LUZON	0	0
2	N LUCKER, Jr	4112	42	MANILA	CELEBES	0	0
3	N LUCKER, Jr	4202	26	JAVA	BARRIER	0	0
4	N LUCKER, Jr	4205	30	BRISBANE	SOLOMONS	0	0
5	N LUCKER, Jr	4206	27	BRISBANE	SOLOMONS	0	0
6	FM GMBCRTA	4208	28	BRISBANE	SOLOMONS	0	0
7	FM GMBCRTA	4210	30	BRISBANE	SOLOMONS	0	0
8	FM GMBRCTA	4306	37	ALASKA	ALASKA	0	0
9	FM GMBRCTA	4307	30	ALASKA	ALASKA	0	0

S-40 did not claim any victories, nor was she credited with any.

The abbreviated name above is Gambacorta.

S-40 was decommissioned on October 27, 1945, stricken from the lists and sold for scrap.

U. S. S. S-41
S. S. 146

S-41 was built by Bethlehem Steel and commissioned on January 15, 1924.

★ ★ ★ ★
S-41'S WARTIME PATROLS

NO.	CAPTAIN	DATE	DUR.	BASE	AREA	CLAIMED	CONFIRMED
1	GM HOLLEY	4112	31	MANILA	S LUZON	0	0
2	GM HOLLEY	4202	34	JAVA	BARRIER	1/1500	0
3	GM HOLLEY	4205	27	BRISBANE	SOLOMONS	0	0
4	IS HARTMAN	4208	25	BRISBANE	SOLOMONS	1/1500	0
5	IS HARTMAN	4209	42	BRISBANE	to PEARL	0	0
6	IS HARTMAN	4305	31	ALASKA	ALASKA	2/6200	1/1036
7	IS HARTMAN	4306	36	ALASKA	ALASKA	0	0
8	IS HARTMAN	4307	39	ALASKA	ALASKA	0	0

S-41'S VICTORY

DATE	VESSEL	SIZE	TYPE	CAPTAIN	LOCATION
430528	SEIKI MARU #4	01036	FREIGHTER	IS HARTMAN	KIRULES

S-41 operated from Brisbane in the tropical heat of the Solomons and was not equipped with an air conditioner. Temperatures ranged from 105 to 120 degrees inside while submerged and men and machinery always dripped with sweat. The boats were showing their age with constant break downs. *S-41* suffered a leak in her pressure hull which was repaired with a pipe plug. During the spring of 1943, *S-41* was sent with six others to Alaska. Crews who previously had barely survived the heat of the tropics, now had to contend with the freezing cold of the Arctic.

S-41 is tied up with sister ship *S-37*, probably at pre-war Cavite.

S-41 was decommissioned on February 13, 1945, stricken from the lists and sold for scrap in 1946.

U. S. S. S-42
S. S. 153

S-42 was built by Bethlehem Steel and commissioned on November 20, 1924.

★
S-42'S WARTIME PATROLS

NO.	CAPTAIN	DATE	DUR.	BASE	AREA	CLAIMED	CONFIRMED
1	OG KIRK	4204	24	BRISBANE	SOLOMONS	1/9800	1/4400
2	OG KIRK	4207	25	BRISBANE	SOLOMONS	0	0
3	NK NAUMAN	4208	29	BRISBANE	SOLOMONS	0	0
4	NK NAUMAN	4210	27	BRISBANE	SOLOMONS	0	0
5	NK NAUMAN	4309	40	ALASKA	ALASKA	0	0
6	PE GLENN	4408	29	BRISBANE	SPL MISSION	0	0

S-42'S VICTORY

DATE	VESSEL	SIZE	TYPE	CAPTAIN	LOCATION
420511	OKINOSHIMA	04400	MINELAYER	OG KIRK	NEW IRELAND

S-42 was one of the six "Sugar" boats of Subdivision 53 that left Panama in early March of 1942 enroute to Australia, 12,000 miles away. Led by the tender *GRIFFIN*, under command of Captain Ralph Cristie, they refueled at Bora Bora and arrived at Brisbane after 42 days at sea. "Sugar" boats operating out of Australia held the line against the enemy for nearly a year in spite of breakdowns, limited range and speed, faulty torpedoes, no air conditioning, and assorted other ills of these World War I vintage craft.

The crew of *S-42* on deck in Norfolk Navy Yard, June 18, 1943.

S-42 was decommissioned on October 25, 1945, stricken from the lists and scrapped the following year.

U. S. S. S-43
S. S. 154

S-43 was built by Bethlehem Steel and commissioned on December 31, 1924.

S-43'S WARTIME PATROLS

NO.	CAPTAIN	DATE	DUR.	BASE	AREA	CLAIMED	CONFIRMED
1	ER HANNON	4205	28	BRISBANE	SOLOMONS	0	0
2	ER HANNON	4207	31	FREMANTLE	SOLOMONS	0	0
3	FE BROWN	4209	35	BRISBANE	SOLOMONS	0	0

S-43 did not claim any victories, nor was she credited with any.

S-43 is shown aff the Weeksville Naval Air Station, June 17, 1943.

S-43 was decommissioned on October 10, 1945, stricken from the lists and sold for scrap.

Axis submarines sank 3,750 Allied vessels during World War II. Over 2,800 of those were sunk by German U-Boats, and the balance by Italian, Japanese, Finnish, Rumanian, and Vichy French boats.

U.S.S. S-44
S.S. 155

S-44 was built by Bethlehem Steel and commissioned on February 16, 1925.

★★

S-44'S WARTIME PATROLS

NO.	CAPTAIN	DATE	DUR.	BASE	AREA	CLAIMED	CONFIRMED
1	JR MOORE	4204	29	BRISBANE	SOLOMONS	1/1900	1/5644
2	JR MOORE	4206	28	BRISBANE	SOLOMONS	1/1100	1/2626
3	JR MOORE	4207	30	BRISBANE	SOLOMONS	1/7100	1/8800
4	RT WHITAKER	4209	28	BRISBANE	SOLOMONS	1/1500	0
5	FE BROWN	4309	00	ALASKA	ALASKA	0	0

S-44'S VICTORIES

DATE	VESSEL	SIZE	TYPE	CAPTAIN	LOCATION
420512	SHOEI	05644	SALVAGE VSL	JR MOORE	BISMARCKS
420621	KEIJO	02626	GUNBOAT	JR MOORE	GUADALCANAL
420710	KAKO	08800	CRUISER	JR MOORE	KAVIENG

S-44 was one of the six "Sugar" boats of Subdivision 53 that left Panama in early March of 1942 enroute to Australia, 12,000 miles away. Led by the tender *GRIFFIN*, under command of Captain Ralph Cristie, they refueled at Bora Bora and arrived at Brisbane after 42 days at sea. Operating out of Australia these "Sugar" boats held the line against the enemy for nearly a year in spite of breakdowns, limited range and speed, faulty torpedoes, and other problems. *S-44* was the only one to have air conditioning (purchased by the crew before they left the States).

S-44 is shown at Coco Solo, Canal Zone on February 6, 1943.

S-44 was sunk by a Japanese destroyer in a surface action on October 7, 1943, near Paramushiro. There were only two survivors.

U.S.S. S-45
S.S. 156

S-45 was built by Bethlehem Steel and commissioned on March 31, 1925.

S-45'S WARTIME PATROLS

NO.	CAPTAIN	DATE	DUR.	BASE	AREA	CLAIMED	CONFIRMED
1	IC EDDY	4205	38	BRISBANE	SOLOMONS	0	0
2	IC EDDY	4208	28	BRISBANE	SOLOMONS	0	0
3	RH CALDWELL	4210	28	BRISBANE	SOLOMONS	0	0
4	RH CALDWELL	4312	28	ALASKA	ALASKA	0	0
5	G CAMPBELL	4312	33	ALASKA	ALASKA	0	0

S-45 did not claim any victories, nor was she credited with any.

S-45 at Mare Island Navy Yard on October 17, 1943.

S-45 was decommissioned on October 31, 1945, stricken from the lists and sold for scrap.

U.S.S. S-46
S.S. 157

S-46 was built by Bethlehem Steel and commissioned on June 6, 1925.

★
S-46'S WARTIME PATROLS

NO.	CAPTAIN	DATE	DUR.	BASE	AREA	CLAIMED	CONFIRMED
1	RC LYNCH, Jr	4205	35	BRISBANE	SOLOMONS	0	0
2	RC LYNCH, Jr	4207	26	BRISBANE	SOLOMONS	0	0
3	ER CRAWFORD	4209	31	BRISBANE	SOLOMONS	0	0
4	ER CRAWFORD	4309	33	ALASKA	ALASKA	0	0

S-46 did not claim any victories, nor were any credited to her.

S-46 is shown off Weeksville Air Station, June 17, 1943.

S-46 was decommissioned on October 25, 1945, stricken from the lists and sold for scrap.

U.S.S. S-47
S.S. 158

S-47 was built at Bethlehem Steel and commissioned on September 16, 1925.

★ ★ ★
S-47'S WARTIME PATROLS

NO.	CAPTAIN	DATE	DUR.	BASE	AREA	CLAIMED	CONFIRMED
1	JW DAVIS	4204	30	BRISBANE	SOLOMONS	0	0
2	JW DAVIS	4206	25	BRISBANE	SOLOMONS	0	0
3	JW DAVIS	4207	56	BRISBANE	SOLOMONS	1/7100	0
4	FE HAYLOR	4210	28	BRISBANE	SOLOMONS	0	0
5	FE HAYLOR	4310	28	ALASKA	ALASKA	0	0
6	FE HAYLOR	4312	26	ALASKA	ALASKA	0	0
7	LV YOUNG	4406	29	BRISBANE	SPL MISSION	0	0

S-47 claimed one victory, but it was not confirmed.

S-47 shown at Mare Island Navy Yard on September 7, 1943.

S-47 was decommissioned on October 25, 1945, stricken from the lists and sold for scrap.

Electric Boat Company of Groton, Connecticut, began production in 1934 when the **U.S.S. CUTTLEFISH (SS 171)** *was launched.*

ARGONAUT CLASS

ARGONAUT was a class by herself, as only one model was built at the Portsmouth Navy Yard. It was the only U.S. submarine designed exclusively for mine-laying. She was based on the *BARRACUDA* Class, but larger as she was 381 feet long and displaced 2710 tons. Launched in 1928, she had a range of 18,000 miles and a top speed of 15 knots. She had four 21-inch torpedo tubes forward, for which she carried 16 torpedoes, and four mine launching tubes aft with space for 36 mines, although she could carry 60 mines. She carried two 6-inch deck guns and two .30 cal anti-aircraft machine guns. The crew compliment was 89. In September of 1942 she was converted to a transport submarine and re-designated *APS-1*. She took part in the Makin raid along with *NAUTILUS* when they landed Carlson's Raiders on Makin Island in the Gilberts on August 17-19, 1942.

U. S. S. ARGONAUT
S. S. 166

U. S. S. ARGONAUT
S. S. 166
ARGONAUT was built at Portsmouth Navy Yard
and commissioned on April 2, 1928.

★ ★
ARGONAUT'S WARTIME PATROLS

NO.	CAPTAIN	DATE	DUR.	BASE	AREA	CLAIMED	CONFIRMED
1	SG BARCHET	4112	59	PEARL	MIDWAY	0	0
2	JR PIERCE	4208	18	PEARL	MAKIN RAID	0	0
3	JR PIERCE	4211	00	PEARL	to BRISBANE	0	0

ARGONAUT did not claim any victories, nor was she credited with any.

ARGONAUT was in process of conducting a defensive war patrol off Midway on the morning of December 7, 1941. She sighted the Japanese force shelling Midway and maneuvered for an attack position. She was detected and forced to go deep before getting off a shot.

In August 1942, *ARGONAUT* and *NAUTILUS* ferried Carlson's Raiders to Makin Island for their famous raid. On her third and last patrol she was forced to surface by three Japanese destroyers' depth charges, and destroyed with all hands by surface fire. This happened on January 10, 1943 between Lae and Rabaul, and proved the folly of sending a boat on a mission for which she was neither designed nor well suited. The *ARGONAUT* was the only U.S. submarine designed specifically for laying mines. This photo was taken on July 18, 1942.

In the German U-Boat service, the two highest scoring boats were U-48 with 53 victories totaling 318,111 tons, and U-99 with 37 victories totaling 242,658 tons. Both were Type VII boats, the backbone of the German U-Boat fleet, of which more than 700 were built. They were around 900 tons, compared to the 1800 tons of the average United States fleet boat.

NARWHAL CLASS

Only two *NARWHAL* Class boats were built: *NARWHAL* and *NAUTILUS*. These largest submarines ever built by the United States Navy were huge ocean-cruiser types inspired by the oversized German U-Cruisers. Built between 1927-30, they were 371 feet long and displaced nearly 3000 tons. Armed with two 6-inch deck guns, six torpedo tubes (four forward and two aft), four more external tubes were added (two fore and two aft). They had a range of 18,000 miles and a top surface speed of 17 knots. Due to their large size they were employed mainly on special missions to re-supply guerillas in the Philippines and to conduct raids of Japanese outposts. They carried a crew of 90.

U. S. S. NARWHAL
S. S. 167

U. S. S. NARWHAL
S. S. 167

NARWHAL was built at the Portsmouth Navy Yard, and commissioned on May 15, 1930.

NARWHAL'S WARTIME PATROLS

NO.	CAPTAIN	DATE	DUR.	BASE		AREA	CLAIMED	CONFIRMED
1	CW WILKINS	4202	54	PEARL		ECHINA SEA	2/12000	1/1244
2	CW WILKINS	4205	15	PEARL		MIDWAY	0	0
3	CW WILKINS	4207	49	PEARL		EMPIRE	4/14500	3/7000
4	FD LATTA	4304	38	PEARL		SPL MISSION	RECON ATTU	
5	FD LATTA	4306	42	PEARL		SPL MISSION	BOMBARD MATSUWA	
6	FD LATTA	4308	31	PEARL	to	FREMANTLE	1/4500	1/4200
7	FD LATTA	4310	31	FREMANTLE		SPL MISSION	SUPPLY MINDORO	
8	FD LATTA	4311	23	FREMANTLE		SPL MISSION	1/4000	1/834
9	FD LATTA	4401	29	FREMANTLE		SPL MISSION	SUPPLY PANAY	
10	FD LATTA	4402	33	FREMANTLE		SPL MISSION	1/1000	1/560
11	JC TITUS	4405	11	FREMANTLE		SPL MISSION	LNDG PARTY SAMAR	
12	JC TITUS	4406	27	FREMANTLE		SPL MISSION	BOMBARD BULA	
13	JC TITUS	4408	27	FREMANTLE		SPL MISSION	LNDG PARTY LUZON	
14	JC TITUS	4409	22	FREMANTLE		SPL MISSION	LNDG PARTY MINDANAO	
15	WG HOLMAN	4410	22	FREMANTLE		SPL MISSION	LNDG PARTY NEGROS	

NARWHAL'S VICTORIES

DATE	VESSEL	SIZE	TYPE	CAPTAIN	LOCATION
420304	TAKI MARU	01244	FREIGHTER	CW WILKINS	AMIMINO
420724	UNKNOWN MARU	01500	FREIGHTER	CW WILKINS	KIRULES
420801	MEIWA MARU	02921	FREIGHTER	CW WILKINS	TSUGARU
420808	BIFUKU MARU	02559	PASS-CARGO	CW WILKINS	TSUGARU
430911	HOKUSHO MARU	04211	FREIGHTER	FD LATTA	MAKASSER
431205	HIMENO MARU	00834	FREIGHTER	FD LATTA	SULU SEA
440303	KARATSU	00560	GUNBOAT	FD LATTA	NEGROS

NARWHAL was one of the five submarines at the base in Pearl Harbor during the Japanese attack on December 7, 1941. She and *TAUTOG* shared credit with a destroyer for shooting down the first Japanese plane in the war. Because of her large size, she was pressed into service ferrying raiders, guerillas, and their required supplies during the last two years of the war, mostly to the Philippines.

Shown is a pre-war photo of the *NARWHAL*.

NARWHAL was decommissioned on April 23, 1945, and sold for scrap that same year.

U.S.S. NAUTILUS
S.S. 168

U. S. S. NAUTILUS
S. S. 168

NAUTILUS was built at Mare Island Navy Yard and commissioned on May 15, 1930.

★ ★ ★ ★ ★ ★ ★ ★ ★

NAUTILUS'S WARTIME PATROLS

NO.	CAPTAIN	DATE	DUR.	BASE		AREA	CLAIMED	CONFIRMED
00	WH BROCKMAN	4206	15	PEARL		MIDWAY	1/30000	0.5/15000
1	WH BROCKMAN	4206	48	PEARL		EMPIRE	3/13200	1/1600
2	WH BROCKMAN	4208	18	PEARL		SPL MISSION - MAKIN RAID		
3	WH BROCKMAN	4209	56	PEARL		EMPIRE	2/10100	3/12000
4	WH BROCKMAN	4212	55	PEARL	to	BRISBANE	1/1000	1/1500
0	WH BROCKMAN	4303	21	BRISBANE	to	PEARL	0	0
5	WH BROCKMAN	4304	36	PEARL		SPL MISSION - ATTU RAID		
6	WD IRVIN	4309	31	PEARL		GILBERTS	0	0
7	WD IRVIN	4311	27	PEARL		GILBERTS	0	0
8	WD IRVIN	4401	57	PEARL		MARIANAS	1/6100	1/6100
9	GA SHARP	4405	13	FREMANTLE		SPL MISSION - MINDANAO		
10	GA SHARP	4406	10	FREMANTLE		SPL MISSION - PHILLIPINES		
11	GA SHARP	4407	27	FREMANTLE		SPL MISSION - PANDAN ISLE		
12	GA SHARP	4409	19	FREMANTLE		SPL MISSION - PANAY		
13	GA SHARP	4410	41	FREMANTLE		SPL MISSION - LUZON		
14	WD MICHAEL	4501	28	FREMANTLE		SPL MISSION - MINDANAO		

NAUTILUS'S VICTORIES

DATE	VESSEL	SIZE	TYPE	CAPTAIN	LOCATION
420604	SORYU	17500	CARRIER	WH BROCKMAN	MIDWAY
	(Shared credit with carrier-based aircraft)				
420625	YAMAKAZI	01580	DESTROYER	WH BROCKMAN	IZU SHICHITO
420828	TAMON MARU #6	04994	FREIGHTER	WH BROCKMAN	HONSHU
421001	TOSEI MARU II	02432	FREIGHTER	WH BROCKMAN	HONSHU
421024	KENUN MARU	04643	FREIGHTER	WH BROCKMAN	HONSHU
430109	YOSHINOGAWA M.	01430	FREIGHTER	WH BROCKMAN	SOLOMONS
440306	AMERICA MARU	06070	TRANSPORT	WD IRVIN	MARIANAS

NAUTILUS received Presidential Unit Citations for Patrols #1, 2, and 3 under command of W.H. Brockman. Because of her large size, she was pressed into service ferrying raiders, guerillas, and their supplies during the last two years of the war, mostly to the Philippines.

An idea of her large size is captured in this close-up photo at Mare Island Navy Yard on August 4, 1943.

NAUTILUS was decommissioned on June 6, 1945, and sold for scrap that same year.

DOLPHIN CLASS

The **DOLPHIN**, an experimental boat built at the Portsmouth Navy Yard in 1932, was a class by itself. It was an outgrowth of a compromise between the much larger **V Class** boats, such as **NAUTILUS** and the much smaller **S-Type** boats. She displaced 1560 tons and was 319 feet long, with a range of 9000 miles and a top surface speed of 17 knots. **DOLPHIN** had four torpedo tubes forward and two tubes aft, and carried a crew of 60. She was disappointing both in performance and endurance. Much of her time was spent in repair yards, due mostly to her Navy-built M.A.N. engines which failed to deliver designed power.

U. S. S. DOLPHIN
S. S. 169

U. S. S. DOLPHIN
S. S. 169

DOLPHIN was built at the Portsmouth Navy Yard
and commissioned on June 1, 1932.

★ ★

DOLPHIN'S WARTIME PATROLS

NO.	CAPTAIN	DATE	DUR.	BASE	AREA	CLAIMED	CONFIRMED
1	GB RAINER	4112	42	PEARL	MARSHALLS	0	0
2	RL RUTTER	4205	15	PEARL	MIDWAY	0	0
3	RL RUTTER	4206	68	PEARL	EMPIRE	0	0
4	RL RUTTER	4210	51	ALASKA	ALASKA	0	0

DOLPHIN did not claim any victories, nor was she credited with any.

DOLPHIN was one of the five submarines moored at Pearl Harbor on the day of the attack. Most of her crew was on liberty and she lay exposed in her berth with hatches open and shore cables connected. Luckily, she and the other subs escaped damage. She departed on her first patrol on Christmas Eve, along with *TAUTOG*, to scout the Marshalls. She was in the scouting line at the Battle of Midway, but got no shooting. Her last patrol was in the Alaskan winter of 1942-43. That spring she was retired to the Mainland to act as a training ship until the end of the war.

DOLPHIN was decommissioned on October 2, 1945, and scrapped the following year.

The first recorded instance of a submarine attack on an enemy ship was that of the TURTLE against the Royal Navy blockading squadron in New York Harbor during the American Revolution. David Bushnell was the inventor of this one-man submarine, constructed of wood and shaped like an egg. It was driven by a screw propeller turned by a hand-operated crank. There was sufficient ballast to keep it upright and it carried a gunpowder mine which would be attached to the bottom of the target vessel by means of an auger. A Sergeant Ezra Lee was given the task of carrying out the attack. Strong tides carried him past his first target, H.M.S. EAGLE, but he managed to get under the next ship, H.M.S. ASIA. He had trouble attaching the mine to the ship's bottom due to the copper sheathing. When discovered by a British patrol boat rowing guard on the Fleet, he released and set the mine and headed for safety. The mine exploded near the river bottom but caused no damage to the British ship. However, it did cause the British Commander to move the squadron farther out into the river.

CACHALOT CLASS

Only two **CACHALOT** Class boats were built as experimental types. They were medium-sized boats where wide-spread use of electric welding was used by the Navy for the first time. Displacement was 1200 tons, length 274 feet, top surface speed was 17 knots and range was 9000 miles. They had four torpedo tubes forward and two tubes aft, and carried a crew of 50. **CACHALOT** and her sister **CUTTLEFISH** were built during 1934-35, one each at Portsmouth Navy Yard, Portsmouth, New Hampshire, and Electric Boat Company of Groton, Connecticut..

U. S. S. CACHALOT
S. S. 170

U. S. S. CACHALOT
S. S. 170

CACHALOT was the first of two in her class and built at Portsmouth Navy Yard.
She was commissioned on December 1, 1933.

★ ★ ★

CACHALOT'S WARTIME PATROLS

NO.	CAPTAIN	DATE	DUR.	BASE	AREA	CLAIMED	CONFIRMED
1	W CHRISTENSEN	4201	66	PEARL	CAROLINES	0	0
2	GA LEWIS	4205	15	PEARL	MIDWAY	0	0
3	GA LEWIS	4206	47	PEARL	EMPIRE	0	0
4	HC STEVENSON	4209	46	PEARL	ALASKA	0	0

CACHALOT did not claim any victories, nor were credited to her.

CACHALOT was undergoing extensive repair at Pearl Harbor on the date of the attack, and was not ready for patrol work until January. After her first patrol, she returned to the yard for another refit. She was able to serve in the screen at the Battle of Midway, but had no shooting opportunities. Her third patrol was also lackluster and her skipper, G.A. Lewis was relieved of duties. It was evident after her fourth patrol that she was worn out, so she was sent to New London, Connecticut, to serve as a school boat.

CACHALOT at sea off the Jersey coast on November 23, 1943.

CACHALOT was decommissioned on October 17, 1945, stricken from the lists and sold for scrap in 1947.

─────────────

*During World War II, 380 U.S. airmen were rescued by 86 different submarines. The most famous rescued airman was LT(jg) George W. Bush when he was picked up by **U.S.S. FINBACK**. At the time, September 1944, he was the youngest carrier pilot in the United States Navy.*

U. S. S. CUTTLEFISH
S. S. 171

CUTTLEFISH was the only other *CACHALOT* Class boat built.
Constructed at Electric Boat Company, she was commissioned on June 8, 1934.

★
CUTTLEFISH'S WARTIME PATROLS

NO.	CAPTAIN	DATE	DUR.	BASE	AREA	CLAIMED	CONFIRMED
1	HP HOTTEL	4201	54	PEARL	MARSHALLS	0	0
2	HP HOTTEL	4204	56	PEARL	MARIANAS	0	0
3	EE MARSHALL	4207	69	PEARL	EMPIRE	2/29000	0
4	HC STEVENSON	4209	46	PEARL	ALASKA	0	0

CUTTLEFISH claimed two victories, but they were not credited to her.

CUTTLEFISH was undergoing extensive repair and modernization at Mare Island Navy Yard on December 7, 1941. She was rushed to Pearl Harbor in time to make her first patrol in January. It was not a huge success as most of the crew became violently ill from cans of cleaning fluid that came open. On her second patrol, the old boat broke down and although she completed her patrol, it was also a disappointment.

CUTTLEFISH had as much trouble keeping the ancient boat running as she did with the enemy. She was withdrawn from active combat and sent to New London, Connecticut to serve as a school boat.

CUTTLEFISH was decommissioned on October 24, 1945, stricken from the lists and sold for scrap.

A total of 206 submarines were launched in the United States between Pearl Harbor Day 1941, and Labor Day 1945.

P - CLASS

The *"P"* or **PORPOISE** Class were the first of the modern Fleet boats, so called because they had the speed and range to operate along with the fleet. They were 300 feet in length and displaced just over 1300 tons. The propulsion system was, for the first time, entirely diesel-electric. The main engines were connected to generators which powered the electric motors which drove the boat. They had four torpedo tubes forward and two aft, and carried a 3-inch deck gun. They had two .50 cal and two .30 cal machine guns for anti-aircraft use. They had a top surface speed of 19 knots, a range of 10,000 miles and carried a crew of 55. A total of ten *"P"* Class boats were built in the mid-1930s.

U. S. S. PORPOISE
S. S. 172

U. S. S. PORPOISE
S. S. 172

PORPOISE was built at Portsmouth Navy Yard
and commissioned on August 15, 1935.

★ ★ ★ ★ ★
PORPOISE'S WARTIME PATROLS

NO.	CAPTAIN	DATE	DUR.	BASE	AREA	CLAIMED	CONFRMEO
1	JA CALAHAN	4112	39	MANILA	W LUZON	0	0
2	JR McKNIGHT	4205	53	FREMANTLE	MIDWAY	0	0
3	JR McKNIGHT	4204	53	FREMANTLE to PEARL		0	0
4	JR McKNIGNT	4211	47	PEARL	EMPIRE	1/5300	1/5000
5	JR McKNIGHT	4302	48	PEARL	TRUK	1/3000	0
6	CL BENNETT	4306	36	PEARL	MARSHALLS	2/17300	2/3000

PORPOISE'S VICTORIES

DATE	VESSEL	SIZE	TYPE	CAPTAIN	LOCATION
430101	RENZAN MARU	04900	FREIGHTER	JR McKNIGHT	HOKKAIDO
430404	KOA MARU	02024	FREIGHTER	CL BENNETT	MARSHALLS
430719	MIKAGE MARU #20	02718	PASS-CARGO	CL BENNETT	KIRULES

PORPOISE took part in the Battle of Midway as all but five of the available boats were pressed into service. The name abbreviated above is J.A. Callaghan.

PORPOISE at Mare Island Navy Yard on October 13, 1942.

PORPOISE was decommissioned on November 15, 1945, stricken from the lists and sold for scrap in 1959.

United States submarines performed a total of 298 special missions which included delivering ammo, money and supplies to guerillas, evacuating key personnel, reporting weather, taking pictures, landing raiding parties, rescuing stranded aviators, doing pre-invasion re-con work, laying mines, bombarding certain areas for G-2, landing secret agents, and sweeping minefields.

U. S. S. PERCH
S. S. 176

PERCH was built at Electric Boat Company
and commissioned on November 19, 1936.

★

PERCH'S WARTIME PATROLS

NO.	CAPTAIN	DATE	DUR.	BASE	AREA	CLAIMED	CONFIRMED
1	DA HURT	4112	38	MANILA	FORMOSA	1/1500	0
2	DA HURT	4202	00	DARWIN	BARRIER	0	0

PERCH claimed one victory, but it was not confirmed.

In a night surface engagement, *PERCH* took a shell in the conning tower which ruptured the antenna trunk and did other damage. Three days later, while moving onto station, she was discovered by two destroyers and forced to dive. A severe depth charging followed which put many of her operating systems out of commission. Though she managed to survive and later surfaced, the boat was badly damaged. The Japanese destroyers managed to locate her again and forced her down once more. This time was even worse but she survivied . While trying to limp away she was discovered yet again, but could no longer dive. Commander Hurt ordered the crew off and the boat scuttled. They were all taken prisoner. All but nine managed to survive the mines of Ashio, Japan, until the war was over.

This photograph of *U.S.S. PERCH* was taken at Portsmouth, New Hampshire, on June 17, 1937.

United States submarines sank 214 Japanese warships during World War II, totaling 577,626 gross registered tons.

U. S. S. PERMIT
S. S. 178

PERMIT was built at Electric Boat Company and commissioned on March 17, 1937

★ ★ ★ ★ ★ ★ ★ ★ ★ ★
PERMIT'S WARTIME PATROLS

NO.	CAPTAIN	DATE	DUR.	BASE	AREA	CLAIMED	CONFIRMED
1	AM HURST	4112	9	MANILA	W LUZON	0	0
2	AM HURST	4112	6	MANILA	LINGAYAN	0	0
3	AM HURST	4112	38	MANILA	CELEBES	0	0
4	JR McKNIGHT	4202	44	JAVA	BARRIER	0	0
5	WG CHAPPLE	4205	38	FREMANTLE	MAKASSER	0	0
6	WG CHAPPLE	4207	50	FREMANTLE	to PEARL	0	0
7	WG CHAPPLE	4302	38	PEARL	EMPIRE	2/10300	1/2700
8	WG CHAPPLE	4304	49	PEARL	TRUK	2/15000	0
9	WG CHAPPLE	4306	37	PEARL	EMPIRE	3/16100	2/3000
10	CL BENNETT	4308	32	PEARL	MARSHALLS	3/27700	0
11	CL BENNETT	4401	74	PEARL	TRUK	0	0
12	DA SHERER	4404	12	PEARL	TRUK	1/2200	0
13	DA SHERER	4406	13	PEARL	to BRISBANE	1/800	0
14	DA SHERER	4409	50	BRISBANE	to PEARL	1/500	0

PERMIT'S VICTORIES

DATE	VESSEL	SIZE	TYPE	CAPTAIN	LOCATION
430308	HISASHIMA MARU	02742	FREIGHTER	WG CHAPPLE	SHICHITO
430706	BANSHU MARU #33	00787	FREIGHTER	WG CHAPPLE	SHICHITO
430707	SHOWA MARU	02212	PASS-CARGO	WG CHAPPLE	SHICHITO

PERMIT made a call at Corregidor during the first weeks of the war where she discharged ammunition and picked up torpedoes and personnel. In July, she was chosen, along with *LAPON* and *PLUNGER* to make the first penetration of the Sea of Japan. It was successful, although *PERMIT* was nearly swamped by accident. She was on the guard line during Operation Flintlock, and later was generally assigned to lifeguard duty as the newer and better-equipped boats took over the offensive roles. *PERMIT* received a Navy Unit Commendation for Patrol #10.

This photograph is prewar since she is wearing her number.

PERMIT was decommissioned on November 15, 1945, stricken from the lists and sold for scrap in 1957.

U. S. S. PICKEREL
S. S. 177

PICKEREL was built at the Electric Boat Company and commissioned on January 26, 1937.

★ ★ ★

PICKEREL'S WARTIME PATROLS

NO.	CAPTAIN	DATE	DUR.	BASE	AREA	CLAIMED	CONFIRMED
1	BE BACON	4112	21	MANILA	INDOCHINA	0	0
2	BE BACON	4112	30	MANILA	CELEBES	2/10000	1/2929
3	BE BACON	4202	41	JAVA	BARRIER	0	0
4	BE BACON	4204	52	FREMANTLE	PHILLIPINES	0	0
5	BE BACON	4207	47	BRISBANE to	PEARL	0	0
6	AH ALSTON	4301	37	PEARL	EMPIRE	1/6100	1/1200
7	AH ALSTON	4303	00	PEARL	EMPIRE	2/2000	2/1553

PICKEREL'S VICTORIES

DATE	VESSEL	SIZE	TYPE	CAPTAIN	LOCATION
420110	KANKO	02919	GUNBOAT	BE BACON	TALLAUD ISL
430215	TATEYAMA MARU	01990	FREIGHTER	AH ALSTON	N HONSHU
430403	SUBCHASER #13	00440	SUBCHASER	AH ALSTON	N HONSHU
430407	FUKEUI MARU	01113	FREIGHTER	AH ALSTON	N HONSHU

PICKEREL was dispatched to the Camranh Bay area at the outbreak of the war. Like so many of the earlier models, she was plagued by faulty torpedoes. She also stood picket in Makassar Strait in an attempt to stem the Japanese juggernaut rolling southward. On her seventh patrol, after scoring two victories in Northern Honshu waters, she went down with all hands near Shiramuka Lighthouse, a victim of small patrol craft.

PICKEREL is shown at Electric Boat Company, Groton, Connecticut, in 1937.

U. S. S. PIKE
S. S. 173

PIKE was built at Portsmouth Navy Yard and commissioned on December 2, 1935.

★ ★ ★ ★

PIKE'S WARTIME PATROLS

NO.	CAPTAIN	DATE	DUR.	BASE	AREA	CLAIMED	CONFIRMED
1	WA NEW	4112	21	MANILA	HONG KONG	0	0
2	WA NEW	4112	25	MANILA	CELEBES	0	0
3	WA NEW	4202	51	DARWIN	BARRIER	0	0
4	WA NEW	4204	35	FREMANTLE to PEARL		0	0
5	WA NEW	4205	11	PEARL	MIDWAY	0	0
6	WA NEW	4212	48	PEARL	EMPIRE	0	0
7	L McGREGOR	4303	40	PEARL	TRUK	0	0
8	L McGREGOR	4307	50	PEARL	MARIANAS	1/5000	1/2022

PIKE'S VICTORY

DATE	VESSEL	SIZE	TYPE	CAPTAIN	LOCATION
430705	SHOJU MARU II	02022	PASS-CARGO	LD McGREGOR	MARIANAS

PIKE was sent to patrol the Hainan area when hostilities broke out and was later relieved by *SNAPPER*. In December 1942, she was part of the trans-oceanic line between Midway and Wake to guide a B-24 strike at Wake and pick up downed airmen. *PIKE* did lifeguard duty at the Battle of Midway and later during Operation Galvanic.

PIKE is shown at Mare Island Navy Yard on October 6, 1942.

PIKE was decommissioned on November 15, 1945, stricken from the lists and sold for scrap in 1957.

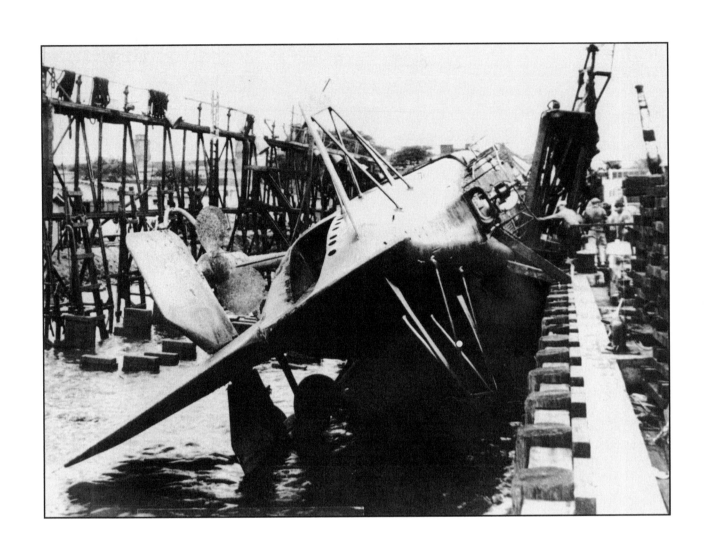

U. S. S. PLUNGER
S. S. 179

U. S. S. PLUNGER
S. S. 179

PLUNGER was built at Portsmouth Navy Yard and commissioned on November 19, 1936.

PLUNGER'S WARTIME PATROLS

NO.	CAPTAIN	DATE	DUR.	BASE	AREA	CLAIMED	CONFIRMED
1	DC WHITE	4112	52	PEARL	EMPIRE	1/7200	1/4700
00	DC WHITE	4205	15	PEARL	MIDWAY	0	0
2	DC WHITE	4206	36	PEARL	E CHINA SEA	2/19000	2/6300
3	DC WHITE	4210	27	PEARL	to BRISBANE	0	0
4	DC WHITE	4122	53	BRISBANE	to PEARL	1/1300	0
5	RH BASS	4302	29	PEARL	MARSHALLS	1/9000	1/1800
6	RH BASS	4304	29	PEARL	MARSHALLS	3/24100	2/15000
7	RH BASS	4306	32	PEARL	EMPIRE	1/1500	1/2500
8	RH BASS	4308	30	PEARL	EMPIRE	2/9000	2/10500
9	RH BASS	4311	42	PEARL	MARSHALLS	0	0
10	RH BASS	4401	55	PEARL	EMPIRE	4/22500	3/9600
11	EJ FAHY	4405	56	PEARL	BONINS	0	0
12	EJ FAHY	4407	51	PEARL	TRUK	1/5000	0

PLUNGER'S VICTORIES

DATE	VESSEL	SIZE	TYPE	CAPTAIN	LOCATION
420118	EIZAN MARU	04703	FREIGHTER	DC WHITE	SHIKOKU
420630	UKAI MARU #5	03882	FREIGHTER	DC WHITE	YELLOW SEA
420702	UNYO MARU #5	02997	FREIGHTER	DC WHITE	YELLOW SEA
430312	TAIHOSAN MARU	01805	WATER CARRIER	RH BASS	CAROLINES
430510	TATSUTAKE MARU	07068	PASS-CARGO	RH BASS	ROTA
430510	KINAI MARU	08360	PASS-CARGO	RH BASS	ROTA
430712	NIJAKA MARU	0247$	PASS-CARGO	RH BASS	HOKKAIDO
430820	SEITAI MARU	03404	FREIGHTER	RH BASS	HOKKAIDO
430822	RYOKAI MARU	04655	FREIGHTER	RH BASS	HOKKAIDO
440202	TOYO MARU #5	02193	FREIGHTER	RH BASS	SHIKOKU
440202	TOYO MARU #8	02191	FREIGHTER	RH BASS	SHIKOKU
440223	KIMISHIMA MARU	05193	FREIGHTER	RH BASS	SHIKOKU

PLUNGER was enroute to Hawaii from San Francisco on December 7, 1941. When she left on her first patrol later that month, she carried the first radar set into battle. She also suffered the very first depth-charging of any U.S. submarine as she probed Empire waters to test enemy defenses. She received Navy Unit Commendations for Patrols #2, 3, and 4 under D.C. White, and for Patrols #6 and 10 under R.H. Bass.

This photo of *PLUNGER*, taken at Pearl Harbor in February 1942, is after she had slipped off oil-soaked blocks in the dry dock.

PLUNGER was decommissioned on November 11, 1945, stricken from the lists and sold for scrap in 1957.

U. S. S. POLLACK
S. S. 180

POLLACK was built at Portsmouth Navy Yard and commissioned on August 15, 1935.

★ ★ ★ ★ ★ ★ ★ ★ ★ ★ ★
POLLACK'S WARTIME PATROLS

NO.	CAPTAIN	DATE	DUR.	BASE	AREA	CLAIMED	CONFIRMED
1	SP MOSELEY	4112	39	PEARL	EMPIRE	2/16000	2/7600
2	SP MOSELEY	4202	49	PEARL	FORMOSA	1/5400	1/1454
3	SP MOSELEY	4205	45	PEARL	EMPIRE	1/900	0
4	RE PALMER	4210	49	PEARL	TRUK	0	0
5	RE PALMER	4212	41	PEARL	EMPIRE	0	0
6	RE PALMER	4303	44	PEARL	MARSHALLS	0	0
7	BE LEWELLEN	4305	46	PEARL	MARSHALLS	2/9300	2/8400
8	BE LEWELLEN	4307	47	PEARL	EMPIRE	0	2/7000
9	BE LEWELLEN	4402	43	PEARL	EMPIRE	4/21400	3/5400
10	BE LEWELLEN	4405	32	PEARL	EMPIRE	1/1500	1/1300
11	EH STEINMETZ	4407	60	PEARL	to BRISBANE	0	0

POLLACK'S VICTORIES

DATE	VESSEL	SIZE	TYPE	CAPTAIN	LOCATION
420107	UNKAI MARU #1	02225	FREIGHTER	SP MOSELEY	HONSHU
420109	TEIAN MARU	05378	FREIGHTER	SP MOSELEY	HONSHU
420311	FUKUSHU MARU	01454	FREIGHTER	SP MOSELEY	E CHINA SEA
430518	TERUSHIMA MARU	03110	GUNBOAT	BE LEWELLEN	WOTJE
430520	BANKOK MARU	05350	AUX-CRUISER	BE LEWELLEN	MAKIN
430727	TAIFUKU MARU	3520	PASS-CARGO	BE LEWELLEN	KYUSHU
430803	TAGONOURA MARU	03521	FREIGHTER	BE LEWELLEN	SHIKOKU
440320	HAKOYO MARU	01327	FREIGHTER	BE LEWELLEN	KYUSHU
440325	SUBCHASER #54	00300	SUB-CHASER	BE LEWELLEN	E CHINA SEA
440403	TOSEI MARU	02814	PASS-CARGO	BE LEWELLEN	SHICHITO
440522	ASANAGI	01270	DESTROYER	BE LEWELLEN	BONINS

POLLACK was enroute to Hawaii from San Francisco on December 7, 1941. On arrival, she was topped off and dispatched to Empire waters on December 13th to test enemy defenses. While there she sank the first Japanese merchantman of the war.

This is probably a prewar builder's photo, with date and location unknown.

POLLACK was decommissioned on September 21, 1945, stricken from the lists and sold for scrap.

U. S. S. POMPANO
S. S. 181

POMPANO was built at Mare Island Navy Yard and commissioned on June 12, 1937

★ ★ ★ ★ ★ ★ ★

POMPANO'S WARTIME PATROLS

NO.	CAPTAIN	DATE	DUR.	BASE	AREA	CLAIMED	CONFRMED
1	LS PARKS	4112	43	PEARL	MARSHALLS	1/1600	0
2	LS PARKS	4204	58	PEARL	E CHINA SEA	2/16400	2/8900
3	WM THOMAS	4207	55	PEARL	EMPIRE	3/9000	3/9600
4	WM THOMAS	4301	44	PEARL	MARSHALLS	0	0
5	WM THOMAS	4303	52	PEARL	EMPIRE	0	0
6	WM THOMAS	4306	52	PEARL	EMPIRE	0	0
7	WM THOMAS	4308	00	PEARL	EMPIRE	0	0

POMPANO'S VICTORIES

DATE	VESSEL	SIZE	TYPE	CAPTAIN	LOCATION
420525	TOKYO MARU #3	00902	TANKER	LS PARKS	E CHINA SEA
420530	ATSUTA MARU	07983	TRANSPORT	LS PARKS	RYUKUS
420812	UNKNOWN MARU	04000	FREIGHTER	WH THOMAS	KYUSHU
430903	AKAMA MARU	05600	FREIGHTER	WH THOMAS	HONSHU
430925	TAIKO MARU	02958	FREIGHTER	WH THOMAS	HONSHU

POMPANO was enroute from San Francisco to Hawaii on December 7, 1941. After stopping at Pearl for fuel, she departed on the 18th to observe the enemy's defenses of the Marshall Islands. On her seventh patrol, repeated radio calls failed to get a response and she was presumed lost with all hands—probably a mine, since no Japanese anti-submarine action was reported in her patrol area.

POMPANO at Mare Island Navy Yard on December 19, 1942.

U. S. S. SHARK
S. S. 174

SHARK was built at Electric Boat Company and commissioned on January 25, 1936.

★
SHARK'S WARTIME PATROLS

NO.	CAPTAIN	DATE	DUR.	BASE	AREA	CLAIMED	CONFIRMED
1	L SHANE, Jr	4112	12	MANILA	S LUZON	0	0
00	L SHANE, Jr	4112	7	MANILA	SPL MISSION	0	0
2	L SHANE, Jr	4201	00	JAVA	CELEBES	0	0

SHARK did not claim any victories, nor was she credited with any.

SHARK was in Division 203 of the Asiatic Fleet at Cavite when war broke out and went on patrol almost immediately. **SHARK** took Admiral Hart out of Manila just before the arrival of the Japanese. His seaplane was bombed and rendered useless. On her third patrol, **SHARK** was depth-charged off Manado on February 11, 1942, and thus became the first U.S. submarine to be lost to enemy surface craft.

This is a prewar builder's photograph, date and location unknown.

———————————

A total of ninety-three Presidential Unit Citations were awarded to thirty-five different boats during World War II.

U. S. S. TARPON
S. S. 175

TARPON was built at the Electric Boat Company and commissioned on March 12, 1936.

★ ★ ★ ★ ★ ★ ★

TARPON'S WARTIME PATROLS

NO.	CAPTAIN	DATE	DUR.	BASE	AREA	CLAIMED	CONFIRMED
1	L WALLACE	4112	33	MANILA	E LUZON	0	0
2	L WALLACE	4201	40	DARWIN	BARRIER	0	0
3	L WALLACE	4203	52	FREMANTLE	to PEARL	0	0
4	L WALLACE	4205	9	PEARL	MIDWAY	0	0
5	TL WOGAN	4210	42	PEARL	TRUK	0	0
6	TL WOGAN	4301	47	PEARL	EMPIRE	2/21000	2/27000
7	TL WOGAN	4303	47	PEARL	TRUK	0	0
8	TL WOGAN	4307	40	PEARL	EMPIRE	1/1000	0
9	TL WOGAN	4310	34	PEARL	EMPIRE	1/10000	GERMAN
10	TL OAKLEY	4312	39	PEARL	MARSHALLS	0	0
11	S FILIPONE	4406	41	PEARL	TRUK	0	0
12	S FILIPONE	4408	45	PEARL	TRUK	0	0

TARPON'S VICTORIES

DATE	VESSEL	SIZE	TYPE	CAPTAIN	LOCATION
430201	FUSHIMI MARU	10335	PASS-CARGO	TL WOGAN	SHIKOKU
430208	TATSUTA MARU	16375	TRANSPORT	TL WOGAN	SHIKOKU

TARPON was stationed at Cavite when war broke out, and was patroling in San Bernadino Strait. She was caught in a bad storm and nearly swamped, shorting much of her electrical gear. Her victories included two of the five largest liners in Japan's inventory. Her sixth patrol was the 13th best on record for total tonnage.

TARPON is shown at Mare Island Navy Yard on September 30, 1942, during a re-fit.

TARPON was removed from active duty in late 1944, decommissioned on December 15, 1945, and sunk as a target on August 26, 1957.

SALMON CLASS

SALMON Class boats were the next step up from the *"P"* Class and were about a hundred tons larger in displacement. They were 310 feet long with four torpedo tubes forward and four aft. Their range was 10,000 miles and the top surface speed was 20 knots. They were armed with a 3-inch deck gun and two .50 cal and two .30 cal machines guns. The crew compliment was 70. Sixteen *SALMON* Class boats were built in the late-1930s.

U.S.S. SALMON
S.S. 182

U. S. S. SALMON
S. S. 182

SALMON was built at Electric Boat Company and commissioned on March 15, 1938.

★ ★ ★ ★ ★ ★ ★ ★ ★
SALMON'S WARTIME PATROLS

NO.	CAPTAIN	DATE	DUR.	BASE	AREA	CLAIMED	CONFIRMED
1	EB McKINNY	4112	55	MANILA	W LUZON	1/1500	0
2	EB McKINNY	4202	31	JAVA	BARRIER	0	0
3	EB McKINNY	4205	52	FREMANTLE	INDOCHINA	2/9800	2/15800
4	EB McKINNY	4207	49	FREMANTLE	S CHINA SEA	0	0
5	EB McKINNY	4210	58	FREMANTLE to PEARL		1/6100	1/5900
6	NJ NICHOLAS	4304	51	PEARL	EMPIRE	0	0
7	NJ NICHOLAS	4307	40	PEARL	EMPIRE	2/11100	1/2500
8	NJ NICHOLAS	4309	51	PEARL	EMPIRE	0	0
9	NJ NICHOLAS	4312	59	PEARL	EMPIRE	0	0
10	HK NAUMAN	4404	51	PEARL	PALAU	0	0
11	HK NAUMAN	4409	38	PEARL	EMPIRE	.3/3300	.3/3333

SALMON'S VICTORIES

DATE	VESSEL	SIZE	TYPE	CAPTAIN	LOCATION
420525	ASAHI	11441	REPAIR SHIP	EB McKINNY	S CHINA SEA
420528	GANGES MARU	04382	PASS-CARGO	EB McKINNY	S CHINA SEA
421117	OREGON MARU	05873	SALVG VESSEL	EB McKINNY	MINDORO
430810	WAKANOURA MARU	02411	PASS-CARGO	NJ NICHOLAS	HOKKAIDO
441030	TAKANE MARU	10021	TANKER	HK NAUMAN	RYUKUS

(Shared credit with *TRIGGER* and *STERLET*)

SALMON was plagued by faulty torpedoes in the early months of the war while she was in the Asiatic Squadron. She received a Presidential Unit Citation for Patrol #11 under H.K. Nauman.

SALMON at Mare Island Navy Yard, March 22, 1943.

SALMON was decommissioned on October 24, 1945, stricken from the lists and sold for scrap in 1946.

A total of seventy-seven United States submarine captains had five or more confirmed sinkings to their credit. Topping the list was Richard O'Kane with twenty-four confirmed sinkings.

U. S. S. SAILFISH
S. S. 192

U. S. S. SAILFISH
S. S. 192

SAILFISH was built at Portsmouth Navy Yard and was originally commissioned in May 1939 as *SQUALUS*. On her trial run she had a diving accident and went to the bottom, killing the 27 men in the engine compartment. The other crew members were rescued and the boat raised, salvaged and overhauled. She was recommissioned as the *SAILFISH* on April 15, 1940.

★ ★ ★ ★ ★ ★ ★ ★ ★
SAILFISH'S WARTIME PATROLS

NO.	CAPTAIN	DATE	DUR.	BASE	AREA	CLAIMED	CONFRMED
1	MC MUMMA, Jr	4112	9	MANILA	W LUZON	1/1500	0
2	RG VOGE	4112	55	MANILA	FORMOSA	0	0
3	RG VOGE	4202	28	JAVA	BARRIER	0	1/6440
4	RG VOGE	4204	28	FREMANTLE	CORREGIDOR	0	0
5	RG VOGE	4206	49	FREMANTLE	INDOCHINA	1/7000	0
6	JR MOORE	4209	49	BRISBANE	SOLOMONS	0	0
7	JR MOORE	4211	53	BRISBANE to	PEARL	0	0
8	JR MOORE	4305	49	PEARL	EMPIRE	2/12000	2/6908
9	WR LEFAVOR	4307	51	PEARL	E CHINA SEA	0	0
10	RE WARD	4311	49	PEARL	EMPIRE	3/35700	3/29571
11	RE WARD	4407	58	PEARL	LUZON STRT	4/13200	1/2100
12	RE WARD	4409	70	PEARL	LUZON STRT	1/800	0

SAILFISH'S VICTORIES

DATE	VESSEL	SIZE	TYPE	CAPTAIN	LOCATION
420302	KAMOGAWA MARU	06440	AIRCFT FERRY	RG VOCE	LOMBOK STRT
430615	SHINJU MARU	03617	FREIGHTER	JR MOORE	HONSHU
430625	IBURI MARU	03291	PASS-CARGO	JR MOORE	HONSHU
431204	CHUYO	20000	AIRC CARRIER	RE WARD	BONINS
431213	TATAI MARU	03195	FREIGHTER	RE WARD	OSMUI ISLE
431221	UYO MARU	06376	FREIGHTER	RE WARD	KYUSHU
440824	TOAN MARU	02110	FREIGHTER	RE WARD	LUZON

SAILFISH received a Presidential Unit Citation for Patrol #10 under R.E. Ward. The Carrier *CHUYO* went down with twenty survivors of the *SCULPIN* that were being transferred from Truk to Japan. In a strange twist of fate, it was *SCULPIN* that had stood by *SQUALUS* while her crew was being rescued when she went to the bottom on her trial run.

SAILFISH undergoing a refit at Mare Island Navy Yard. Photo taken April 13, 1943.

SAILFISH, dubbed *SQUAILFISH* by her crewmen, was decommissioned on October 27, 1946, and sold for scrap in 1948.

U. S. S. SARGO
S. S. 188

SARGO was built at Electric Boat Company and commissioned on February 7, 1938.

★ ★ ★ ★ ★ ★ ★ ★

SARGO'S WARTIME PATROLS

NO.	CAPTAIN	DATE	DUR.	BASE	AREA	CLAIMED	CONFRMED
1	TD JACOBS	4112	48	MANILA	INDOCHINA	0	0
2	TD JACOBS	4202	25	JAVA	SPL MISSION	DELV AMMO MINDANAO	
3	RV GREGORY	4203	52	FREMANTLE	INDOCHINA	0	0
4	RV GREGORY	4206	56	FREMANTLE	S CHINA SEA	0	0
5	RV GREGORY	4208	59	FREMANTLE	CELEBES	1/7000	1/4500
6	ES CARMICK	4211	53	BRISBANE to PEARL		0	0
7	ES CARMICK	4305	43	PEARL	TRUK	1/6600	1/5300
8	ES CARMICK	4308	46	PEARL	TRUK	0	0
9	PW GARNETT	4310	55	PEARL	E CHINA SEA	2/15900	2/6419
10	PW GARNETT	4401	46	PEARL	PALAU	1/7000	2/11800
11	PW GARNETT	4404	49	PEARL	EMPIRE	1/5000	1/4800
12	PW GARNETT	4410	63	PEARL	BONINS	0	0

SARGO'S VICTORIES

DATE	VESSEL	SIZE	TYPE	CAPTAIN	LOCATION
420925	TEIBO MARU	04472	FREIGHTER	RV GREGORY	S CHINA SEA
430613	KONAN MARU	05226	PASS-CARGO	ES CARMICK	PALAU
431109	TAGA MARU	02868	FREIGHTER	PW GARNETT	PHILIPPINE SEA
431111	KOSEI MARU #3	03551	PASS-CARGO	PW GARNETT	RYUKUS
440217	NICHIRO MARU	06534	PASS-CARGO	PW GARNETT	PALAU
440229	UCHIDE MARU	05275	PASS-CARGO	PW GARNETT	PALAU
440426	WAZAN MARU	04851	FREIGHTER	PW GARNETT	KYUSHU

   SARGO was at Cavite as part of the Asiatic Squadron when the war broke out. During the first ten days of the war, SARGO made eight attacks, firing thirteen torpedos with zero kills; a common result in those days. Pressed into service as freight hauler, *SARGO* carried over a million rounds of ammo from Sarabaja to Mindanao and the hard-pressed forces there. Returning from this mission, she narrowly escaped being sunk by a "friendly" Australian aircraft.

Photograph taken at Mare Island Navy Yard on August 24, 1944.

SARGO was decommissioned on June 22, 1946, stricken from the lists and sold for scrap in 1947.

U. S. S. SAURY
S. S. 189

SAURY was built at Electric Boat Company and commissioned on March 31, 1938.

★ ★ ★ ★ ★ ★ ★

SAURY'S WARTIME PATROLS

NO.	CAFTAIN	DATE	DUR.	BASE	AREA	CLAIMED	CONFIRMED
1	JL BURNSIDE	4112	53	MANILA	W LUZON	0	0
2	JL BURNSIDE	4202	38	JAVA	BARRIER	0	0
3	JL BURNSIDE	4204	vl	FREMANTLE	DAVAO	0	0
4	JL BURNSIDE	4205	61	FREMANTLE	MANILA	0	0
5	LS MEWHINEY	4207	51	FREMANTLE	MANILA	1/10000	1/8600
6	LS MEWHINEY	4210	51	FREMANTLE to PEARL		0	0
7	AH DROPP	4305	38	PEARL	E CHINA SEA	3/24900	4/20000
8	AH DROPP	4307	30	PEARL	EMPIRE	0	0
9	AH DROPP	4310	53	PEARL	TRUK	0	0
10	AH DROPP	4312	62	PEARL	E CHINA SEA	0	0
11	AH DROPP	4406	54	PEARL	PHILPPINE SEA	0	0
12	AH DROPP	4409	65	PEARL	EMPIRE	0	0

SAURY'S VICTORIES

DATE	VESSEL	SIZE	TYPE	CAPTAIN	LOCATION
420911	KANTO MARU	08606	AIRCFT FERRY	LS MEWHINEY	JAVA SEA
430526	KAGI MARU	02343	TRANSPORT	AH DROPP	RYUKUS
430568	AKATSUKI MARU	10216	TANKER	AH DROPP	RYUKUS
430530	TAMAMISAN MARU	01992	FREIGHTER	AH DROPP	E CHINA SEA
430530	SHOKO MARU	05385	FREIGHTER	AH DROPP	E CHINA SEA

SAURY was stationed at Cavite as part of the Asiatic Squadron when war broke out. She conducted the sea tests of the Mark 14 Torpedo that proved they were running ten feet deeper than set. In July 1943, *SAURY* had a scrape (*literally*) with a Japanese destroyer, when the Japanese tried to ram the partially submerged submarine and damaged her conning tower and periscope shears. In February 1944, she was overtaken and nearly swamped by a large tidal wave while running on the surface.

SAURY on April 4, 1943 during a re-fit at Mare Island Navy Yard.

SAURY was decommissioned on June 22, 1946, stricken from the lists and sold for scrap in 1951.

U. S. S. SCULPIN
S. S. 191

SCULPIN was built at Portsmouth Navy Yard and commissioned on January 16, 1939.

★ ★ ★ ★ ★ ★ ★ ★
SCULPIN'S WARTIME PATROLS

NO.	CAPTAIN	DATE	DUR.	BASE	AREA	CLAIMED	CONFIRMED
1	LH CHAPPELL	4112	45	MANILA	E LUZON	1/1500	0
2	LH CHAPPELL	4201	29	JAVA	BARRIER	1/1500	0
3	LH CHAPPELL	4203	45	FREMANTLE	BANDA SEA	0	0
4	LH CHAPPELL	4205	78	FREMANTLE	S CHINA SEA	1/1700	0
5	LH CHAPPELL	4209	54	BRISBANE	SOLOMONS	3/24100	2/6652
6	LH CHAPPELL	4211	52	BRISBANE to	PEARL	0	0
7	LH CHAPPELL	4305	41	PEARL	EMPIRE	0	0
8	LH CHAPPELL	4307	54	PEARL	E CHINA SEA	1/4500	1/3183
9	F CONNAWAY	4311	00	PEARL	TRUK	0	0

SCULPIN'S VICTORIES

DATE	VESSEL	SIZE	TYPE	CAPTAIN	LOCATION
421007	NAMINOUE MARU	04731	TRANSPORT	LH CHAPPELL	BISMARCKS
421014	SUMIYOSHI MARU	01921	FREIGHTER	LH CHAPPELL	BISMARCKS
430709	SEKKO MARU	03183	PASS-CARGO	LH CHAPPELL	FORMOSA

SCULPIN was in the Asiatic Squadron at Cavite when war broke out and, along with *SEAWOLF*, left at once with a southbound convoy. On her first patrols she suffered torpedo failures like most of the other older boats already on station. *SCULPIN* got into a surface action during Operation Galvanic (Tarawa Invasion) and her crew was forced to abandon ship when her skipper and gunnery officer were killed and the boat fatally hit. Captain J.P. Cromwell, acting as pack commander, chose to go down with the boat rather than subject himself to possible torture to extract important information, and received a Congressional Medal of Honor posthumously. The rest of the crew were taken prisoner by the Japanese. Some were embarked for Japan aboard the Japanese carrier *CHUYO*. In an ironic twist of fate, *CHUYO* was sunk on her homeward voyage by *SAILFISH* and only one of the *SCULPIN* survivors aboard her was saved. It had been *SCULPIN* that had discovered *SQUALUS* when she sank after a diving accident off New Hampshire in 1938, and had stood by while *SQUALUS'* crew was rescued. *SQUALUS* was salvaged and renamed *SAILFISH*.

SCULPIN on acceptance trials at the Portsmouth, New Hampshire, Navy Yard, April 6, 1939.

U. S. S. SEADRAGON
S. S. 194

SEADRAGON was built at Electric Boat Company and commissioned on October 23, 1939.

★ ★ ★ ★ ★ ★ ★ ★ ★ ★ ★
SEADRAGON'S WARTIME PATROLS

NO.	CAPTAIN	DATE	DUR.	BASE	AREA	CLAIMED	CONFRMED
1	WE FERRALL	4112	45	MANILA	INDOCHINA	2/10000	1/6441
2	WE FERRALL	4203	39	FREMANTLE	CORREGIDOR	0	0
3	WE FERRALL	4206	52	FREMANTLE	INDOCHINA	3/18100	3/15900
4	WE FERRALL	4208	55	FREMANTLE	INDOCHINA	2/12500	1/2500
5	WE FERRALL	4211	52	BRISBANE to	PEARL	2/7400	1/2000
6	RL RUTTER	4305	43	PEARL	TRUK	0	0
7	RL RUTTER	4307	49	PEARL	MARSHALLS	0	0
8	RL RUTTER	4309	42	PEARL	MARSHALLS	1/8200	0
9	RL RUTTER	4312	46	PEARL	TRUK	1/7400	0
10	JH ASHLEY	4404	54	PEARL	EMPIRE	0	1/1300
11	JH ASHLEY	4409	44	PEARL	LUZON STRT	3/13500	3/15700
12	JH ASHLEY	4412	60	PEARL	BONINS	0	0

SEADRAGON'S VICTORIES

DATE	VESSEL	SIZE	TYPE	CAPTAIN	LOCATION
420202	TAMAGAWA MARU	06441	PASS-CARGO	WE FERRALL	LINGAYAN
420712	HIYAMA MARU	06171	FREIGHTER	WE FERRALL	S CHINA SEA
420713	SHINYO MARU II	04163	PASS-CARGO	WE FERRALL	S CHINA SEA
420716	HAKODATE MARU	05302	FREIGHTER	WE FERRALL	S CHINA SEA
421010	SHIGURE MARU	02445	FREIGHTER	JH ASHLEY	MOLUCCA STRT
421220	I-4	01995	SUBMARINE	JH ASHLEY	BISMARCKS
430328	SUWA MARU	10673	TRANSPORT	JH ASHLEY	off WAKE

(Shared credit with ***FINBACK*** and ***TUNNY***)

DATE	VESSEL	SIZE	TYPE	CAPTAIN	LOCATION
440423	DAIJU MARU	01279	FREIGHTER	JH ASHLEY	SHIKOKU
441023	EIKO MARU	01843	FREIGHTER	JH ASHLEY	S CHINA SEA
441024	TAITEN MARU	06442	PASS-CARGO	JH ASHLEY	S CHINA SEA
441024	KOKURYU MARU	07369	PASS-CARGO	JH ASHLEY	S CHINA SEA

   SEADRAGON, narrowly escaping destruction when the Japanese bombed Cavite, was more than slightly damaged. Patchwork repairs were necessary so she could move Admiral Hart's staff out of Manila. On her trip to Corregidor, she delivered ammunition and took off torpedoes and spare parts as well as key personnel. In September 1942, a successful apendectomy was performed aboard ***SEADRAGON***. It was the first of three to be performed aboard U.S. subs during the war. Tokyo Rose dubbed her the "Red Pirate" because of the red lead under her damaged outer coat of paint. The nickname was cheerfully adopted by her crewmen.

   SEADRAGON at Mare Island Navy Yard undergoing re-fit on August 5, 1944.

   SEADRAGON was decommissioned on November 15, 1945, stricken from the lists and sold for scrap in 1952.

U. S. S. SEAL
S. S. 183

SEAL was built at Electric Boat Company and commissioned on April 30, 1937.

★ ★ ★ ★ ★ ★ ★ ★ ★ ★
SEAL'S WARTIME PATROLS

NO.	CAPTAIN	DATE	DUR.	BASE	AREA	CLAIMED	CONFRMED
1	KC HURD	4112	53	MANILA	W LUZON	1/1500	1/856
2	KC HURD	4202	48	JAVA	BARRIER	2/10000	0
3	KC HURD	4205	53	FREMANTLE	INDOCHINA	1/5000	1/2000
4	KC HURD	4208	53	FREMANTLE	INDOCHINA	0	0
5	KC HURD	4210	37	FREMANTLE	to PEARL	1/5500	1/5500
6	HB DODGE	4304	50	PEARL	PALAU	1/10200	1/7254
7	HB DODGE	4306	30	PEARL	EMPIRE	0	0
8	HB DODGE	4308	50	PEARL	EMPIRE	0	0
9	HB DODGE	4311	42	PEARL	MARSHALLS	0	0
10	HB DODGE	4401	50	PEARL	TRUK	0	0
11	JH TURNER	4408	41	PEARL	POLAR CIRC	3/7700	2/6330
12	JH TURNER	4410	50	PEARL	POLAR CIRC	2/10000	1/5700

SEAL'S VICTORIES

DATE	VESSEL	SIZE	TYPE	CAPTAIN	LOCATION
411223	HAYATAKA MARU	00856	FREIGHTER	KC HURD	LUZON
420528	TATSUFUKU MARU	01946	FREIGHTER	KC HURD	PALAWAN
421116	BOSTON MARU	05477	TRANSPORT	KC HURD	PALAU
430504	SAN CLEMENTE M.	07354	TANKER	HB DODGE	PALAU
440724	TOSEI MARU #5	00531	FREIGHTER	JH TURNER	HONSHU
440909	SHONAN MARU #3	05859	PASS-CARGO	JH TURNER	KIRULES
441025	HAKUYO MARU	05742	FREIGHTER	JH TURNER	KIRULES

SEAL was rammed by a merchant ship just after dispatching the ***BOSTON MARU***, and both of her periscopes were put out of commission. She took part in Operation Galvanic during the occupation of Tarawa in the Gilberts. During Operation Flintlock, she served as photo recon for the invasion of the Marshalls.

Shown at Mare Island Navy Yard during re-fit, June 22, 1944.

SEAL was decommissioned on November 15, 1945, stricken from the lists and sold for scrap in 1956.

U. S. S. SEARAVEN
S. S. 196
SEARAVEN was built at Portsmouth Navy Yard and commissioned on October 2, 1939.

★ ★ ★ ★ ★ ★ ★ ★ ★ ★

SEARAVEN'S WARTIME PATROLS

NO.	CAPTAIN	DATE	DUR.	BASE	AREA	CLAIMED	CONFIRMED
1	TC AYLWARD	4112	41	MANILA	FORMOSA	0	0
2	TC AYLWARD	4201	43	DARWIN	INDOCHINA	1/1500	0
3	H CASSEDY	4204	23	FREMANTLE	TIMOR	0	0
4	H CASSEDY	4206	40	FREMANTLE	KENDARI	0	0
5	H CASSEDY	4209	58	FREMANTLE	S CHINA SEA	2/21900	0
6	H CASSEDY	4212	55	FREMANTLE to PEARL		1 / 5900	1/5700
7	H CASSEDY	4306	43	PEARL	MARIANAS	0	0
8	H CASSEDY	4308	47	PEARL	EMPIRE	0	0
9	MH DRY	4311	49	PEARL	TRUK	1/10100	1/10000
10	MH DRY	4401	47	PEARL	TRUK	0	0
11	MH DRY	4403	45	PEARL	BONINS	2/6500	0
12	MH DRY	4408	52	PEARL	POLAR CIRC	1/5100	1/4700
13	R BERTHRONG	4411	52	PEARL	S CHINA SEA	2.5/25800	0

SEARAVEN'S VICTORIES

DATE	VESSEL	SIZE	TYPE	CAPTAIN	LOCATION
430114	SHIRAHA MARU	05693	FREIGHTER	H CASSEDY	MINDANAO
431125	TOA MARU	10052	TANKER	MH DRY	CAROLINES
440921	RIZAN MARU	04747	FREIGHTER	MH DRY	MINDANAO

SEARAVEN left on patrol as soon as the news of Pearl Harbor reached Manila. She later rescued 33 Australian soldiers from Timor under the noses of the Japanese. Like other early boats, she was plagued by faulty torpedoes. During Operation Galvanic, she worked with nine other boats to clear the way for the capture of Tarawa. Later she would do the same during Operation Flintlock in the Marshalls.

SEARAVEN at Mare Island Navy Yard after decommissioning.

SEARAVEN was decommissioned on December 11, 1945, stricken from the lists and sold for scrap in 1948.

U. S. S. SEAWOLF
S. S. 197

U.S.S. SEAWOLF
S.S. 197

SEAWOLF was built at Portsmouth Navy Yard and commissioned on December 15, 1937.

SEAWOLF'S WARTIME PATROLS

NO.	CAPTAIN	DATE	DUR.	BASE	AREA	CLAIMED	CONFIRMED
1	FB WARDER	4112	18	MANILA	E LUZON	0	0
2	FB WARDER	4112	10	MANILA	SFL MISSION	0	0
3	FB WARDER	4201	22	DARWIN	SFL MISSION	0	0
4	FB WARDER	4202	51	JAVA	BARRIER	3/14000	0
5	FB WARDER	4205	51	FREMANTLE	MANILA	0	1/1200
6	FB WARDER	4207	52	FREMANTLE	CELEBES	2/8100	2/4462
7	FB WARDER	4210	55	FREMANTLE to PEARL		3/16800	3/13000
8	RL GROSS	4304	30	PEARL	E CHINA SEA	3/13100	2/5300
9	RL GROSS	4305	56	PEARL	E CHINA SEA	1/4300	1/4700
10	RL GROSS	4308	32	PEARL	E CHINA SEA	2/15300	3/13000
11	RL GROSS	4310	53	PEARL	E CHINA SEA	2/14000	2/6399
12	RL GROSS	4312	36	PEARL	E CHINA SEA	4/24000	4.5/35793
13	RB LYNCH	4406	32	PEARL	PALAU	0	0
14	AM BONTIER	4408	24	FREMANTLE to BRISBANE		0	0
15	AM BONTIER	4409	00	BRISBANE	SPL MISSION	0	0

SEAWOLF'S VICTORIES

DATE	VESSEL	SIZE	TYPE	CAPTAIN	LOCATION
420615	NAMPO	01206	GUNBOAT	FB WARDER	MINDORO
420814	HACHIGEN MARU	03113	PASS-CARGO	FB WARDER	CELEBES
420825	SHOWA MARU II	01349	FREIGHTER	FB WARDER	CELEBES
421102	GIFU MARU	02933	FREIGHTER	FB WARDER	TALAUD ISL
421103	SAGAMI MARU	07189	PASS-CARGO	FB WARDER	SULU ARCH
421108	KEIKO MARU	02929	GUNBOAT	FB WARDER	SULU ARCH
430415	KAIHEI MARU	04575	FREIGHTER	RL GROSS	MARIANAS
430423	PATROL BOAT #39	00820	FRIGATE	RL GROSS	RYUKUS
430620	SHOJUN MARU	04739	FREIGHTER	RL GROSS	FORMOSA
430831	SHOTO MARU	05254	PASS-CARGO	RL GROSS	E CHINA SEA
430831	KOKKO MARU	05486	FREIGHTER	RL GROSS	E CHINA SEA
430901	FUSEI MARU	02256	PASS-CARGO	RL GROSS	E CHINA SEA
431029	WUHU MARU	03222	FREIGHTER	RL GROSS	HAINAN
431104	KAIFUKU MARU	03177	PASS-CARGO	RL GROSS	S CHINA SEA
440110	ASUKA MARU	07523	FREIGHTER	RL GROSS	E CHINA SEA
440110	GETSUYO MARU	06440	FREIGHTER	RL GROSS	E CHINA SEA
440111	YAHIKO MARU	05747	FREIGHTER	RL GROSS	E CHINA SEA
440114	YAMATSURU MARU	04865	FREIGHTER	RL GROSS	PHILIPPINE SEA

(Shared credit with *WHALE*)

SEAWOLF received Navy Unit Commendations for Patrols #4 and 7 under F.B. Warder, and for Patrols #10 and 12 under R.L. Gross. She tied for 7th in number of vessels sunk and stood 14th in enemy tonnage destroyed.

An aerial photo taken at sea on May 20, 1940.

SEAWOLF was sunk in error by *U.S.S. ROWELL* on October 3, 1944.

U. S. S. SKIPJACK
S. S. 184

SKIPJACK was built at Electric Boat Company and commissioned on June 30, 1938.

★ ★ ★ ★ ★ ★ ★ ★

SKIPJACK'S WARTIME PATROLS

NO.	CAPTAIN	DATE	DUR.	BASE	AREA	CLAIMED	CONFRMED
1	CL FREEMAN	4112	36	MANILA	E LUZON	0	0
2	CL FREEMAN	4201	40	DARWIN	CELEBES	0	0
3	JW COE	4204	50	FREMANTLE	CAMRAN BAY	4/280000	3/12800
4	JW COE	4207	49	FREMANTLE	JAVA SEA	0	0
5	JW COE	4209	60	FREMANTLE	to PEARL	1/7000	1/6800
6	HF STONER	4304	45	PEARL	MARSHALLS	0	0
7	HF STONER	4307	49	PEARL	EMPIRE	0	0
8	GG MOLUMPHY	4309	43	PEARL	MARSHALLS	0	0
9	GG MOLUMPHY	4401	57	PEARL	MARIANAS	2/8400	2/8200
10	RS ANDREWS	4410	49	PEARL	POLAR CIRC	0	0

SKIPJACK'S VICTORIES

DATE	VESSEL	SIZE	TYPE	CAPTAIN	LOCATION
420506	KANAN MARU #3	02567	FREIGHTER	JW COE	S CHINA SEA
420508	BUJUN MARU	04804	FREIGHTER	JW COE	S CHINA SEA
420517	TAZAN MARU	05478	PASS-CARGO	JW COE	MALAY
421014	SHUNKO MARU	06781	FREIGHTER	JW COE	PALAU
440126	OKITSU MARU	06666	TENDER	GG MOLUMPHY	CAROLINES
4401126	SUZUKAZE	01580	DESTROYER	GG MOLUMPHY	CAROLINES

SKIPJACK was enroute to Manila from Pearl Harbor during November and reached Cavite on the 18th. When war broke out, she was sent on patrol at once. She made the sea tests of the Mark 14 torpedo at Albany, Australia, were it was found to be definitely defective.

SKIPJACK at Mare Island Navy Yard during a re-fit, March 22, 1943.

SKIPJACK was decommissioned on July 28, 1946, stricken from the lists and sunk as a target in August 1948.

U. S. S. SNAPPER
S. S. 185

SNAPPER was built at Portsmouth Navy Yard and commissioned on December 15, 1937.

★ ★ ★ ★ ★ ★
SNAPPER'S WARTIME PATROLS

NO.	CAPTAIN	DATE	DUR.	BASE	AREA	CLAIMED	CONFIRMED
1	HL STONE	4112	53	MANILA	HONG KONG	4/31700	1/8662
2	HL STONE	4203	50	FREMANTLE	CORREGIDOR	1/3000	0
3	HE BAKER	4205	49	FREMANTLE	CELEBES	0	0
4	HE BAKER	4208	79	FREMANTLE	S CHINA SEA	0	0
5	AR ST ANGELO	4210	64	FREMANTLE	SOLOMONS	0	0
6	AR ST ANGELO	4301	46	BRISBANE	to PEARL	0	.5/4150
7	MK CLEMENTSON	4307	54	PEARL	TRUK	2/10400	1/860
8	MK CLEMENTSON	4310	56	PEARL	EMPIRE	3/20300	1/4575
9	WW WALKER	4403	57	PEARL	BONINS	0	0
10	WW WALKER	4405	56	PEARL	TRUK	0	0
11	WW WALKER	4409	52	PEARL	BONINS	1/4000	2/2720

SNAPPER'S VICTORIES

DATE	VESSEL	SIZE	TYPE	CAPTAIN	LOCATION
420330	UNKNOWN MARU	08662	AUX CRUISER	HL STONE	DAVAO
430126	TOKAI MARU	08358	PASS-CARGO	AR ST ANGELO	PALAU
	(Shared credit with *FLYINGFISH*)				
430902	MUTSURE	00860	FRIGATE	MK CLEMENTSON	CAROLINES
431129	KENRYU MARU	04575	FREIGHTER	MK CLEMENTSON	SHIKOKU
441001	SEISAN MARU	01990	PASS-CARGO	WW WALKER	BONINS
441001	AJIRO	00720	MINELAYER	WW WALKER	BONINS

SNAPPER was plagued by faulty torpedoes in the early months of the war. She delivered over 50 tons of food to the Corregidor defenders and took off some key personnel shortly before the island fell.

Photograph at Mare Island Navy Yard during a re-fit, February 24, 1945.

SNAPPER was decommissioned on November 15, 1945, stricken from the lists and sold for scrap in 1948.

U. S. S. SPEARFISH
S. S. 190

SPEARFISH was built at Electric Boat Company and commissioned on August 19, 1939.

★ ★ ★ ★ ★ ★ ★ ★ ★ ★ ★

SPEARFISH'S WARTIME PATROLS

NO.	CAPTAIN	DATE	DUR.	BASE	AREA	CLAIMED	CONFRMED
1	RF PRYCE	4112	51	MANILA	INDOCHINA	0	0
2	RF PRYCE	4202	27	JAVA	BARRIER	0	0
3	JC DEMPSEY	4203	54	FREMANTLE	CORREGIDOR	2/10000	2/10995
4	JC DEMPSEY	4206	52	FREMANTLE	S CHINA SEA	1/12000	0
5	JC DEMPSEY	4209	64	FREMANTLE	MANILA	1/3000	0
6	JC DEMPSEY	4212	55	BRISBANE	to PEARL	0	0
7	GA SHARP	4306	57	PEARL	TRUK	0	0
8	JW WILLIAMS	4308	47	PEARL	EMPIRE	2/12600	0
9	JW WILLIAMS	4311	41	PEARL	MARSHALLS	0	0
10	JW WILLIAMS	4401	43	PEARL	LUZON STRT	4/21800	1/3600
11	JW WILLIAMS	4404	58	PEARL	E CHINA SEA	2/14900	1/2500
12	CC COLE	4412	64	PEARL	EMPIRE	0	0

SPEARFISH'S VICTORIES

DATE	VESSEL	SIZE	TYPE	CAPTAIN	LOCATION
420417	UNKNOWN MARU	04000	FREIGHTER	JC DEMPSEY	SULU SEA
420425	TOBA MARU	06995	FREIGHTER	JC DEMPSEY	LUZON
440130	TAMASHIMA MARU	03560	PASS-CARGO	JW WILLIAMS	MARIANAS
440506	TOYOURA MARU	02510	FREIGHTER	JW WILLIAMS	E CHINA SEA

SPEARFISH was in the Philippines when war broke out and, like all of the early boats, was plagued by faulty torpedoes. She was the last sub to visit Corregidor with supplies and also evacuated key personnel, including eleven Army Nurses. Later she took part in Operation Galvanic which included the capture of Tarawa. She did recon work in Operation Flintlock in the Marshalls, and still later took pictures for the Iwo Jima Campaign.

SPEARFISH during a re-fit at Mare Island Navy Yard, May 8, 1943.

SPEARFISH was decommissioned on June 22, 1946, stricken from the lists and sold for scrap in 1947.

U. S. S. STINGRAY
S. S. 186

STINGRAY was built at Portsmouth Navy Yard and commissioned on March 15, 1938

★ ★ ★ ★ ★ ★
★ ★ ★ ★ ★ ★

STINGRAY'S WARTIME PATROLS

NO.	CAPTAIN	DATE	DUR.	BASE	AREA	CLAIMED	CONFRMED
1	RS LAMB	4112	13	MANILA	W LUZON	0	0
2	RJ MOORE	4112	44	MANILA	INDOCHINA	1/10700	1/5167
3	RJ MOORE	4203	48	FREMANTLE	JAVA SEA	0	0
4	RJ MOORE	4205	50	FREMANTLE	to PEARL	0	1/1300
5	RJ MOORE	4210	55	PEARL	TRUK	0	0
6	OJ EARLE	4301	55	PEARL	TRUK	0	0
7	OJ EARLE	4304	46	PEARL	E CHINA SEA	1/7500	1/8156
8	OJ EARLE	4306	50	PEARL	to BRISBANE	0	0
9	OJ EARLE	4308	50	BRISBANE	to PEARL	0	0
10	SC LOOMIS	4403	54	PEARL	MARIANAS	1/8600	1/3900
11	SC LOOMIS	4405	45	PEARL	MARIANAS	0	0
12	SC LOOMIS	4408	35	FREMANTLE	to BRISBANE	0	0
13	SC LOOMIS	4409	9	FREMANTLE	SPL MISSION	0	0
14	SC LOOMIS	4409	22	FREMANTLE	to BRISBANE	0	0
15	HF STONER	4412	27	BRISBANE	SPL MISSION	0	0
16	HF STONER	4501	34	FREMANTLE	SPL MISSION	0	0

STINGRAY'S VICTORIES

DATE	VESSEL	SIZE	TYPE	CAPTAIN	LOCATION
420110	HARBIN MARU	05167	TRANSPORT	RJ MOORE	S CHINA SEA
420628	SAIKYO MARU	01292	GUNBOAT	RJ MOORE	PALAU
430502	TAMON MARU	08156	FREIGHTER	OJ EARLE	E CHINA SEA
440330	IKUSHIMA MARU	03943	FREIGHTER	SC LOOMIS	MARIANAS

STINGRAY was dispatched to Lingayen from Cavite when war broke out and found Japanese invasion forces already there. Later she would lay mines in the East China Sea along the Japanese supply lines. She participated in Operation Forager ahead of the Saipan landings. She carried supplies and ammunition to Philippine guerrillas. In June 1944, she rescued an aviator off Guam under the noses of Japanese shore batteries by submerging and allowing the pilot to hook onto the periscope and be hauled out of range by that means.

STINGRAY at Mare Island Navy Yard during a refit, January 26, 1944.

STINGRAY was decommissioned on October 17, 1945, stricken from the lists and sold for scrap in 1947.

U. S. S. SWORDFISH
S. S. 193

U. S. S. SWORDFISH
S. S. 193

SWORDFISH was built at Mare Island Navy Yard and commissioned on July 22, 1939.

★ ★ ★ ★ ★ ★ ★ ★

SWORDFISH'S WARTIME PATROLS

NO.	CAPTAIN	DATE	DUR.	BASE	AREA	CLAIMED	CONFRMED
1	CC SMITH	4112	19	MANILA	INDOCHINA	0	1/8162
00	CC SMITH	4112	8	MANILA	SPL MISSION	0	0
2	CC SMITH	4201	52	JAVA	CELEBES	4/20000	1/4124
3	CC SMITH	4204	31	FREMANTLE	CORREGIDOR	0	0
4	CC SMITH	4205	50	FREMANTLE	S CHINA SEA	2/11900	2/6500
5	AC BURROWS	4207	55	FREMANTLE	CELEBES	0	0
6	CC SMITH	4210	50	BRISBANE	SOLOMONS	1/4400	0
7	JH LEWIS	4301	46	BRISBANE	SOLOMONS	1/4200	1/4200
8	FM PARKER	4307	57	PEARL	PALAU	1/7000	2/6000
9	FL BARROWS	4310	42	PEARL	EMPIRE	0	0
10	KG HENSEL	4312	40	PEARL	EMPIRE	2/15200	3/12543
11	KE MONTROSS	4403	46	PEARL	MARIANAS	0	0
12	KE MONTROSS	4405	49	PEARL	BONINS	2/7000	2/5100
13	KE MONTROSS	4412	00	PEARL	EMPIRE	0	0

SWORDFISH'S VICTORIES

DATE	VESSEL	SIZE	TYPE	CAPTAIN	LOCATION
411216	ATSUTASAN MARU	08662	FREIGHTER	CC SMITH	S CHINA SEA
420124	MYCKEN MARU	04124	FREIGHTER	CC SMITH	CELEBES
420529	UNKNOWN MARU	01900	FREIGHTER	CC SMITH	CELEBES
420612	BURMA MARU	04584	FREIGHTER	CC SMITH	MALAY
430119	MYOHO MARU	04122	FREIGHTER	JH LEWIS	SOLOMONS
430722	NISHIYAMA MARU	03016	FREIGHTER	FM PARKER	PALAU
430905	TENKAI MARU	03203	FREIGHTER	FM PARKER	PALAU
440114	YAMAKUNI MARU	06921	PASS-CARGO	KG HENSEL	SHIKOKU
440116	DELHI MARU	02182	GUNBOAT	KG HENSEL	SHIKOKU
440127	KASAGI MARU	03140	SALVG VESL	KG HENSEL	SHIKOKU
440609	MATSUKAZE	01270	DESTROYER	KE MONTROSS	BONINS
440615	KANSEISHI MARU	04804	FREIGHTER	KE MONTROSS	BONINS

SWORDFISH was stationed at Cavite when war broke out. She has been credited with the first confirmed sinking of a Japanese ship in World War II. She left on her 13th patrol on December 22, 1944, to carry out a photo recon mission off Okinawa. Whether she struck a mine or was the victim of an unrecorded anti-submarine attack is not known, but she was not heard from again.

SWORDFISH docking at Mare Island Navy Yard for a re-fit, June 13, 1943.

U. S. S. STURGEON
S. S. 187

STURGEON was built at Mare Island Navy Yard and commissioned on June 25, 1938.

★ ★ ★ ★ ★ ★ ★ ★ ★ ★

STURGEON'S WARTIME PATROLS

NO.	CAPTAIN	DATE	DUR.	BASE	AREA	CLAIMED	CONFRMED
1	WL WRIGHT	4112	17	MANILA	FORMOSA	0	0
2	WL WRIGHT	4112	46	MANILA	CELEBES	3/20000	0
3	WL WRIGHT	4203	53	FREMANTLE	JAVA SEA	2/6500	2/1592
4	WL WRIGHT	4206	47	FREMANTLE	MANILA	1/10000	1/7300
5	HA PZNKWSKI	4209	51	BRISBANE	SOLOMONS	1/17000	1/8033
6	HA PZNKWSKI	4211	51	BRISBANE	to PEARL	0	0
7	HA PZNKWSKI	4306	51	PEARL	EMPIRE	0	0
8	CL MURPHY	4308	59	PEARL	EMPIRE	0	0
9	CL MURPHY	4312	55	PEARL	EMPIRE	3/19200	2/8603
10	CL MURPHY	4404	50	PEARL	BONINS	3/15400	1/2000
11	CL MURPHY	4406	55	PEARL	EMPIRE	2/18600	2/14000

STURGEON'S VICTORIES

DATE	VESSEL	SIZE	TYPE	CAPTAIN	LOCATION
420330	CHOKO MARU #4	00842	FREIGHTER	WL WRIGHT	MOLUCCA STRT
420403	UNKNOWN	00750	FRIGATE	WL WRIGHT	MOLUCCA STRT
420701	MONTEVIDEO MARU	07267	TRANSPORT	WL WRIGHT	LUZON
421001	KATSURAGI MARU	08033	ARCF FERRY	HA PZNKWSKI	BISMARCKS
440111	ERIE MARU	05493	FREIGHTER	CL MURPHY	KYUSHU
440124	CHOSEN MARU	03110	FREIGHTER	CL MURPHY	KYUSHU
440411	SEIRYU MARU	01904	FREIGHTER	CL MURPHY	BONINS
440629	TOYAMA MARU	07089	PASS-CARGO	CL MURPHY	E CHINA SEA
440703	TAIRIN MARU	06862	FREIGHTER	CL MURPHY	KYUSHU

STURGEON made her first patrol from Cavite and covered the Formosa area. Like all the Asiatic Squadron boats, she suffered from faulty torpedoes. The abbreviated name on Patrols 6 and 7 is Pieczentkowski.

STURGEON at Mare Island Navy Yard during a re-fit, May 3, 1943.

STURGEON was decommissioned on November 15, 1945, and sold for scrap in 1948.

TAMBOR CLASS

"T" or ***TAMBOR*** Class boats evolved from the ***SALMON*** Class. Although they were slightly smaller, the number of torpedo tubes was increased to ten (six forward and four aft). Top surface speed was 20 knots and range was 10,000 miles. Twelve were built during the late thirties and early forties. A *"T"* Class boat, ***TAUTOG***, scored the highest number of confirmed sinkings in World War II (26) for an American submarine.

U. S. S. TAMBOR
S. S. 198

U. S. S. TAMBOR
S. S. 198

TAMBOR was built at Electric Boat Company and commissioned on June 3, 1940.

TAMBOR'S WARTIME PATROLS

NO.	CAPTAIN	DATE	DUR.	BASE	AREA	CLAIMED	CONFIRMED
1	JW MURPHY	4112	35	PEARL	WAKE	0	0
2	JW MURPHY	4203	58	PEARL	MARSHALLS	1/7000	0
00	JW MURPHY	4205	15	PEARL	MIDWAY	0	0
3	SH AMBRUSTER	4207	57	PEARL	to FREMANTLE	2/12000	2/5800
4	SH AMBRUSTER	4210	38	FREMANTLE	INDOCHINA	1/10000	1/2500
5	SH AMBRUSTER	4212	41	FREMANTLE	SUNDS STRT	0	0
6	SH AMBRUSTER	4302	55	FREMANTLE	DAVAO	0	0
7	R KEFAUVER	4305	50	FREMANTLE	INDOCHINA	3/170C0	1/2500
8	R KEFAUVER	4306	55	FREMANTLE	to PEARL	1/4400	0
9	R KEFAUVER	4401	60	PEARL	E CHINA SEA	4/30100	4/18400
10	R KEFAUVER	4404	54	PEARL	MARIANAS	1/6700	1/650
11	WJ GMRHASN	4407	47	PEARL	POLAR CIRC	1/4000	1/2300
12	WJ GMRHASN	4410	55	PEARL	EMPIRE	2/5200	1/1200

TAMBOR'S VICTORIES

DATE	VESSEL	SIZE	TYPE	CAPTAIN	LOCATION
420707	SHOFUKU	00871	TENDER	SH AMBRUSTER	MARSHALLS
420721	SHINSEI MARU #6	04928	PASS-CARGO	SH AMBRUSTER	CAROLINES
421103	CHIKUGO MARU	02461	FREIGHTER	SH AMBRUSTER	S CHINA SEA
430529	EISHO MARU	02486	FREIGHTER	SH AMBRUSTER	S CHINA SEA
440129	SHUNTAI MARU	02253	FREIGHTER	R KEFAUVER	RYUKUS
440203	ARIAKE MARU	05000	FREIGHTER	R KEFAUVER	E CHINA SEA
440203	GOYO MARU	08436	TANKER	R KEFAUVER	E CHINA SEA
440212	RONSAN MARU	02735	PASS-CARGO	R KEFAUVER	RYUKUS
440526	CHIYO MARU #3	00657	FREIGHTER	R KEFAUVER	PHILIPN SEA
440713	TOEI MARU #4	02324	FREIGHTER	W GERMERSHAUSEN	KIRULES
441102	EIKA MARU	01248	PASS-CARGO	W GERMERSHAUSEN	TONKIN GULF

TAMBOR was already conducting a war patrol off Wake when war broke out and she was recalled to Pearl. Her covering operation at Midway was not counted as a patrol. She was the indirect cause of damage to two Japanese cruisers as they collided trying to take evasive action. She made deliveries of ammunition and money to Philippine guerrillas and took part in Operation Hotfoot to sweep Task Force 38's route to Japan proper.

At sea off Provincetown, Massachusetts, April 8, 1940.

TAMBOR was decommissioned on December 10, 1945, stricken from the lists and sold for scrap in 1959.

U. S. S. GAR
S. S. 206

U. S. S. GAR
S. S. 206

GAR was built at Electric Boat Company and commissioned on April 14, 1941.

GAR'S WARTIME PATROLS

NO.	CAPTAIN	DATE	DUR.	BASE		AREA	CLAIMED	CONFIRMELD
1	D McGREGOR	4202	54	PEARL		EMPIRE	1/10000	1/1520
2	D McGREGOR	4204	50	PEARL	to	FREMANTLE	1/4000	0
3	D McGREGOR	4207	50	FREMANTLE		S CHINA SEA	0	0
4	D McGREGOR	4209	51	FREMANTLE		S CHINA SEA	0	0
5	PD QUIRK	4211	53	FREMANTLE		MANILA	0	1/600
6	PD QUIRK	4302	53	FREMANTLE		S CHINA SEA	0	0
7	PD QUIRK	4304	34	FREMANTLE		MANILA	5/10500	3/8000
8	PD QUIRK	4306	34	FREMANTLE		JAVA SEA	0	0
9	GW LAUTRUP	4308	37	FREMANTLE		CELEBES	1/4000	1/1000
10	GW LAUTRUP	4312	55	FREMANTLE	to	PEARL	3/2 1500	2/9000
11	GW LAUTRUP	4403	49	PEARL		PALAU	0	0
12	GW LAUTRUP	4405	47	PEARL		BONINS	1/900	0
13	M FERRARA	4408	54	PEARL	to	BRISBANE	0	0
14	M FERRARA	4411	26	BRISBANE		SPL MISSION	1/1000	0
15	M FERRARA	4412	24	BRISBANE	to	PEARL	0	0

GAR'S VICTORIES

DATE	VESSEL	SIZE	TYPE	CAPTAIN	LOCATION
420313	CHICHIBU MARU	01520	FREIGHTER	C McGREGOR	HONSHU
421208	HEINAN MARU	00661	FREIGHTER	PD QUIRK	MAKASSAR
430509	ASO MARU #3	00703	FREIGHTER	PD QUIRK	SULU SEA
430515	MEIKAI MARU	03197	PASS-CARGO	PD QUIRK	SAMAR
430515	INDUS MARU	04361	PASS-CARGO	PD QUIRK	SAMAR
430720	SEIZAN MARU #7	00955	FREIGHTER	GW LAUTRUP	MAKASSAR
440120	KOYU MARU	05325	FREIGHTER	GW LAUTRUP	PALAU
440123	TAINAN MARU #3	03625	FREIGHTER	GW LAUTRUP	PALAU

GAR was assigned, along with five other boats, to mine the waters around the Gulf of Siam. They planted the first U.S. mines laid during the war. She later pulled lifeguard duty during Operation Desecrate and rescued eight fliers, a record up to that time.

GAR, shown at rest, probably at Mare Island Navy Yard.

GAR was decommissioned on December 12, 1945, stricken from the lists and sold for scrap in May 1959.

U.S.S. GRAMPUS
S.S. 207

GRAMPUS was built at Electric Boat Company and commissioned on May 23, 1941.

★ ★ ★
GRAMPUS'S WARTIME PATROLS

NO.	CAPTAIN	DATE	DUR.	BASE	AREA	CLAIMED	CONFIRMED
1	E HUTCHINSON	4202	48	PEARL	MARSHALLS	2/20000	1/8636
2	E HUTCHINSON	4204	51	PEARL	TRUK	0	0
3	E HUTCHINSON	4207	54	FREMANTLE	MANILA	0	0
4	JR CRAIG	4210	58	BRISBANE	SOLOMONS	1/1400	0
5	JR CRAIG	4212	37	BRISBANE	SOLOMONS	3/24000	0
6	JR CRAIG	4302	00	BRISBANE	SOLOMONS	0	0

GRAMPUS'S VICTORIES

DATE	VESSEL	SIZE	TYPE	CAPTAIN	LOCATION
420501	KAIJO MARU #2	08636	TANKER	E HUTCHINSON	CAROLINES

GRAMPUS took part in the Guadalcanal Campaign along with *GRAYBACK* and *GROWLER.* She landed coast watchers on Vella LaVella and Choisuel Islands. On February 14 she was ordered to patrol the Buka-Shortland-Rabaul area, and a week later, Bougainville. She was warned of the presence of two Japanese destroyers entering Blackett Strait. It is generally believed that *GRAMPUS* went down in a night surface action with those two destroyers.

GRAMPUS at Electric Boat Company, Groton, Connecticut, March 26, 1941.

U. S. S. GRAYBACK
S. S. 208

GRAYBACK was built at Electric Boat Company and commissioned on June 30, 1941.

★ ★ ★ ★ ★ ★ ★ ★
GRAYBACK'S WARTIME PATROLS

NO.	CAPTAIN	DATE	DUR.	BASE	AREA	CLAIMED	CONFIRMED
1	WA SAUNDERS	4202	54	PEARL	MARIANAS	2/111800	1/3291
2	WA SAUNDERS	4205	50	PEARL	to FREMANTLE	0	0
3	WA SAUNDERS	4207	51	FREMANTLE	INDOCHINA	0	0
4	JR CRAIG	4210	41	BRISBANE	SOLOMONS	2/15200	0
5	EC STEPHAN	4212	47	BRISBANE	SOLOMONS	1/2C00	1/2000
6	EC STEPHAN	4302	47	BRISBANE	SOLOMONS	1/0400	0
7	EC STEPHAN	4304	36	BRISBANE	to PEARL	0	2/12300
8	JA MOORE	4305	45	PEARL	E CHINA SEA	2.5/18700	2.5/19000
9	JA MOORE	4312	33	PEARL	E CHINA SEA	6/24000	4/10000
10	JA MOORE	4401	00	PEARL	E CHINA SEA	4/20800	4/16689

GRAYBACK'S VICTORIES

DATE	VESSEL	SIIZE	TYPE	CAPTAIN	LOCATION
420317	ISHIKAR MARU	03251	FREIGHTER	WA SAUNDERS	BONINS
430102	I-18	02180	SUBMARINE	EC STEPHAN	SOLOMONS
430511	YODOGAWA MARU	06441	FREIGHTER	EC STEPHAN	MUSSAU
430517	ENGLAND MARU	05830	FREIGHTER	EC STEPHAN	MANUS
431014	KOZUI MARU	07072	PASS-CARGO	JA MOORE	RYUKYUS
431022	AWATA MARU	07397	CRUISER	JA MOORE	E CHINA SEA
431027	FUJI MARU	09138	TRANSPORT	JA MOORE	E CHINA SEA
	(Shared credit with **SHAD**).				
431218	GYOKUREI MARU	05588	FREIGHTER	JA MOORE	RYUKYUS
431219	NUMIKAZI	01300	DESTROYER	JA MOORE	OKINAWA
431221	KONAN MARU II	02027	FREIGHTER	JA MOORE	OSUMI ISL
431221	KASHIWA MARU	00515	TENDER	JA MOORE	OSUMI ISL
440219	TAIKEI MARU	04735	FREIGHTER	JA MOORE	PESCADORES
440219	TOSHIN MARU	01917	FREIGHTER	JA MOORE	PESCADORES
440224	NAMPO MARU	10033	TANKER	JA MOORE	FORMOSA
440227	CEYLON MARU	04905	FREIGHTER	JA MOORE	KYUSHU

GRAYBACK received Navy Unit Commendations for Patrol #7 under E.C. Stephan, and for Patrols #8, 9, and 10 under J.A. Moore. On February 27, 1944, a Japanese carrier plane surprised **GRAYBACK** on the surface. The first bomb was a direct hit. The boat exploded and sank immediately. A wartime appendectomy was performed aboard her

GRAYBACK, at Mare Island Navy Yard during a re-fit on August 26, 1943.

At Pearl Harbor on 31 December 1941 hoisted 4-star
Admiral flag on U.S.S. Grayling reassumed took
Command of U. S. Pacific Fleet.

C.W. Nimitz, Fleet Admiral, USN

U. S. S. GRAYLING
S. S. 209

U.S.S. GRAYLING
S.S. 209

GRAYLING was built at Portsmouth Navy Yard and commissioned on March 1, 1941.

★ ★ ★ ★ ★ ★

GRAYLING'S WARTIME PATROLS

NO.	CAPTAIN	DATE	DUR.	BASE		AREA	CLAIMED	CONFRMED
1	E OLSEN	4201	61	PEARL		CAROLINES	0	0
2	E OLSEN	4203	51	PEARL		EMPIRE	1/6000	1/6343
00	FW FENNO	4205	15	PEARL		MIDWAY	0	0
3	E OLSEN	4207	43	PEARL		TRUK	1/10000	0
4	JE LEE	4210	55	PEARL	to	FREMANTLE	1/5300	1/4000
5	JE LEE	4301	49	FREMANTLE		MANILA	3/14400	1/750
6	JE LEE	4303	38	FREMANTLE		MANILA	3/14600	1/4000
7	JE LEE	4305	50	FREMANTLE		S CHINA SEA	1/5600	0
8	RM BRINKER	4306	00	FREMANTLE	to	PEARL	1/5500	1/5500

GRAYLING'S VICTORIES

DATE	VESSEL	SIZE	TYPE	CAPTAIN	LOCATION
420513	RYUJIN MARU	06243	FREIGHTER	E OLSEN	KYUSHU
421110	UNKNOWN MARU	04000	FREIGHTER	JE LEE	CAROLINES
430126	USHIO MARU	00749	FREIGHTER	JE LEE	CAROLINES
430509	SHANGHAI MARU	04103	FREIGHTER	JE LEE	CAROLINES
430727	MEIZAN MARU	05480	PASS-CARGO	RM BRINKER	CAROLINES

GRAYLING took part in the Battle of Midway screening action. During this operation, **GRAYLING** was mistakenly bombed by a flight of American B-17s who reported sinking a Japanese cruiser in 15 seconds. Fortunately, their aim in this instance was as bad as during the battle, as **GRAYLING** executed a crash dive and escaped. In July 1943, **GRAYLING** made supply deliveries to the Philippines, completing the mission on August 23. The first week in September, she failed to answer calls from base. On September 30, 1943, she was reported lost with all hands.

This historic pre-war builder's photo was signed by Admiral Chester W. Nimitz when he took command of the Pacific Fleet. The inscription reads: "At Pearl Harbor on 31 December 1941 hoisted 4-star Admiral's flag on U.S.S. Grayling and took command of the U.S. Pacific Fleet."

———————————

At the end of World War II, when Allied designers were able to access German and Japanese submarine plans, they discovered they were "embarrassingly better than ours."

U. S. S. GRENADIER
S. S. 210

GRENADIER was built at Portsmouth Navy Yard and commissioned on May 1, 1941.

★ ★ ★ ★

GRENADIER'S WARTIME PATROLS

NO.	CAPTAIN	DATE	DUR.	BASE	AREA	CLAIMED	CONFRMED
1	AR JOYCE	4202	48	PEARL	EMPIRE	0	0
2	WA LENT	4204	59	PEARL	E CHINA SEA	2/24000	1/14500
3	BL CARR	4207	67	PEARL to	FREMANTLE	1/15000	0
4	BL CARR	4210	58	FREMANTLE	INDOCHINA	0	0
5	J FITZGERALD	4301	51	FREMANTLE	JAVA SEA	2/1300	0
6	J FITZGERALD	4303	00	FREMANTLE	MALACCA STR	0	0

GRENADIER'S VICTORY

DATE	VESSEL	SIZE	TYPE	CAPTAIN	LOCATION
420508	TAIYO MARU	14457	TRANSPORT	WA LENT	E CHINA SEA

GRENADIER was deployed in the screen at the Battle of Midway, but had no opportunity for shooting. She was also part of the Truk Blockade, and participated in the first mining by submarines operation in the war. On April 21, 1943, on her sixth patrol in the Penang area, she was struck by an aircraft bomb and badly damaged. Despite heroic efforts on the part of all the ship's company, the boat could not be saved. Her crew were taken prisoner. All but four survived Japanese mistreatment to see war's end and freedom.

Photo taken at Portsmouth Navy Yard on December 27, 1941.

U. S. S. GUDGEON
S. S. 211

GUDGEON was built at Mare Island Navy Yard and commissioned on April 21, 1941.

★ ★ ★ ★ ★ ★ ★ ★ ★ ★ ★
GUDGEON'S WARTIME PATROLS

NO.	CAPTAIN	DATE	DUR.	BASE	AREA	CLAIMED	CONFIRM
1	EW GRENFELL	4112	50	PEARL	EMPIRE	2/6500	1/1800
2	EW GRENFELL	4202	52	PEARL	E CHINA SEA	2/15000	2/8000
3	HB LYON	4204	20	PEARL	MIDWAY	0	0
4	WS STOVALL	4207	53	PEARL to	FREMANTLE	4135000	1/4900
5	WS STOVALL	4210	54	BRISBANE	SOLOMONS	3122000	1/6783
6	WS STOVALL	4212	53	BRISBANE	MANILA	0	0
7	WS POST, Jr	4303	24	FREMANTLE	JAVA SEA	4/29600	2/15000
8	WS POST, Jr	4304	41	FREMANTLE to PEARL		3119600	2/23000
9	WS POST, Jr	4309	37	PEARL	MARIANAS	2/15000	1/3158
10	WS POST, Jr	4310	41	PEARL	E CHINA SEA	3/13700	2/7644
11	WS POST, Jr	4401	49	PEARL	E CHINA SEA	1/10000	0
12	RA BONIN	4404	00	PEARL	MARIANAS	0	0

GUDGEON'S VICTORIES

DATE	VESSEL	SIZE	TYPE	CAPTAIN	LOCATION
420127	I-173	01785	SUBMARINE	EW GRENFELL	N LYSAN IS
420326	UNKNOWN MARU	04000	FREIGHTER	EW GRENFELL	SHICHITO
420327	UNKNOWN MARU	04000	FREIGHTER	EW GRENFELL	SHICHITO
420703	NANIWA MARU	04850	FREIGHTER	WS STOVALL	MARSHALLS
421021	CHOKO MARU	06783	PASS-CARGO	WS STOVALL	BISMARCKS
430322	MEIGEN MARU	05434	FREIGHTER	WS POST, Jr	JAVA SEA
430329	TOHO MARU	09997	TANKER	WS POST, Jr	MAKASSER
430428	KAMAKURA MARU	17526	TRANSPORT	WS POST, Jr	SULU SEA
430512	SUMATRA MARU	05862	FREIGHTER	WS POST, Jr	SAMAR
430828	TAINAN MARU II	03158	PASS-CARGO	WS POST, Jr	MARIANAS
431123	NEKKA MARU	06784	TRANSPORT	WS POST, Jr	E CHINA SEA
431123	WAKAMIYA	00860	FRIGATE	WS POST, Jr	E CHINA SEA

GUDGEON was conducting training exercises off Maui on the morning of December 7, 1941. She conducted the first patrol of the war with *PLUNGER* and headed for Empire waters. She made history by sinking the first enemy warship to go down from the fire of a U.S. submarine. On April 18, 1944, the Japanese reported making two direct hits on a U.S. submarine during an air attack. This was probably *GUDGEON* as she failed to report in after that date. *GUDGEON* received Presidential Unit Citations for Patrols #1 and 2 under E.W. Grenfell, for Patrol #3 under H.B. Lyon, and Patrols #4, 5, 6, 7, and 8 under W.S. Post, Jr.

U. S. S. TAUTOG
S. S. 199

U. S. S. TAUTOG
S. S. 199

TAUTOG was built at Electric Boat Company and commissioned on July 3, 1940.

★ ★ ★ ★
★ ★ ★ ★ ★ ★ ★ ★ ★ ★

TAUTOG'S WARTIME PATROLS

NO.	CAPTAIN	DATE	DUR.	BASE	AREA	CLAIMED	CONFIRMED
1	JH WILINGHM	4112	41	PEARL	MARSHALLS	0	0
2	JH WILINGHM	4204	47	PEARL	to FREMANTLE	6/19500	3/7500
3	JH WILINGHM	4207	57	FREMANTLE	CELEBES	1/7000	1/5900
4	JH WILINGHM	4210	44	FREMANTLE	INDOCHINA	1/5100	1/4000
5	WB SIEGLAFF	4212	46	FREMANTLE	JAVA SEA	2/6900	2/2900
6	WB SIEGLAFF	4302	53	FREMANTLE	FLORES SEA	2/6800	2/7000
7	WB SIEGLAFF	4305	53	FREMANTLE	to PEARL	2/14300	2/5300
8	WB SIEGLAFF	4310	41	PEARL	PALAU	1/3800	1/100
9	WB SIEGLAFF	4312	49	PEARL	EMPIRE	2/9700	2/6000
10	WB SIEGLAFF	4402	28	PEARL	POLAR CIRC	5/17700	4/11277
11	TS BASKETT	4404	35	PEARL	POLAR CIRC	4/20500	4/16100
12	TS BASKETT	4406	48	PEARL	EMPIRE	2/4300	2/2787
13	TS BASKETT	4412	42	PEARL	E CHINA SEA	3/8500	2/3300

TAUTOG'S VICTORIES

DATE	VESSEL	SIZE	TYPE	CAPTAIN	LOCATION
420426	RO-30	00965	SUBMARINE	J WILLINGHAM	MARSHALLS
420517	I-28	02212	SUBMARINE	J WILLINGHAM	CAROLINES
420525	SHOKA MARU	04467	FREIGHTER	J WILLINGHAM	CAROLINES
420706	OHIO MARU	05867	PASS-CARGO	J WILLINGHAM	S CHINA SEA
421027	UNKNOWN MARU	04000	PASS-CARGO	J WILLINGHAM	S CHINA SEA
421225	BANSHU MARU #2	01000	FREIGHTER	WB SIEGLAFF	TIMOR
430122	HASSHU MARU	01873	PASS-CARGO	WB SIEGLAFF	FLORES SEA
430409	ISONAMI	01950	DESTROYER	WB S1EGLAFF	BANDA SEA
430419	PENANG MARU	05214	FREIGHTER	WB SIEGLAFF	BANDA SEA
430606	SHINEI MARU #3	00973	FREIGHTER	WB SIEGLAFF	CELEBES
430620	MEITEN MARU	04474	FREIGHTER	WB SIEGLAFF	PHILIPPINE SEA
431104	SUBCHASER #30	00100	SUB CHASER	WB SIEGLAFF	PALAU
440103	SAISHU MARU	02082	FREIGHTER	WB SIEGLAFF	SHIKOKU
440103	U S A MARU	03943	FREIGHTER	WB SIEGLAFF	SHIKOKU
440313	RYUA MARU	01925	FREIGHTER	WB SIEGLAFF	KIRULES
440313	SHOJUN MARU II	01942	FREIGHTER	WB SIEGLAFF	KIRULES
440316	SHIRAKUMO	01950	DESTROYER	WB SIEGLAFF	KIRULES
440316	NICHIREN MARU	05460	FREIGHTER	WB SIEGLAFF	KIRULES
440502	RYOYO MARU	05973	PASS-CARGO	TS BASKETT	KIRULES
440503	FUSHIMI MARU II	04935	PASS-CARGO	TS BASKETT	KIRULES
440508	MIYAZAKI MARU	03944	PASS-CARGO	TS BASKETT	KIRULES
440512	BANEI MARU #2	01186	FREIGHTER	TS BASKETT	HONSHU
440708	MATSU MARU	00887	FREIGHTER	TS BASKETT	HONSHU
440702	KONEI MARU II	01922	FREIGHTER	TS BASKETT	SHIKOKU
450117	TRANSPORT #15	01500	LANDING CRFT	TS BASKETT	RYUKUS
450120	SHURI MARU	01857	TENDER	TS BASKETT	E CHINA SEA

TAUTOG received Navy Unit Commendations for Patrols #2, 3, 4, 5, 6, 8, 9, 10, and 11. She was 1st in vessels sunk and 11th in total tonnage destroyed.

TAUTOG during a re-fit at Hunters Point, California, September 16, 1943.

TAUTOG was decommissioned on December 8, 1945, stricken from the lists and sold for scrap in 1959.

U. S. S. THRESHER
S. S. 200

U. S. S. THRESHER
S. S. 200

THRESHER was built at Electric Boat Company and commissioned on August 27, 1940.

THRESHER'S WARTIME PATROLS

NO.	CAPTAIN	DATE	DUR.	BASE	AREA	CLAIMED	CONFIRMED
1	WL ANDERSON	4112	22	PEARL	WAKE	0	0
2	WL ANDERSON	4112	58	PEARL	MARSHALLS	1/4500	0
3	WL ANDERSON	4203	37	PEARL	DOOLITLE RAID	1/5000	1/3039
4	WJ MILLICAN	4206	50	PEARL to	FREMANTLE	1/6000	1/4800
5	WJ MILLICAN	4209	61	FREMANTLE	S CHINA SEA	1/3000	1/3000
6	WJ MILLICAN	4212	25	FREMANTLE	JAVA SEA	2/17000	1/2700
7	WJ MILLICAN	4301	45	FREMANTLE	SUNDS STRT	2/14000	2/11000
8	H HULL	4304	50	FREMANTLE	JAVA SEA	0	0
9	H HULL	4306	42	FREMANTLE to	PEARL	2/20000	1/1500
10	H HULL	4311	29	PEARL	TRUK	1/5600	1/4862
11	D MacMILLEN	4312	54	PEARL	E CHINA SEA	2/26300	4/14523
12	D MacMILLEN	4403	51	PEARL	TRUK	0	0
13	D MacMILLEN	4406	44	PEARL	LUZON STRT	6/35100	2/7700
14	J MIDDLETON	4408	50	PEARL	E CHINA SEA	3/20600	3/9170
15	J MIDDLETON	4501	82	PEARL	LUZON STRT	0	0

THRESHER'S VICTORIES

DATE	VESSEL	SIZE	TYPE	CAPTAIN	LOCATION
420410	SADO MARU	03039	FREIGHTER	WL ANDERSON	SHIKOKU
420709	SHINSHO MARU	04836	TENDER	WJ MILLICAN	EBON ISL
421031	UNKNOWN MARU	03000	FREIGHTER	WJ MILLICAN	FLORES SEA
421229	HACHIAN MARU	02733	FREIGHTER	WJ MILLICAN	JAVA SEA
430221	KUWAYAMA MARU	05724	FREIGHTER	WJ MILLICAN	SUNDA ISLES
430302	TOEN MARU	05232	TANKER	WJ MILLICAN	JAVA SEA
430701	YONEYAMA MARU	05274	PASS-CARGO	H HULL	MAKASSAR STR
431113	MUKO MARU	04862	TRANSPORT	H HULL	CAROLINES
440115	TATSUNO MARU	06960	FREIGHTER	DC MacMILLAN	LUZON
440115	TOHO MARU II	04092	FREIGHTER	DC MacMILLAN	LUZON
440127	KIKUZUKI MARU	01266	FREIGHTER	DC MacMILLEN	S CHINA SEA
440127	KOSEI MARU #5	02205	FREIGHTER	DC MacMILLEN	S CHINA SEA
440717	SAINEI MARU	04916	FREIGHTER	DC MacMILLEN	LUZON
440717	SHOZAN MARU II	02838	FREIGHTER	DC MacMILLEN	LUZON
440918	GYOKU MARU	06854	FREIGHTER	J MIDDLETON	YELLOW SEA
440925	NISSEI MARU	01468	FREIGHTER	J MIDDLETON	YELLOW SEA
440926	KOETSU MARU	00873	FREIGHTER	J MIDDLETON	YELLOW SEA

THRESHER received a Navy Unit Commendation for Patrol #13 under D.C. McMillen. She was at sea during the Pearl Harbor attack and was attacked by a U.S. destroyer and again by U.S. planes on her way in. She made the trip to Japan to play forecaster and observer for the Doolittle Raid. *THRESHER* tied for 12th in number of vessels sunk and stood 18th in tonnage destroyed.

A pre-war builder's photo taken at Electric Boat Company, August 1940.

THRESHER was decommissioned on December 13, 1945, stricken from the lists and sold for scrap in 1948.

U. S. S. TRITON
S. S. 201

TRITON was built at Portsmouth Navy Yard and commissioned on August 15, 1940.

★ ★ ★ ★ ★
TRITON'S WARTIME PATROLS

NO.	CAPTAIN	DATE	DUR	BASE	AREA	CLAIMED	CONFIRMED
1	WA LENT	4112	42	PEARL	WAKE	0	0
2	WA LENT	4201	52	PEARL	E CHINA SEA	2/12000	2/5982
3	C KIRKPATRICK	4204	52	PEARL	E CHINA SEA	5/24200	5/15843
4	C KIRKPATRICK	4206	60	PEARL	ALASKA	2/3100	1/1600
5	C KIRKPATRICK	4212	40	PEARL	to BRISBANE	3/17300	2/5300
6	GK MacKENZIE	4302	00	BRISBANE	SOLOMONS	2/8000	1/3000

TRITON'S VICTORIES

DATE	VESSEL	SIZE	TYPE	CAPTAIN	LOCATION
420217	SHINYO MARU #3	01498	FREIGHTER	WA LENT	E CHINA SEA
420221	SHOKYO MARU	04484	FREIGHTER	WA LENT	E CHINA SEA
420423	UNKNOWN MARU	01000	TRAWLER	C KIRKPATRICK	BONINS
420501	CALCUTTA MARU	05339	PASS-CARGO	C KIRKPATRICK	E CHINA SEA
420506	TAIEI MARU	02209	FREIGHTER	C KIRKPATRICK	E CHINA SEA
420506	TAIGEN MARU	05660	PASS-CARGO	C KIRKPATRICK	E CHINA SEA
420517	I-164	01635	SUBMARINE	C KIRKPATRICK	KYUKUS
420704	NENOHI	01600	DESTROYER	C KIRKPATRICK	KIRULES
421224	AMAKASU MARU	01913	TANKER	C KIRKPATRICK	WAKE
421228	OMI MARU	03393	PASS-CARGO	C KIRKPATRICK	CAROLINES
430306	KIRIHA MARU	03057	FREIGHTER	GK MacKENZIE	CAROLINES

TRITON was patrolling off Wake when war broke out and was a witness to the attack on that island. She was in the guide line from Midway to Wake to mark the way for the mid-December, 1942, B-25 attack on Wake. On March 11, 1943, she sent her last message—she was attacking a convoy. Three Japanese destroyers forced her down deep and worked her over. They later reported oil, cork and other flotsam coming up as the *TRITON* was lost with all hands.

This wartime photo of *TRITON* was taken at Anchorage, Alaska.

U. S. S. Trout
S. S. 202

TROUT was built at Portsmouth Navy Yard and commissioned on November 15, 1940.

★ ★ ★ ★ ★ ★ ★ ★ ★ ★ ★

TROUT'S WARTIME PATROLS

NO.	CAPTAIN	DATE	DUR.	BASE		AREA	CLAIMED	CONFIRMED
1	FW FENNO	4112	22	PEARL		MIDWAY	0	0
2	FW FENNO	4201	5C	PEARL		CORREGIDOR	1/1520	1/2719
3	FW FENNO	4203	54	PEARL		EMPIRE	5/31000	2/7133
4	FW FENNO	4205	15	PEARL		MIDWAY	0	0
5	LP RAMAGE	4208	47	PEARL	to	BRISBANE	1/8200	1/900
6	LP RAMAGE	4210	28	BRISBANE		SOLOMONS	0	0
7	LP RAMAGE	4212	58	FREMANTLE		INDOCHINA	2/10800	2/4900
8	LP RAMAGE	4303	42	FREMANTLE		S CHINA SEA	0	0
9	AH CLARK	4305	59	FREMANTLE		INDOCHINA	3/17200	2/5800
10	AH CLARK	4308	54	FREMANTLE	to	PEARL	3/15000	3/12542
11	AH CLARK	4402	00	PEARL		E CHINA SEA	1/9200	1/7100

TROUT'S VICTORIES

DATE	VESSEL	SIZE	TYPE	CAPTAIN	LOCATION
420210	CHUWA MARU	02719	FREIGHTER	FW FENNO	FORMOSA
420402	UZAN MARU	05014	FREIGHTER	FW FENNO	SHIKOKU
420504	KONGOSAN MARU	02119	GUNBOAT	FW FENNO	SHIKOKU
420921	KOEI MARU	00863	TENDER	LP RAMAGE	CAROLINES
430121	UNKNOWN MARU	02984	FREIGHTER	LP RAMAGE	S CHINA SEA
430214	HIROTAMA MARU	01911	GUNBOAT	LP RAMAGE	MAKASSAR STR
430615	SANRAKU MARU	03000	TANKER	AH CLARK	CELEBES
430702	ISUZU MARU	02866	FREIGHTER	AH CLARK	MINDORO
430909	I-182	01630	SUBMARINE	AH CLARK	SULU SEA
430923	RYOTOKU MARU	03483	FREIGHTER	AH CLARK	MARIANAS
430923	YAMASHIRO MARU	03429	PASS-CARGO	AH CLARK	MARIANAS
440229	SAKITO MARU	07126	PASS-CARGO	AH CLARK	PHILIPN SEA

TROUT received Presidential Unit Citations for Patrols #2 and 3 under F.W. Fenno, and for Patrol #5 under L.P. Ramage. She was on patrol off Midway when war broke out. She carried anti-aircraft ammunition to Corregidor and on the return trip hauled two tons of gold bars and eighteen tons of silver coins to safety. While attacking a convoy in her patrol area, she was sunk with all hands by a hunter-killer group.

TROUT, during a re-fit at Hunter's Point, California, December 11, 1943.

U. S. S. TUNA
S. S. 203

TUNA was built at Mare Island Navy Yard and commissioned on January 1, 1941.

★ ★ ★ ★ ★ ★ ★
TUNA'S WARTIME PATROLS

NO.	CAPTAIN	DATE	DUR.	BASE		AREA	CLAIMED	CONFIRMED
1	JL DeTAR	4201	54	PEARL		EMPIRE	1/6000	1/4000
2	JL DeTAR	4204	60	PEARL		E CHINA SEA	1/8000	1/800
3	AH HOLTZ	4207	42	PEARL		ALASKA	0	0
4	AH HOLTZ	4211	48	PEARL	to	BRISBANE	0	0
5	AH HOLTZ	4301	31	BRISBANE		SOLOMONS	0	0
6	AH HOLTZ	4303	47	BRISBANE		SOLOMONS	1/8500	1/5000
7	AH HOLTZ	4305	47	BRISBANE		SOLOMONS	0	0
8	AH HOLTZ	4308	54	FREMANTLE		S CHINA SEA	0	0
9	JT HARDIN	4311	56	FREMANTLE	to	PEARL	0	1/5484
10	JT HARDIN	4404	56	PEARL		PALAU	0	0
11	JT HARDIN	4407	51	PEARL		EMPIRE	0	0
12	E STEFNADA	4410	52	PEARL	to	BRISBANE	0	0
13	E STEFNADA	4501	64	BRISBANE		SPL MISSION	0	0

TUNA'S VICTORIES

DATE	VESSEL	SIZE	TYPE	CAPTAIN	LOCATION
420301	UNKNOWN MARU	04000	FREIGHTER	JL DeTAR	KYUSHU
420515	TOYOHARA MARU	00805	FREIGHTER	JL DeTAR	KYUSHU
430330	KUROHIME MARU	04697	FREIGHTER	AH HOLTZ	MARIANAS
440131	TOSEI MARU	00584	FREIGHTER	JT HARDIN	MOLUCCA PASG

TUNA was being overhauled at Mare Island when war broke out. Rushed to Pearl as soon as possible, she was among the first boats to enter Empire waters. She would later participate in Operation King Two which kept the Japanese supply line snipped during the Battle of Leyte Gulf. The name abbreviated above is E.F. Steffanides.

TUNA was decommissioned on December 11, 1946, stricken from the lists and sunk off the West Coast on October 21, 1948.

GATO CLASS

The **GATO** Class boats were the result of all the experimenting with other classes up to that time and, with only slight alterations, became the standard Navy fleet boat of World War II. They were 311 feet long, displaced 1825 tons, had a top surface speed of 20 knots, and a range of 11,800 miles. They had six torpedo tubes forward and four tubes aft and carried a total of 24 torpedoes. The crew compliment was 72. A total of 72 **GATO** Class boats were built, most of them at the Electric Boat Company of Groton, Connecticut.

U.S.S. GATO
S.S. 212

U.S.S. GATO
S. S. 212

GATO was the first of her class, and the boat for which the class was named.
She was built at the Electric Boat Company and commissioned on December 31, 1941.

GATO'S WARTIME PATROLS

NO.	CAPTAIN	DATE	DUR.	BASE		AREA	CLAIMED	CONFIRMED
1	WG MYERS	4204	51	PEARL		MARSHALLS	0	0
2	WG MYERS	4207	50	PEARL		ALASKA	1/9300	0
3	RJ FOLEY	4211	58	PEARL	to	BRISBANE	0	0
4	RJ FOLEY	4301	44	BRISBANE		SOLOMONS	4/27800	3.5/1150
5	RJ FOLEY	4303	72	BRISBANE	to	PEARL	0	0
6	RJ FOLEY	4309	50	PEARL	to	BRISBANE	0	0
7	RJ FOLEY	4311	54	BRISBANE		BISMARCKS	3/21000	2/8544
8	RJ FOLEY	4402	60	BRISBANE	to	PEARL	3/17300	2/8070
9	RM FARRELL	4404	48	PEARL		TRUK	0	0
10	RM FARRELL	4407	49	PEARL		BONINS	0	0
11	RM FARRELL	4501	45	PEARL		E CHINA SEA	2/4700	2/3125
12	R HOLDEN	4504	52	PEARL		EMPIRE	0	0
13	R HOLDEN	4507	61	PEARL		EMPIRE	1/800	0

GATO'S VICTORIES

DATE	VESSEL	SIZE	TYPE	CAPTAIN	LOCATION
430121	KENKON MARU	04575	TRANSPORT	RJ FOLEY	BISMARCKS
430129	NICHIUN MARU	02723	FREIGHTER	RJ FOLEY	BISMARCKS
430215	SURUGA MARU	00991	FREIGHTER	RJ FOLEY	BISMARCKS
430219	HIBARI MARU	06550	FREIGHTER	RJ FOLEY	BISMARCKS
	(Shared credit with land-based aircraft)				
431130	COLUMBIA MARU	05618	PASS-CARGO	RJ FOLEY	ANCHORITE
431220	TSUNESHIMA MARU	02926	FREIGHTER	RJ FOLEY	ANCHORITE
440226	DAIGEN MARU #3	05056	PASS-CARGO	RJ FOLEY	N NEW GUINEA
440312	OKINOYAMA MARU	00871	FREIGHTER	RJ FOLEY	MANOKWARI
450214	COAST DEF #9	00800	FRIGATE	RM FARRELL	YELLOW SEA
450221	TAIRIKU MARU	02325	FREIGHTER	RM FARRELL	YELLOW SEA

GATO saw picket duty for the Battle of Midway and later for Aleutian defense. She was sent to Brisbane with some of the new fleet boats to replace the *"S"* types which had been withdrawn and sent to the States for training duties. *GATO* received Presidential Unit Citations for Patrols #4, 5, 6, 7, and 8 under R.J. Foley.

GATO, the first of her class, being launched at Groton, Connecticut on August 21, 1941.

GATO was decommissioned on March 16, 1946, stricken from the lists and sold for scrap in 1960.

U.S.S. ALBACORE
S.S. 218

ALBACORE was built at the Electric Boat Company and commissioned on June 1, 1942.

★ ★ ★ ★ ★ ★ ★ ★ ★
ALBACORE'S WARTIME PATROLS

NO.	CAPTAIN	DATE	DUR.	BASE	AREA	CLAIMED	CONFIRMED
1	RC LAKE	4208	53	PEARL	TRUK	0	0
2	RC LAKE	4211	43	PEARL to	BRISBANE	2/3200	1/3300
3	RC LAKE	4301	50	BRISBANE	SOLOMONS	1/1300	2/2500
4	RC LAKE	4304	50	BRISBANE	SOLOMONS	0	0
5	OE HAGBERG	4306	45	BRISBANE	BISMARCKS	0	0
6	OE HAGBERG	4308	26	BRISBANE	BISMARCKS	1/4200	1/2600
7	OE HAGBERG	4310	54	BRISBANE	BISMARCKS	1/9000	1/4700
8	JW BLANCHARD	4312	53	BRISBANE to PEARL		2/6800	2/4500
9	JW BLANCHARD	4405	48	PEARL	PHLPN SEA	2/30800	1/32000
10	JW BLANCHARD	4408	49	PEARL	EMPIRE	3/11000	2/1050
11	HR RIMMER	4410	00	PEARL	EMPIRE	0	0

ALBACORE'S VICTORIES

DATE	VESSEL	SIZE	TYPE	CAPTAIN	LOCATION
421218	TENRYU	03300	CRUISER	RC LAKE	CAROLINES
430220	OSHIO	01850	DESTROYER	RC LAKE	N PAPUA
430220	UNKNOWN	00750	FRIGATE	RC LAKE	N PAPUA
430904	HEIJO MARU	02627	GUNBOAT	OE HAGBERG	CAROLINES
431125	KENZAN MARU	04705	FREIGHTER	OE HAGBERG	CAROLINES
440112	CHOKO	02629	GUNBOAT	JW BLANCHARD	S CAROLINES
440114	SAZANAMI	01350	DESTROYER	JW BLANCHARD	PALAU
440619	TAIHO	31000	CARRIER	JW BLANCHARD	N YAP ISL
440905	SHIGETSU MARU	00880	FREIGHTER	JW BLANCHARD	KYUSHU
440911	SUBCHAER #165	00170	SUB CHASER	JW BLANCHARD	off NAGASAKI

ALBACORE holds the record for Japanese warships sunk with ten vessels. She sank the *TAIHO,* one of only four first-line Japanese carriers to fall victim to U.S. subs. She received Presidential Unit Citations for Patrols #2, and 3 under R.C. Lake and for Patrols #7 and 8 under J.W. Blanchard. On her eleventh patrol, she was running submerged to avoid enemy patrol craft while covering the approaches to Hakodate and Ominato. She struck a mine on November 7, 1944, and went down with all hands off Northern Hokkaido.

ALBACORE during a re-fit at Mare Island Navy Yard, April 28, 1944.

U.S.S. AMBERJACK
S. S. 219

AMBERJACK was built at the Electric Boat Company and commissioned on June 19, 1942.

★ ★ ★

AMBERJACK'S WARTIME PATROLS

NO.	CAPTAIN	DATE	DUR.	BASE	AREA	CLAIMED	CONFIRMED
1	JA BOLE	4209	57	PEARL to	BRISBANE	3/28500	2/5200
2	JA BOLE	4211	51	BRISBANE	SOLOMONS	0	0
3	JA BOLE	4302	00	BRISBANE	SOLOMONS	1/4000	0

AMBERJACK'S VICTORIES

DATE	VESSEL	SIZE	TYPE	CAPTAIN	LOCATION
420919	SHIROGANE MARU	03130	PASS-CARGO	JA BOLE	TRUK
421007	SENKAI MARU	02095	PASS-CARGO	JA BOLE	MICRONESIA

AMBERJACK was one of the fleet boats assigned to Brisbane after the older *"S"* boats were retired to training roles stateside. After her victories, *AMBERJACK* was assigned to deliver 9000 gallons of aviation gas, 200 aircraft bombs and 15 aviators to Guadalcanal. Following several harrowing squeaks she delivered this touchy cargo at Tulagi. On her third patrol, *AMBERJACK* engaged a munitions freighter in a surface attack and reported blowing her up. After undergoing an air attack by enemy planes and depth charging by two destroyers, *AMBERJACK* was finally sunk on February 16, 1943, by the Japanese torpedo boat *HAYADORI*, assisted by *Sub Chaser #18*.

This builder's photograph was taken at Electric Boat Company, Groton, Connecticut, May 30, 1942.

U.S.S. ANGLER
S.S. 240

ANGLER was built at Electric Boat Company and commissioned on October 1, 1943.

★ ★ ★ ★ ★ ★

ANGLER'S WARTIME PATROLS

NO.	CAPTAIN	DATE	DUR.	BASE		AREA	CLAIMED	CONFIRMED
1	RI OLSEN	4401	25	PEARL		MARIANAS	1/8700	1/890
2	RI OLSEN	4402	53	PEARL	to	FREMANTLE	0	0
3	RI OLSEN	4405	27	FREMANTLE		SUNDA STR	1/5700	1/2100
4	FG HESS	4406	54	FREMANTLE		S CHINA SEA	0	0
5	FG HESS	4409	50	FREMANTLE		MANILA	1/4000	1/2400
6	H BISSELL	4412	72	FREMANTLE	to	PEARL	0	0
7	H BISSELL	4506	56	PEARL		EMPIRE	0	0

ANGLER'S VICTORIES

DATE	VESSEL	SIZE	TYPE	CAPTAIN	LOCATION
440129	SHUKO MARU	00889	TENDER	RI OLSEN	BONINS
440520	OTORI MARU	02105	FREIGHTER	RI OLSEN	off SUMATRA
441014	NANREI MARU	02407	TRANSPORT	FG HESS	S CHINA SEA

On her second patrol, *ANGLER* evacuated 58 Philippine civilian refugees, 16 of whom were women and children. The boat was forced on two meals a day until the undernourished passengers could be disembarked in Australia. *ANGLER* also came to the assistance of the *BERGALL* after that boat had a surface engagement with a Japanese cruiser. Unable to submerge due to damage, the *BERGALL* was escorted home by *ANGLER.*

ANGLER entering an undisclosed harbor on June 12, 1945.

ANGLER was decommissioned on February 12, 1946, stricken from the lists and scrapped in 1971.

U. S. S. BASHAW
S. S. 241

BASHAW was built at the Electric Boat Company and commissioned on October 25, 1943.

★ ★ ★ ★ ★
BASHAW'S WARTIME PATROLS

NO.	CAPTAIN	DATE	DUR.	BASE	AREA	CLAIMED	CONFIRMED
1	RE NICHOLS	4403	60	BRISBANE	DAVAO	0	0
2	RE NICHOLS	4405	50	BRISBANE	HALMAHERA	1/5700	1/6440
3	RE NICHOLS	4408	55	BRISBANE	DAVAO	1/7700	1/2800
4	RE NICHOLS	4410	63	BRISBANE	S CHINA SEA	0	0
5	HS SIMPSON	4501	47	FREMANTLE	S CHINA SEA	1/10700	1/10016
6	HS SIMPSON	4503	33	FREMANTLE	S CHINA SEA	0	0

BASHAW'S VICTORIES

DATE	VESSEL	SIZE	TYPE	CAPTAIN	LOCATION
440625	YAMAMAIYA MARU	06440	FREIGHTER	RE NICHOLS	off MOROTAI
440908	YANAGIGAWA MARU	02854	FREIGHTER	RE NICHOLS	off LUZON
450305	RYOEI MARU	10016	TANKER	HS SIMPSON	KARAMATA STR

BASHAW and eleven other boats stood as interceptors from the late March air strikes on the Palaus. On her way home from this action, she was mistakenly bombed by a U.S. B-24. She was also among the twenty-two boats sent out to sink the battleships *ISE* and *HYUGA*, but, like the others, she was outrun by the faster Japanese warships.

This beam shot of *BASHAW* was taken during the war.

BASHAW was decommissioned on June 20, 1949, stricken from the lists and sunk as a target in 1969.

U. S. S. BARB
S. S. 220

U.S.S. BARB
S.S. 220

BARB was built at the Electric Boat Company and commissioned on July 8, 1942.

★ ★ ★ ★ ★ ★ ★ ★ ★
BARB'S WARTIME PATROLS

NO.	CAPTAIN	DATE	DUR.	BASE	AREA	CLAIMED	CONFIRMED
1	J WATERMAN	4210	36	BRIT ISLES	EUROPE	0	0
2	J WATERMAN	4212	31	BRIT ISLES	EUROPE	0	0
3	J WATERMAN	4302	3	BRIT ISLES	EUROPE	0	0
4	N LUCKER	4304	44	BRIT ISLES	EUROPE	0	0
5	J WATERMAN	4306	41	BRIT ISLES	EUROPE	0	0
6	J WATERMAN	4309	53	PEARL	E CHINA SEA	1/01800	0
7	J WATERMAN	4403	55	PEARL	MARIANAS	1/02200	1/02200
8	E FLUCKEY	4405	49	PEARL	POLAR CIRC	5/37500	5/15472
9	E FLUCKEY	4408	59	PEARL	LUZON STR	4/42100	3/36800
10	E FLUCKEY	4410	30	PEARL	E CHINA SEA	5/28900	2/15200
11	E FLUCKEY	4412	56	PEARL	E CHINA SEA	8/60000	4.3/24197
12	E FLUCKEY	4506	54	PEARL	EMPIRE	3/11200	2/03620

BARB'S VICTORIES

DATE	VESSEL	SIZE	TYPE	CAPTAIN	LOCATION
440328	FUKUSEI MARU	02219	FREIGHTER	J WATERMAN	RYUKYUS
440531	KOTO MARU II	01053	FREIGHTER	E FLUCKEY	KURILS
440531	MADRAS MARU	03802	PASS-CARGO	E FLUCKEY	KURILS
440611	TOTEN MARU	03823	FREIGHTER	E FLUCKEY	HOKKAIDO
440611	CHIHAYA MARU II	01161	FREIGHTER	E FLUCKEY	HOKKAIDO
440613	TAKASHIMA MARU	05633	PASS-CARGO	E FLUCKEY	HOKKAIDO
440731	OKUNI MARU	05633	FREIGHTER	E FLUCKEY	FORMOSA
440916	AZUSA	11177	TANKER	E FLUCKEY	S CHINA SEA
440916	UNYO	20000	ESC CARRIER	E FLUCKEY	S CHINA SEA
441110	GOKOKU MARU	10438	LT CRUISER	E FLUCKEY	KYUSHU
441112	NARUO MARU	04823	FREIGHTER	E FLUCKEY	KYUSHU
450108	SHINYO MARU	05892	FREIGHTER	E FLUCKEY	E CHINA SEA
450108	ANYO MARU	09256	PASS-CARGO	E FLUCKEY	E CHINA SEA
450108	SANYO MARU II	02854	TANKER	E FLUCKEY	E CHINA SEA
450108	HIKOSHIMA MARU	02854	TANKER	E FLUCKEY	E CHINA SEA

(Shared credit with *PICUDA* and *QUEENFISH*)

DATE	VESSEL	SIZE	TYPE	CAPTAIN	LOCATION
450123	TAIKYO MARU	05244	FREIGHTER	E FLUCKEY	E CHINA SEA
450705	SAPPORO MARU	02820	FREIGHTER	E FLUCKEY	SEA OF JAPAN
450718	CST DEF #112	00800	FRIGATE	E FLUCKEY	HOKKAIDO

BARB stands third in total tonnage sunk (even though she spent her first five patrols in the unproductive waters of Europe) and tied for eighth in number of vessels. She received Presidential Unit Citations for Patrols #8, 9, 10, and 11, and a Navy Unit Commendation for Patrol #12.

BARB at Mare Island Navy Yard.

BARB was decommissioned on February 12, 1947, and transferred to the Italian Navy as the ***ENRICO TAZZOLI*** in 1955.

U. S. S. BLACKFISH
S. S. 221

U. S. S. BLACKFISH
S. S. 221

BLACKFISH was built at the Electric Boat Company and commissioned on July 22, 1942.

★ ★ ★ ★ ★ ★ ★ ★
BLACKFISH'S WARTIME PATROLS

NO.	CAPTAIN	DATE	DUR.	BASE	AREA	CLAIMED	CONFIRMED
1	JF DAVIDSON	4210	37	SCOTLAND	N AFRICA	0	0
2	JF DAVIDSON	4212	29	SCOTLAND	BAY OF BISCAY	0	0
3	JF DAVIDSON	4302	22	SCOTLAND	BAY OF BISCAY	0	0
4	JF DAVIDSON	4304	39	SCOTLAND	ENG CHANNEL	0	0
5	JF DAVIDSON	4306	48	SCOTLAND	BAY OF BISCAY	0	0
6	JF DAVIDSON	4310	47	BRISBANE	BISMARCKS	1/4500	0
7	JF DAVIDSON	4312	50	BRISBANE	BISMARCKS	1/6000	1/2000
8	RF SELLARS	4403	80	BRISBANE to	PEARL	0	0
9	RF SELLARS	4409	60	PEARL	LUZON STRT	0	0
10	RF SELLARS	4501	50	PEARL	S CHINA SEA	0	0
11	RF SELLARS	4503	50	PEARL	S CHINA SEA	0	0
12	RC GILLETT	4506	57	PEARL	E CHINA SEA	0	0

BLACKFISH'S VICTORY

DATE	VESSEL	SIZE	TYPE	CAPTAIN	LOCATION
440116	KAIKA MARU	02087	FREIGHTER	JF DAVIDSON	BISMARCKS

BLACKFISH was assigned to Squadron 50, stationed off Dakar, Senegal, which covered the Allied invasion of North Africa. On November 8, 1942, *BLACKFISH* damaged a French freighter off Point Alemadies, but did not claim a sinking. From her base at Roseneath, Scotland, *BLACKFISH* made four more patrols off the European coast before being sent back to the United States in mid-1943. Re-assigned to the Pacific Theater, she joined "Blakley's Behemoths," and took part in Operation King Two in Philippine waters.

This postwar photograph is circa 1945.

BLACKFISH was decommissioned on May 11, 1946, stricken from the lists and sold for scrap in 1959.

———————

A German freighter, running the blockade, was sunk in error by a German U-Boat during World War II.

U. S. S. BLUEFISH
S. S. 222

U. S. S. BLUEFISH
S. S. 222

BLUEFISH was built at the Electric Boat Company and commissioned on May 24, 1943.

★ ★ ★ ★ ★ ★ ★ ★ ★ ★

BLUEFISH'S WARTIME PATROLS

NO.	CAPTAIN	DATE	DUR.	BASE	AREA	CLAIMED	CONFIRMED
1	GE PORTER	4309	29	FREMANTLE	S CHINA SEA	4/16200	2/3822
2	GE PORTER	4310	32	FREMANTLE	S CHINA SEA	2/22800	2/11390
3	GE PORTER	4312	27	FREMANTLE	S CHINA SEA	2/20100	2/11000
4	CM HENDERSON	4401	58	FREMANTLE	S CHINA SEA	1/7500	1/10500
5	CM HENDERSON	4405	53	FREMANTLE	CELEBES	2/7000	2/4700
6	CM HENDERSON	4407	54	FREMANTLE to	PEARL	2.5/34500	1.5/9067
7	CM HENDERSON	4502	42	PEARL	EMPIRE	0	0
8	GW FORBES	4504	38	PEARL to	FREMANTLE	0	0
9	GW FORBES	4506	33	FREMANTLE	S CHINA SEA	1/1200	2/2750

BLUEFISH'S VICTORIES

DATE	VESSEL	SIZE	TYPE	CAPTAIN	LOCATION
430826	KASASAGI	00595	MTS	GE PORTER	FLORES SEA
430826	AKASHI MARU	03227	FREIGHTER	GE PORTER	BANDA SEA
431108	KYOKUEI MARU	10570	TANKER	GE PORTER	LINGAYEN
431118	SANAYE	00820	DESTROYER	GE PORTER	CELEBES
431230	ICHIYE MARU	05061	TANKER	GE PORTER	CELEBES
440104	HAKKO MARU #5	06046	TANKER	GE PORTER	N BORNEO
440304	OMINISAN MARU	10536	TANKER	CM HENDERSON	NATUNA ISLE
440616	NANSHIN MARU #12	01422	PASS-CARGO	CM HENDERSON	CELEBES
440621	KANAN MARU	03312	FREIGHTER	CM HENDERSON	MAKASSAR ST
440712	SHIMPO MARU	05135	TANKER	CM HENDERSON	MINDORO
	(Shared credit with **PUFFER**)				
440719	HAYASUE	06500	TANKER	CM HENDERSON off LUZON	
450709	SUBCHASER #50	00100	SUB CHASER	GW FORBES	SINGAPORE
450714	I-351	02650	SUBMARINE	GW FORBES	BURNEI

G.E. Porter ranked 30th among the 77 submarine skippers who sank five or more ships. He had a confirmed total of nine vessels of 30,940 tons. Part of this record was on the **SENNET**.

BLUEFISH and another boat tied up at dock in 1945.

BLUEFISH was decommissioned on February 12, 1947, stricken from the lists and sold for scrap in 1959.

U.S.S. BLUEGILL
S.S. 242

BLUEGILL was built at the Electric Boat Company and commissioned on November 11, 1943.

★ ★ ★ ★
BLUEGILL'S WARTIME PATROLS

NO.	CAPTAIN	DATE	DUR.	BASE	AREA	CLAIMED	CONFIRMED
1	EL BARR	4404	67	BRISBANE	DAVAO	3/13600	3/14100
2	EL BARR	4407	49	BRISBANE	DAVAO	3/8600	3/6950
3	EL BARR	4409	64	FREMANTLE	MANILA	5/23300	3/19630
4	EL BARR	4412	52	FREMANTLE	S CHINA SEA	0	0
5	EL BARR	4503	37	FREMANTLE	S CHINA SEA	1/5700	1/5542
6	EL BARR	4504	41	FREMANTLE	S CHINA SEA	0	0

BLUEGILL'S VICTORIES

DATE	VESSEL	SIZE	TYPE	CAPTAIN	LOCATION
440427	YUBARO	03500	LT CRUISER	EL BARR	SONDORAL
440501	ASOSAN MARU	08812	FREIGHTER	EL BARR	SPRATLEY ISL
440520	MIYAURA MARU	01856	FREIGHTER	EL BARR	CELEBES
440707	SANJU MARU	04642	FREIGHTER	EL BARR	ANAMBAS ISL
440712	SUBCHASER #12	00300	SUB CHASER	EL BARR	BRUNE I
440713	KOJUN MARU	01931	FREIGHTER	EL BARR	BRUNE I
441018	ARABIA MARU	09480	TRANSPORT	EL BARR	NW MINDORO
441018	CHINZEI MARU	01999	FREIGHTER	EL BARR	NW MINDORO
441018	HAKUSHIKA MARU	08150	PASS-CARGO	EL BARR	NW MINDORO
440328	HONAN MARU	05542	TANKER	EL BARR	INDO-CHINA

Whenever Barr found slim pickings, he would surface and destroy small native craft throught to be working for the Japanese before the policy was changed to forbid this type of action. As targets became more scarce, Barr landed a "commando" party on Pratas Island, SW of Hong Kong and captured it. *BLUEGILL* received Presidential Unit Citations for Patrols #1 and 3.

An aerial photo of *BLUEGILL* taken just before Christmas 1943 just off the Jersey coast.

BLUEGILL was decommissioned on March 1, 1946, and scuttled for training purposes in 1970.

U. S. S. BREAM
S. S. 243

BREAM was built at the Electric Boat Company and commissioned on January 24, 1944.

★ ★ ★ ★

BREAM'S WARTIME PATROLS

NO.	CAPTAIN	DATE	DUR.	BASE	AREA	CLAIMED	CONFIRMED
1	WG CHAPPLE	4406	29	BRISBANE	DAVAO	0	1/5700
2	WG CHAPPLE	4407	48	BRISBANE	DAVAO	0	0
3	WG CHAPPLE	4410	50	FREMANTLE	S CHINA SEA	.5/5000	.3/2270
4	JL McCALLUM	4412	52	FREMANTLE	S CHINA SEA	0	0
5	JL McCALLUM	4503	16	FREMANTLE	JAVA SEA	1/2600	0
6	JL McCALLUM	4505	54	FREMANTLE to PEARL		1/10000	1/1230

BREAM'S VICTORIES

DATE	VESSEL	SIZE	TYPE	CAPTAIN	LOCATION
440616	YUKU MARU	05704	FREIGHTER	WG CHAPPLE	HALMAHERA
441104	KAGI MARU	06806	PASS-CARGO	WG CHAPPLE	off LUZON
	(Shared credit with **RAY** and **GUITARRO**)				
450529	TEISHU MARU	01230	TENDER	JL McCALLUM	KARAMATA STR

BREAM took part in Operation King Two and was part of the line formed up to intercept Japanese warships coming to and fleeing the Leyte Gulf Operation. **BREAM** so crippled the heavy cruiser **AOBA** that she could not take part in the battle. **BREAM** also heavily damaged the heavy cruiser **KUMANO**, and drove her aground where she was later destroyed by aircraft.

BREAM shown from broad on her port beam.

BREAM was decommissioned on January 31, 1946, and sunk as a target in 1969.

U. S. S. BONEFISH
S. S. 223

U. S. S. BONEFISH
S. S. 223

BONEFISH was built at the Electric Boat Company and commissioned on May 31, 1943.

★ ★ ★ ★ ★ ★ ★
BONEFISH'S WARTIME PATROLS

NO.	CAPTAIN	DATE	DUR.	BASE	AREA	CLAIMED	CONFIRMED
1	TW HOGAN	4309	45	FREMANTLE	S CHINA SEA	6/40200	3/24206
2	TW HOGAN	4311	27	FREMANTLE	CELEBES	3/16600	2/7367
3	TW HOGAN	4401	60	FREMANTLE	S CHINA SEA	2/21300	0
4	TW HOGAN	4404	48	FREMANTLE	CELEBES	4/27400	2/2756
5	LL EDGE	4406	49	FREMANTLE	SULU SEA	2/12800	1/10000
6	LL EDGE	4409	62	FREMANTLE	to PEARL	3/22000	2/4500
7	LL EDGE	4504	31	PEARL	E CHINA SEA	0	0
8	LL EDGE	4505	00	PEARL	SEA OF JAPAN	2/14000	2/12380

BONEFISH'S VICTORIES

DATE	VESSEL	SIZE	TYPE	CAPTAIN	LOCATION
430827	KASHIMA MARU	09908	TRANSPORT	TW HOGAN	off HAINAN
431010	TEIBI MARU	10086	TRANSPORT	TW HOGAN	off DANANG
431010	ISUZUGAWA	04212	FREIGHTER	TW HOGAN	off DANANG
431129	SUEZ MARU	04646	FREIGHTER	TW HOGAN	MAKASSAR STR
431201	NICHIRYO MARU	02721	PASS-CARGO	TW HOGAN	CELEBES
440426	TOKIWA MARU II	00806	PASS-CARGO	TW HOGAN	TALAUD ISLES
440514	INAZUMA	01950	DESTROYER	TW HOGAN	CELEBES
440730	KOKUYU MARU II	10026	TANKER	LL EDGE	CELEBES
440828	ANJO MARU	02068	TANKER	LL EDGE	MINDORO
441014	FUSHIMI MARU #5	02542	FREIGHTER	LL EDGE	LINGAYAN
450613	OSHIKAYAMA MARU	06892	FREIGHTER	LL EDGE	SEA OF JAPAN
450619	KONZAN MARU	05488	PASS-CARGO	LL EDGE	TOYAMA BAY

BONEFISH received Navy Unit Commendations for Patrols #1, 3, and 4, under T.W. Hogan, and for Patrols #5 and 6, under L.L. Edge. She is ranked #22 of the top 25 boats in tonnage destroyed with 61,345. *BONEFISH*, operating as a pack member with *TUNNY* and *SKATE*, received permission to enter Toyama Bay after a target. She found the target but was spotted by Japanese destroyers and sunk by repeated depth charges. There were no survivors.

BONEFISH at her launching at Electric Boat Company in Groton, Connecticut, March 7, 1943.

U. S. S. CAVALLA
S. S. 244

CAVALLA was built at the Electric Boat Company and commissioned on February 29, 1944.

★ ★ ★ ★
CAVALLA'S WARTIME PATROLS

NO.	CAPTAIN	DATE	DUR.	BASE		AREA	CLAIMED	CONFIRMED
1	HJ KOSSLER	4406	64	PEARL		PHILIPN SEA	1/29900	1/30000
2	HJ KOSSLER	4408	52	PEARL	to	FREMANTLE	0	0
3	HJ KOSSLER	4411	60	FREMANTLE		S CHINA SEA	3/6300	3/4180
4	HJ KOSSLER	4502	46	FREMANTLE		S CHINA SEA	0	0
5	HJ KOSSLER	4505	38	FREMANTLE	to	PEARL	0	0
6	HJ KOSSLER	4508	36	PEARL		EMPIRE	0	0

CAVALLA'S VICTORIES

DATE	VESSEL	SIZE	TYPE	CAPTAIN	LOCATION
440619	SHOKAKU	30000	CARRIER	HJ KOSSLER	nr YAP
441125	SHIMOTSUKI	02300	DESTROYER	HJ KOSSLER	off SINGAPORE
450105	SHUNSEN MARU	00971	FREIGHTER	HJ KOSSLER	JAVA SEA
450105	KANKO MARU #3	00909	FREIGHTER	HJ KOSSLER	JAVA SEA

CAVALLA sank one of Japan's first-line carriers on her fist patrol and received a Presidential Unit Citation for that action. *SHOKAKU* was one of the two remaining flat-tops of the six that attacked Pearl Harbor. *CAVALLA* participated in Operation Forager during the Marianas Operation and was honored by being one of the twelve fleet boats present at the Japanese surrender in Tokyo Bay.

CAVALLA at the Electric Boat Company dock, Groton, Connecticut, February 25, 1944.

CAVALLA was decommissioned on March 16, 1946, and is now a historic ship exhibit at Galveston, Texas.

U.S.S. CERO
S.S. 225

CERO was built at the Electric Boat Company and commissioned on July 4, 1943.

★ ★ ★ ★ ★ ★ ★

CERO'S WARTIME PATROLS

NO.	CAPTAIN	DATE	DUR.	BASE	AREA	CLAIMED	CONFIRMED
1	DC WHITE	4309	52	PEARL	E CHINA SEA	1/1600	0
2	EF DISSETTE	4312	29	PEARL to	BRISBANE	0	0
3	EF DISSETTE	4402	23	BRISBANE	BISMARCKS	1/1600	0
4	EF DISSETTE	4404	60	BRISBANE	DAVAO	0	1/2800
5	EF DISSETTE	4406	56	BRISBANE	DAVAO	1/8000	1/5600
6	EF DISSETTE	4409	62	BRISBANE to	PEARL	0	0
7	R BERTHRONG	4503	56	PEARL	EMPIRE	4/9800	3/8834
8	R BERTHRONG	4506	33	PEARL	EMPIRE	0	0

CERO'S VICTORIES

DATE	VESSEL	SIZE	TYPE	CAPTAIN	LOCATION
440523	TAIJUN MARU	02825	FREIGHTER	DC WHITE	HALMAHERA
440705	TSURUMI	06500	TANKER	EF DISSETTE	ANAMBAS
450429	TAISHU MARU	06925	FREIGHTER	R BERTHRONG	HONSHU
450504	SHINPEN MARU	00884	FREIGHTER	R BERTHRONG	HONSHU
450513	KANKO MARU II	00909	TENDER	R BERTHRONG	HONSHU

CERO was in the first American wolf-pack employed in the Pacific, along with *SHAD* and *GRAYBACK*. She carried Captain Momsen as Pack Commander. Later she participated in Operation King Two in support of the Leyte Gulf Operation.

Photograph taken at Mare Island Naval Ship Yards, February 13, 1945.

CERO was decommissioned on June 8, 1946, stricken from the lists on June 30, 1967, and sold for scrap in October 1970.

U.S.S. COD
S.S. 224

COD was built at the Electric Boat Company and commissioned on June 21, 1943.

★ ★ ★ ★ ★ ★ ★

COD'S WARTIME PATROLS

NO.	CAPTAIN	DATE	DUR.	BASE		AREA	CLAIMED	CONFIRMED
1	JC DEMPSEY	4310	63	FREMANTLE		S CHINA SEA	1/7100	0
2	JC DEMPSEY	4401	62	FREMANTLE		HALMAHERA	2/9900	2/9823
3	JC DEMPSEY	4404	56	FREMANTLE		MANILA	2/10100	2/8076
4	JA ADKINS	4407	53	FREMANTLE		S CHINA S EA	4/9000	2/1708
5	JA ADKINS	4409	59	FREMANTLE	to	PEARL	1/10000	1/6900
6	JA ADKINS	4503	65	PEARL	to	FREMANTLE	3/5000	1/492
7	EM WESTBROOK	4506	47	FREMANTLE		S CHINA SEA	0	0

COD'S VICTORIES

DATE	VESSEL	SIZE	TYPE	CAPTAIN	LOCATION
440223	OGUTS MARU #3	07350	TANKER	JC DEMPSEY	MOROTAI
440227	TAISOKU MARU	02473	FREIGHTER	JC DEMPSEY	HALMAHERA
440510	KARUKAYA	00820	DESTROYER	JC DEMPSEY	LINGAYAN
440510	SHOHEI MARU	07256	FREIGHTER	JC DEMPSEY	LINGAYAN
440703	SEIKO MARU	00708	TENDER	JA ADKINS	MOLUCCA PSG
440714	TRANSPORT #129	01000	LST	JA ADKINS	SULA ISL
441005	TATSHUSHIRO MARU	06886	FREIGHTER	JA ADKINS	MINDORO
450425	MINESWEEPER #41	00492	MINESWEEPER	JA ADKINS	TAIWAN

COD took part in Operation King Two which set a line from North Borneo to Northern Luzon and guarded against Japanese reinforcements for the Battle of Leyte Gulf. She also did lifeguard duty on the air route from Iwo Jima to Japan.

COD at Mare Island Naval Ship Yard.

COD was decommissioned on June 22, 1946, and is now a historic ship exhibit in Cleveland, Ohio.

U.S.S. COBIA
S.S. 245

COBIA was built at the Electric Boat Company and commissioned on March 29, 1944.

★ ★ ★ ★
COBIA'S WARTIME PATROLS

NO.	CAPTAIN	DATE	DUR.	BASE		AREA	CLAIMED	CONFIRMED
1	AL BECKER	4406	49	PEARL		BONINS	5/24300	3/11455
2	AL BECKER	4409	57	PEARL	to	FREMANTLE	0	0
3	AL BECKER	4412	54	FREMANTLE		S CHINA SEA	1/700	1/720
4	AL BECKER	4502	51	FREMANTLE		S CHINA SEA	0	0
5	AL BECKER	4504	40	FREMANTLE		S CHINA SEA	2/15100	2/4675
6	FN RUSSELL	4507	34	FREMANTLE		S CHINA SEA	0	0

COBIA'S VICTORIES

DATE	VESSEL	SIZE	TYPE	CAPTAIN	LOCATION
440713	TAISHI MARU	02825	FREIGHTER	AL BECKER	BONINS
440718	UNKAI MARU #10	00855	GUNBOAT	AL BECKER	BONINS
440718	NISSHU MARU	07785	FREIGHTER	AL BECKER	BONINS
450114	YURISHIMA	00720	MINELAYER	AL BECKER	MALAY PENIN
450608	NANSHIN MARU #22	00834	TANKER	AL BECKER	S CHINA SEA
450608	HAKUSA	03841	LANDING SHIP	AL BECKER	S CHINA SEA

COBIA took part in Operation King Two in support of the invasion of Leyte, and stood guard with other boats to pick off those Japanese ships fleeing the action there.

COBIA going down the ways at Electric Boat Company, Groton, Connecticut, November 28, 1943.

COBIA was decommissioned on May 22, 1946, and is now a historic ship exhibit in Manitowoc, Wisconsin.

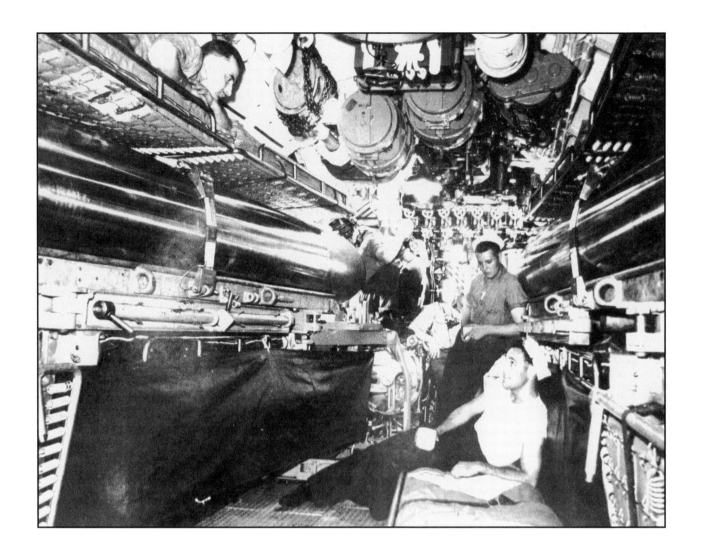

U. S. S. CORVINA
S. S. 226

CORVINA was built at Electric Boat Company and commissioned on August 6, 1943.

CORVINA'S WARTIME PATROL

NO.	CAPTAIN	DATE	DUR.	BASE	AREA	CLAIMED	CONFIRMED
1	RS ROONEY	4311	00	PEARL	TRUK	1/1600	0

CORVINA claimed one sinking but it could not be confirmed.

CORVINA was sent with *DRUM* to patrol south of Truk. They were to rendezvous with *BLACKFISH* and intercept a Japanese sub that was known to be in the area. *BLACKFISH* spotted a sub but could not be sure of her identity until daylight. By then the Japanese boat had escaped, but not before sinking *CORVINA* with a three fish spread. She went down with all hands on November 16, 1943, ironically sunk by the sub (*I-176*) she had been dispatched to destroy.

Crewmen relax in torpedo room while at the sub base, New London, Connecticut, August 1943.

U. S. S. CROAKER
S. S. 246

CROAKER was built at Electric Boat Company and commissioned on April 21, 1944.

★ ★ ★

CROAKER'S WARTIME PATROLS

NO.	CAPTAIN	DATE	DUR.	BASE	AREA	CLAIMED	CONFIRMED
1	JE LEE	4407	43	PEARL	E CHINA SEA	4/17600	3/13900
2	JE LEE	4409	48	PEARL	E CHINA SEA	4/16600	3/5800
3	WB THOMAS	4412	60	PEARL	to FREMANTLE	0	0
4	WB THOMAS	4503	42	FREMANTLE	S CHINA SEA	0	0
5	WB THOMAS	4504	22	FREMANTLE	JAVA SEA	2/5800	0
6	WB THOMAS	4507	47	FREMANTLE	S CHINA SEA	0	0

CROAKER'S VICTORIES

DATE	VESSEL	SIZE	TYPE	CAPTAIN	LOCATION
440707	NAGARA	05700	CRUISER	JE LEE	off NAGASAKI
440714	DAIGEN MARU #7	01289	GUNBOAT	JE LEE	TUSHIMA STR
440717	SANSHO MARU	06862	FREIGHTER	JE LEE	TUSHIMA STR
441009	SHINKI MARU	02211	FREIGHTER	JE LEE	KYUSHU
441023	BYAKURAN MARU	00887	FREIGHTER	JE LEE	KYUSHU
441024	MIKAGE MARU II	02761	FREIGHTER	JE LEE	KYUSHU

CROAKER received a Navy Unit Commendation for Patrol #1 under J.E. Lee

This aerial photograph of ***CROAKER*** was taken May 12, 1944, off the Jersey coast.

CROAKER was decommissioned on May 15, 1946, and is now a historic ship exhibit at the Naval and Servicemen's Park in Buffalo, New York.

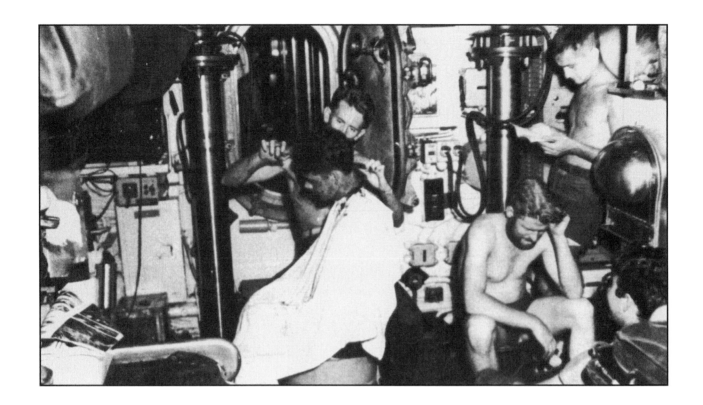

U.S.S. DACE
S.S. 247

DACE was built at the Electric Boat Company and commissioned on July 23, 1943.

★ ★ ★ ★ ★ ★ ★
DACE'S WARTIME PATROLS

NO.	CAPTAIN	DATE	DUR.	BASE		AREA	CLAIMED	CONFIRMED
1	JF ENRIGHT	4310	49	PEARL		EMPIRE	0	0
2	BD CLAGETT	4401	48	PEARL	to	BRISBANE	0	0
3	BD CLAGETT	4403	55	BRISBANE		DAVAO	0	0
4	BD CLAGETT	4406	60	BRISBANE		DAVAO	2/3200	1/1100
5	BD CLAGETT	4409	60	BRISBANE		S CHINA SEA	3/30000	3/25141
6	OR COLE, Jr	4412	56	FREMANTLE	to	PEARL	1/4000	1/1000
7	OR COLE, Jr	4505	46	PEARL		POLAR CIRC	1/4400	1/1391

DACE'S VICTORIES

DATE	VESSEL	SIZE	TYPE	CAPTAIN	LOCATION
440727	KYOEI MARU #7	01157	TANKER	BD CLAGGETT	CELEBES
441014	NITTETSU MARU	05993	FREIGHTER	BD CLAGGETT	N BORNEO
441014	EIKYO MARU	06948	FREIGHTER	BD CLAGGETT	N BORNEO
441023	MAYA	12200	CRUISER	BD CLAGGETT	PALAWAN
441228	NOZAKI	01000	SUPPLY SHIP	OR COLE, Jr	S CHINA SEA
450610	HAKUYO MARU III	01391	FREIGHTER	OR COLE, Jr	KIRULES

DACE escorted *SCAMP* to the Admiralties after the latter's brush with a Japanese patrol plane. She also took part in Operation Hailstone to cut off ships fleeing the Truk Operation. Teamed with *DARTER*, *DACE* sank the heavy cruiser *MAYA* in the Leyte Gulf Operation, and later had to rescue the entire crew of *DARTER* after she ran up on a reef while doing an end-around maneuver. *DACE* received a Navy Unit Commendation for Patrol #5 under B.D. Claggett.

Hair cut time in *DACE's* cramped quarters.

DACE was decommissioned on February 12, 1947, and transferred to the Italian Navy in 1955 as the *LEONARDO DA VINCI.*

U. S. S. DARTER
S. S. 227

DARTER was built at the Electric Boat Company and commissioned on September 7, 1943.

★ ★ ★ ★

DARTER'S WARTIME PATROLS

NO.	CAPTAIN	DATE	DUR.	BASE	AREA	CLAIMED	CONFIRMED
1	WS STOVALL	4312	66	PEARL to	BRISBANE	0	0
2	WS STOVALL	4403	63	BRISBANE	DAVAO	1/6800	1/2800
3	WS STOVALL	4406	48	BRISBANE	DAVAO	1/4400	1/4400
4	DH McCLINTOCK	4409	00	BRISBANE	S CHINA SEA	1/12500	1/12000

DARTER'S VICTORIES

DATE	VESSEL	SIZE	TYPE	CAPTAIN	LOCATION
440330	FUJIKAWA MARU	02829	FREIGHTER	WS STOVAL	MAPIA ISLE
440629	TSUGARU	04400	MINELAYER	WS STOVAL	MOLUCCA
441023	ATAGO	12000	CRUISER	DH McCLINTOCK	PALAWAN

DARTER took part in Operation Hailstone which attempted to cut off fleeing Japanese warships after the Truk Operation. She played a similar role in Operation King Two, during and after the Battle of Leyte Gulf. In concert with **DACE** she sank the heavy cruiser **ATAGO** and while doing an end around for a crack at another, **DARTER** ran aground on Bombay Shoal. Despite repeated attempts, **DARTER** could not be freed. **DACE** moved in and rescued the crew of **DARTER** who had set scuttling charges before leaving. The charges proved ineffective, so **DACE** attempted to torpedo her and succeeded only in blowing up more of the surrounding reef. **ROCK** was dispatched to torpedo her but had the same result. Finally, **NAUTILUS** was ordered to use her 6-inch deck guns on **DARTER** and used 55 shells to destroy **DARTER**. **DARTER** was awarded a Navy Unit Commendation for this action.

DARTER aground on Bombay Shoal off S.W. Palawan. She was destroyed by **NAUTILUS'** big guns.

U. S. S. DRUM
S. S. 228

U.S.S. DRUM
S.S. 228

DRUM was built at the Portsmouth Navy Yard and commissioned on November 1, 1941.

★ ★ ★ ★ ★ ★
★ ★ ★ ★ ★ ★

DRUM'S WARTIME PATROLS

NO.	CAPTAIN	DATE	DUR.	BASE	AREA	CLAIMED	CONFIRMED
1	RH RICE	4204	56	PEARL	EMPIRE	4/24000	4/20000
2	RH RICE	4207	54	PEARL	TRUK	0	0
3	RH RICE	4209	46	PEARL	EMPIRE	3/19000	3/13200
4	BF McMAHON	4211	49	PEARL	EMPIRE	0	0
5	BF McMAHON	4302	47	PEARL to BRISBANE	1/15900	2/10000
6	BF McMAHON	4306	49	BRISBANE	BISMARCK	1/8700	1/5000
7	BF McMAHON	4308	51	BRISBANE	BISMARCK	3/12900	1/1334
8	DF WILLIAMSON	4311	34	BRISBANE to PEARL	1/11900	1/11621
9	DF WILLIAMSON	4404	50	PEARL	BONINS	0	0
10	MH RINDSKOPF	4406	51	PEARL	PALAU	0	0
11	MH RINDSKOPF	4409	59	PEARL	LUZON STR	4/25100	3/18500
12	FM EDDY	4412	42	PEARL	EMPIRE	0	0
13	FM EDDY	4502	51	PEARL	EMPIRE	0	0

DRUM'S VICTORIES

DATE	VESSEL	SIZE	TYPE	CAPTAIN	LOCATION
420502	MIZUHO	09000	TENDER	RH RICE	OSAKA
420509	UNKNOWN MARU	04000	FREIGHTER	RH RICE	OSAKA
420513	SHONAN MARU	05264	FREIGHTER	RH RICE	OSAKA
420525	KITAKATA MARU	02380	FREIGHTER	RH RICE	OSAKA
421008	HAGUE MARU	05641	PASS-CARGO	RH RICE	HOHSHU
421009	HACHIMANZAN M.	02461	FREIGHTER	RH RICE	HONSHU
421020	RYUNAN MARU	05136	FREIGHTER	RH RICE	HONSHU
430409	OYAMA MARU	03809	FREIGHTER	BF McMAHON	BISMARCKS
430518	NISSHUN MARU	06380	FREIGHTER	BF McMAHON	BISMARCKS
430617	MYOKO MARU	05087	PASS-CARGO	BF McMAHON	BISMARCKS
430908	HAKUTETSU M. #13	01334	FREIGHTER	BF McMAHON	BISMARCKS
431117	HIE MARU	11621	SUPPLY SHIP	DF WILLIAMSON	ANCHORITE
441024	SHIKISAN MARU	04725	PASS-CARGO	MH RINDSKOPF	S CHINA SEA
441026	TAISHO MARU	06886	FREIGHTER	MH RINDSKOPF	S CHINA SEA
441026	TAIHAKU MARU	06886	FREIGHTER	MH RINDSKOPF	S CHINA SEA

During December 1942, *DRUM* planted mines in the Bungo Suido Passage. *DRUM* stands eighth in total tonnage and tied for tenth in number of vessels sunk.

DRUM at Mare Island Navy Yard during a re-fit, March 22, 1944.

DRUM was decommissioned on February 16, 1946, and is now a historic ship exhibit in Mobile, Alabama.

U. S. S. FINBACK
S. S. 230

U. S. S. FINBACK
S. S. 230

FINBACK was built at the Portsmouth Navy Yard and commissioned on January 31, 1942.

FINBACK'S WARTIME PATROLS

NO.	CAPTAIN	DATE	DUR.	BASE		AREA	CLAIMED	CONFIRMED
00	JL HULL	4205	15	PEARL		MIDWAY	0	0
1	JL HULL	4206	48	ALASKA		ALASKA	0	0
2	JL HULL	4209	58	PEARL		E CHINA SEA	2/14100	3/22000
3	JL HULL	4212	52	PEARL		EMPIRE	1/200	0
4	JA TYREE	4302	44	PEARL		TRUK	.5/5300	.3/3557
5	JA TYREE	4305	44	PEARL	to	FREMANTLE	4/23200	3/11000
6	JA TYREE	4306	56	FREMANTLE	to	PEARL	3/17000	3/11000
7	JA TYREE	4312	58	PEARL		E CHINA SEA	1/10200	1/10000
8	JA TYREE	4403	55	PEARL		TRUK	0	0
9	JL JORDAN	4405	50	PEARL		PHILIPN SEA	0	0
10	RR WILLIAMS	4408	50	PEARL		BONINS	2/1900	2/1390
11	RR WILLIAMS	4411	50	PEARL		BONINS	1/5000	1/2100
12	RR WILLIAMS	4501	62	PEARL		E CHINA SEA	0	0

FINBACK'S VICTORIES

DATE	VESSEL	SIZE	TYPE	CAPTAIN	LOCATION
421014	TIESON MARU	07007	TRANSPORT	JL HULL	E CHINA SEA
421020	YAMAFUJI MARU	05259	FREIGHTER	JL HULL	E CHINA SEA
421020	AFRICA MARU	09475	FREIGHTER	JL HULL	E CHINA SEA
430328	SUWA MARU	10672	TRANSPORT	JA TYREE	BONINS

(Shared credit with *TUNNY* and *SEADRAGON*)

DATE	VESSEL	SIZE	TYPE	CAPTAIN	LOCATION
430527	KOCHI MARU	02910	FREIGHTER	JA TYREE	PALAU
430608	KAHOKU MARU	03350	GUNBOAT	JA TYREE	PALAU
430611	GENOA MARU	06785	FREIGHTER	JA TYREE	PALAU
430630	RYUZAN MARU	04720	FREIGHTER	JA TYREE	JAVA SEA
430803	KAISHO MARU	06070	PASS-CARGO	JA TYREE	JAVA SEA
430819	SUBCHASER #103	00200	SUBCHASER	JA TYREE	MOLUCCA PSG
440102	ISSHIN MARU	10000	TANKER	JA TYREE	E CHINA SEA
440911	HAKUUN MARU	00860	FREIGHTER	RR WILLIAMS	BONINS
440911	HASSHO MARU	00536	FREIGHTER	RR WILLIAMS	BONINS
441216	JUSAN MARU	02111	FREIGHTER	RR WILLIAMS	BONINS

FINBACK'S record would probably have been better if she had not been plagued by faulty torpedoes on her early patrols (as were most other boats at that time). Commander Hull reported 13 misses out of 20 shots in October 1942. While ***FINBACK*** was on lifeguard duty later in the war, she picked up Lt. (jg) George Herbert Walker Bush, who was at that time, the youngest pilot in the U.S. Navy.

This photograph was taken shortly after the end of the war off New London, Connecticut.

FINBACK was decommissioned on April 21, 1950, stricken from the lists and sold for scrap in 1959.

U. S. S. FLASHER
S. S. 249

U. S. S. FLASHER
S. S. 249

FLASHER was built at the Electric Boat Company and commissioned on September 25, 1943.

★ ★ ★ ★ ★ ★

FLASHER'S WARTIME PATROLS

NO.	CAPTAIN	DATE	DUR.	BASE	AREA	CLAIMED	CONFIRMED
1	RT WHITAKER	4401	53	PEARL	to FREMANTLE	4/26500	4/10528
2	RT WHITAKER	4404	54	FREMANTLE	S CHINA SEA	3/12600	3/6709
3	RT WHITAKER	4406	49	FREMANTLE	S CHINA SEA	6.5/47900	4.5/24949
4	RT WHITAKER	4409	51	FREMANTLE	MANILA	4/23000	3/18610
5	GW GRIDER	4411	48	FREMANTLE	S CHINA SEA	5/41700	6/42800
6	GW GRIDER	4501	75	FREMANTLE	S CHINA SEA	1/2100	1/850

FLASHER'S VICTORIES

DATE	VESSEL	SIZE	TYPE	CAPTAIN	LOCATION
440118	YOSHIDA	02900	GUNBOAT	RT WHITAKER	W BONINS
440205	TAISHIN MARU	01723	FREIGHTER	RT WHITAKER	MINDORO
440214	MINRYO MARU	02193	FREIGHTER	RT WHITAKER	MINDORO
440214	HOKUAN MARU	03712	FREIGHTER	RT WHITAKER	MINDORO
440429	TAHURE	00644	GUNBOAT	RT WHITAKER	S CHINA SEA
440429	SONG GIANG MARU	01065	FREIGHTER	RT WHITAKER	S CHINA SEA
440503	TEISEN MARU	05050	FREIGHTER	RT WHITAKER	PALAWAN
440629	NIPPO MARU #3	06079	FREIGHTER	RT WHITAKER	KAMARATA
440707	KOTO MARU	03557	FREIGHTER	RT WHITAKER	S CHINA SEA
440719	OI	05700	CRUISER	RT WHITAKER	S CHINA SEA
440726	OTORIYAMA MARU	05280	TANKER	RT WHITAKER	S CHINA SEA
440726	TOSAN MARU	08666	PASS-CARGO	RT WHITAKER	S CHINA SEA
	(Shared credit with *CREVALLE*)				
440818	SAIGON MARU	05350	CRUISER	RT WHITAKER	MINDORO
440827	URAL MARU	06374	TRANSPORT	RT WHITAKER	S CHINA SEA
441004	TAIBIN MARU	06886	FREIGHTER	RT WHITAKER	S CHINA SEA
441204	KISHINAMI	02100	DESTROYER	GW GRIDER	S CHINA SEA
441204	IWANAMI	02100	DESTROYER	GW GRIDER	S CHINA SEA
441204	HAKKO MARU	10022	TANKER	GW GRIDER	S CHINA SEA
441222	OMURISAN MARU	09204	TANKER	GW GRIDER	S CHINA SEA
441222	OTOWASAN MARU	09204	TANKER	GW GRIDER	S CHINA SEA
441222	ARITA MARU	10238	TANKER	GW GRIDER	S CHINA SEA
450225	KOHO MARU II	00850	FREIGHTER	GW GRIDER	S CHINA SEA

FLASHER holds the record for tonnage and is the only boat to sink over 100,000 tons. *FLASHER* earned Presidential Unit Citations for Patrols #3 and 4 under R.T. Whitaker and for Patrol #5 under G.W. Grider.

This aerial photograph was taken November 23, 1943, off the Jersey coast.

FLASHER was decommissioned on March 3, 1946, stricken from the lists and sold for scrap in 1963.

U.S.S. FLOUNDER
S.S. 251

FLOUNDER was built at the Electric Boat company and commissioned on November 29, 1943.

★ ★

FLOUNDER'S WARTIME PATROLS

NO.	CAPTAIN	DATE	DUR.	BASE	AREA	CLAIMED	CONFIRMED
1	CA JOHNSON	4403	54	BRISBANE	HALMEHERA	0	0
2	JE STEVENS	4406	39	BRISBANE	DAVAO	1/4000	1/2680
3	JE STEVENS	4408	61	BRISBANE	DAVAO	0	0
4	JE STEVENS	4410	46	BRISBANE	S CHINA SEA	1/700	1.5/2849
5	JE STEVENS	4501	42	FREMANTLE	S CHINA SEA	0	0
6	JE STEVENS	4503	38	FREMANTLE	S CHINA SEA	0	0

FLOUNDER'S VICTORIES

DATE	VESSEL	SIZE	TYPE	CAPTAIN	LOCATION
440617	NIPPONKAI MARU	02681	TENDER	JE STEVENS	MINDANAO
441110	NAZI U-537	01200	SUBMARINE	JE STEVENS	JAVA SEA
441121	GYOSAN MARU	05698	FREIGHTER	JE STEVENS	S CHINA SEA

(Shared credit with *GUAVINA*)

While cruising at periscope depth near Pulo Kambir, *FLOUNDER* had an underwater collision with *U.S.S. HOE* and suffered considerable damage. This was the only underwater collision between U.S. boats on record. *HOE* had merely scraped paint, but *FLOUNDER* had to return to base for repairs.

FLOUNDER is off Mare Island Navy Yard in this July 24, 1945 photograph.

FLOUNDER was decommissioned on February 12, 1947, stricken from the lists and sold for scrap in 1963.

U. S. S. FLIER
S. S. 250

FLIER was built at the Electric Boat Company and commissioned on October 18, 1943.

★

FLIER'S WARTIME PATROLS

NO.	CAPTAIN	DATE	DUR.	BASE	AREA	CLAIMED	CONFIRMED
1	JD CROWLEY	4405	44	PEARL	to FREMANTLE	4/19500	1/10400
2	JD CROWLEY	4408	00	FREMANTLE	S CHINA SEA	0	0

FLIER'S VICTORY

DATE	VESSEL	SIZE	TYPE	CAPTAIN	LOCATION
440604	HAKUSAM MARU	10380	TRANSPORT	JD CROWLEY	PHILIPPINE SEA

On her second patrol, while transiting the Balabac Straits, *FLIER* struck a mine and went under while still making 15 knots. Thirteen of her crew, including the captain, J.D. Crowley, survived after swimming all night to a small island. Friendly natives guided them to U.S. Army Coast-watchers after a five-day stay on their first island. The *REDFIN* eventually picked up the survivors and returned them to base.

FLIER photographed at Mare Island Navy Yard, April 20, 1944.

---

*The longest patrol made by a United States submarine in World War II was by the **GUITARRO** on her third run. It was 83 days.*

U. S. S. FLYINGFISH
S. S. 229

U. S. S. FLYINGFISH
S. S. 229

FLYINGFISH was built at the Portsmouth Navy Yard and commissioned on December 10, 1941.

★ ★ ★ ★ ★ ★
★ ★ ★ ★ ★ ★

FLYINGFISH'S WARTIME PATROLS

NO.	CAPTAIN	DATE	DUR.	BASE	AREA	CLAIMED	COMFIRMED
00	GR DONAHO	4205	15	PEARL	MIDWAY	0	0
1	GR DONAHO	4206	51	PEARL	E CHINA SEA	0	0
2	GR DONAHO	4208	31	PEARL	TRUK	1/400	0
3	GR DONAHO	4209	50	PEARL	to BRISBANE	2/3000	0
4	GR DONAHO	4301	54	BRISBANE	to PEARL	2/1300	1.5/5000
5	GR DONAHO	4303	48	PEARL	EMPIRE	4/28000	3/7500
6	FT WATKINS	4306	55	PEARL	E CHINA SEA	1/8700	1/2820
7	GR DONAHO	4310	34	PEARL	PALAU	1/7000	1/6500
8	RD RISSER	4311	50	PEARL	E CHINA SEA	2/15800	2/18784
9	RD RISSER	4402	49	PEARL	E CHINA SEA	3/10500	3/9928
10	RD RISSER	4405	61	PEARL	to BRISBANE	1/4000	2/8200
11	RD RISSER	4408	80	BRISBANE	to PEARL	0	0
12	RD RISSER	4505	36	PEARL	SEA OF JAPAN	2/3200	2/4113

FLYINGFISH'S VICTORIES

DATE	VESSEL	SIZE	TYPE	CAPTAIN	LOCATION
430126	TOKAI MARU	0$358	PASS-CARGO	GR DONAHO	GUAM
	(Shared with *SNAPPER*)				
430216	HYUGA MARU	00994	FREIGHTER	GR DONAHO	MARIANAS
430412	SAPPORA MARU #12	02865	FREIGHTER	GR DONAHO	HONSHU
430517	AMAHO MARU	02769	FREIGHTER	GR DONAHO	HONSHU
430527	KASAGA MARU	01377	FREIGHTER	GR DONAHO	HONSHU
430702	CANTON MARU	02820	FREIGHTER	FT WATKINS	FORMOSA
431027	NANMAN MARU	06550	FREIGHTER	GR DONAHO	PALAU
431216	GINYO MARU	08613	FREIGHTER	RD RISSER	S CHINA SEA
431227	KYUEI MARU	10171	TANKER	RD RISSER	S CHINA SEA
440312	TAIJIN MARU II	01937	FREIGHTER	RD RISSER	RYUKUS
440316	ANZAN MARU	05493	PASS-CARGO	RD RISSER	RYUKUS
440401	NINAMI MARU	02398	FREIGHTER	RD RISSER	RYUKUS
440525	TAITO MARU	04466	PASS-CARGO	RD RISSER	PALAU
440525	OSAKA MARU	03740	PASS-CARGO	RD RISSER	PALAU
450610	TAGA MARU #3	02220	FREIGHTER	RD RISSER	SEA OF JAPAN
450611	MEISEI MARU	01893	PASS-CARGO	RD RISSER	SEA OF JAPAN

FLYINGFISH ranks 21st of all U.S. boats in number of vessels sunk. Robert D. Risser ranks 27th of 77 skippers with five or more victories.

FLYINGFISH at Hunter's Point Naval Base, February 27, 1945.

FLYINGFISH was decommissioned April 28, 1954, stricken from the lists and sold for scrap in 1959.

U.S.S. GABILAN
S. S. 252

GABILAN was built at the Electric Boat company and commissioned on December 28, 1943

★ ★ ★ ★
GABILAN'S WARTIME PATROLS

NO.	CAPTAIN	DATE	DUR.	BASE	AREA	CLAIMED	CONFIRMED
1	KR WHELAND	4404	46	PEARL	MARIANAS	0	0
2	KR WHELAND	4406	49	PEARL	EMPIRE	1/1700	1/492
3	KR WHELAND	4409	46	PEARL	EMPIRE	1/2200	1/100
4	WB PARHAM	4412	48	BRISBANE	S CHINA S EA	0	0
5	WB PARHAM	4503	60	FREMANTLE to PEARL		3/6800	1.5/3612
6	WB PARHAM	4506	56	PEARL	EMPIRE	0	0

GABILAN'S VICTORIES

DATE	VESSEL	SIZE	TYPE	CAPTAIN	LOCATION
440717	MINESWEEPER #25	00492	MINESWEEPER	KR WHELAND	HONSHU
441031	KAIYO MARU	00100	AUXILIARY	KR WHELAND	HONSHU
450407	ISUZU	05700	CRUISER	WB PARHAM	BIMA BAY
	(Shared credit with *CHARR*)				
450414	KAKO MARU	00762	FREIGHTER	WB PARHAM	JAVA SEA

ISUZU was Japan's last light cruiser and she had been pressed into transport service when *GABILAN* and *CHARR* teamed up to send her down.

GABILAN preparing to dock on June 24, 1945.

GABILAN was decommissioned on February 23, 1946, stricken from the lists and sold for scrap in 1959.

U. S. S. GROUPER
S. S. 214

GROUPER was built at the Electric Boat Company and commissioned on February 12, 1942.

★ ★ ★ ★ ★ ★ ★ ★ ★ ★

GROUPER'S WARTIME PATROLS

NO.	CAPTAIN	DATE	DUR.	BASE	AREA	CLAIMED	CONFIRMED
00	CE DUKE	4205	15	PEARL	MIDWAY	0	0
1	CE DUKE	4206	56	PEARL	E CHINA SEA	0	0
2	R McGREGOR	4208	53	PEARL	E CHINA SEA	2/12000	2/11000
3	R McGREGOR	4211	49	PEARL	to BRISBANE	1/8400	1/4000
4	R McGREGOR	4301	56	BRISBANE	SOLOMONS	0	0
5	MP HOTTEL	4304	47	BRISBANE	SOLOMONS	0	0
6	MP HOTTEL	4306	46	BRISBANE	BISMARCKS	0	0
7	MP HOTTEL	4308	47	BRISBANE	to PEARL	0	0
8	FH WAHLIG	4403	59	PEARL	LUZON STRT	0	0
9	FH WAHLIG	4405	50	PEARL	EMPIRE	1/3500	1/2800
10	FH WAHLIG	4408	62	PEARL	PALAU	0	0
11	FH WAHLIG	4411	54	PEARL	EMPIRE	0	0
12	FH WAHLIG	4503	54	PEARL	E CHINA SEA	0	0

GROUPER'S VICTORIES

DATE	VESSEL	SIZE	TYPE	CAPTAIN	LOCATION
420821	TONE MARU	04070	FREIGHTER	R McGREGOR	E CHINA SEA
421001	LISBON MARU	07053	TRANSPORT	R McGREGOR	E CHINA SEA
421217	BANDOENG MARU	04003	PASS-CARGO	R McGREGOR	BISMARCKS
440624	KUMANOYAMA M.	02857	FREIGHTER	FH WAHLIG	SE HONSHU

GROUPER took part in the screening action at the Battle of Midway and was also in the group of fleet boats sent to Brisbane to relieve the older *"S"* boats. Like many boats at this time, *GROUPER* was plagued by faulty torpedos and, otherwise, might have had a high score.

GROUPER off Hunter's Point Naval Base, December 22, 1943.

GROUPER was decommissioned on December 2, 1968, stricken from the lists and sold for scrap in 1970.

U. S. S. GREENLING
S. S. 213

U. S. S. GREENLING
S. S. 213

GREENLING was built at the Electric Boat Company and commissioned on January 21, 1942.

★ ★ ★ ★ ★ ★ ★ ★ ★ ★
GREENLING'S WARTIME PATROLS

NO.	CAPTAIN	DATE	DUR.	BASE	AREA	CLAIMED	CONFIRMED
1	HC BRUTON	4204	57	PEARL	E CHINA SEA	1/5800	1/3300
2	HC BRUTON	4207	53	PEARL	TRUK	2/24000	2/17250
3	HC BRUTON	4209	41	PEARL	EMPIRE	4/32100	4/21400
4	HC BRUTON	4212	52	PEARL	to BRISBANE	4/20700	4/14000
5	JD GRANT	4302	64	BRISBANE	SOLOMONS	0	0
6	JD GRANT	4305	52	BRISBANE	SOLOMONS	1/5400	0
7	JD GRANT	4307	51	BRISBANE	to PEARL	0	0
8	JD GRANT	4312	39	PEARL	TRUK	1/1900	1/1936
9	JD GRANT	4403	53	PEARL	MARIANAS	0	0
10	J GERWICK	4407	63	PEARL	LUZON STRT	0	0
11	J GERWICK	4410	48	PEARL	EMPIRE	3/9900	3/2695
12	J GERWICK	4412	45	PEARL	EMPIRE	0	0

GREENLING'S VICTORIES

DATE	VESSEL	SIZE	TYPE	CAPTAIN	LOCATION
420504	KINJOSAN MARU	03262	FREIGHTER	HC BRUTON	CAROLINES
420705	BRASIL MARU	12752	TRANSPORT	H C BRUTON	TRUK
420706	PALAO MARU	04495	PASS-CARGO	HC BRUTON	TRUK
421003	KINKAI MARU	05852	FREIGHTER	HC BRUTON	HONSHU
421004	SETSUYO MARU	04117	FREIGHTER	HC BRUTON	HONSHU
421014	TAKUSEI MARU	03515	FREIGHTER	HC BRUTON	HONSHU
421018	HAKONESAN MARU	06673	FREIGHTER	HC BRUTON	HONSHU
421222	PATROL BOAT #35	00750	DESTROYER	HC BRUTON	BISMARCKS
421230	UNKNOWN MARU	04000	FREIGHTER	HC BRUTON	ANCHORITE
421230	HITERU MARU	05857	FREIGHTER	HC BRUTON	ANCHORITE
430116	KINPOSAN MARU	03261	FREIGHTER	HC BRUTON	GUADALCANAL
431231	SHOKO MARU	01936	FREIGHTER	JD GRANT	SOLOMONS
441107	KIRI MARU #8	00939	FREIGHTER	J GERWICK	SE HONSHU
441107	KOTAI MARU	00975	TANKER	J GERWICK	SE HONSHU
441110	PATROL BOAT #46	00820	DESTROYER	J GERWICK	SE HONSHU

GREENLING received Presidential Unit Citations for Patrols #1, 2, and 3 under H.C. Bruton. She tied for 10th overall in number of vessels sunk.

GREENLING at Mare Island Navy Yard, May 8, 1945.

GREENLING was decommissioned on October 16, 1946, stricken from the lists and scrapped in 1960.

U. S. S. GROWLER
S. S. 215

U. S. S. GROWLER
S. S. 215

GROWLER was built at the Electric Boat company and commissioned on March 20, 1942.

★ ★ ★ ★ ★ ★ ★ ★

GROWLER'S WARTIME PATROLS

NO.	CAPTAIN	DATE	DUR.	BASE	AREA	CLAIMED	CONFIRMED
00	HW GILMORE	4205	15	PEARL	MIDWAY	0	0
1	HW GILMORE	4206	27	PEARL	ALASKA	2/3400	1/1500
2	HW GILMORE	4208	49	PEARL	E CHINA SEA	4/26000	4/15000
3	HW GILMORE	4210	49	PEARL	to BRISBANE	0	0
4	HW GILMORE	4301	48	BRISBANE	SOLOMONS	2/7900	1/5900
5	AF SCHADE	4305	48	BRISBANE	SOLOMONS	1/4500	1/5200
6	AF SCHADE	4307	53	BRISBANE	BISMARCKS	0	0
7	AF SCHADE	4310	35	BRISBANE	to PEARL	0	0
8	AF SCHADE	4402	55	PEARL	E CHINA SEA	0	0
9	TB OAKLEY, Jr	4405	64	PEARL	PHIPPN SEA	1/10000	1/2000
10	TB OAKLEY, Jr	4408	45	PEARL	to FREMANTLE	5/22800	2/2800
11	TB OAKLEY, Jr	4410	00	FREMANTLE	CELEBES	0	0

GROWLER'S VICTORIES

DATE	VESSEL	SIZE	TYPE	CAPTAIN	LOCATION
420705	ARARE	01850	DESTROYER	HW GILMORE	off KISKA
420825	SENYO MARU	02904	GUNBOAT	HW GILMORE	FORMOSA
420831	EIFUKU MARU	05866	FREIGHTER	HW GILMORE	FORMOSA
420904	KASHINO	04000	SUPPLY SHIP	HW GILMORE	FORMOSA
420907	TAIKA MARU II	02204	FREIGHTER	HW GILMORE	FORMOSA
430116	CHIFUKU MARU	05857	PASS-CARGO	AF SCHADE	RABAUL
430619	MIYADONA MARU	05196	PASS-CARGO	AF SCHADE	RABAUL
440629	KATORU MARU	01920	FREIGHTER	AF SCHADE	FORMOSA
440912	SHIKINAMI	01950	DESTROYER	TB OAKLEY, Jr	HAINAN
440912	HIRADO	00860	FRIGATE	TB OAKLEY, Jr	HAINAN

GROWLER saw duty in the screen at the Battle of Midway. In a night surface action with a Japanese gunboat, *GROWLER* rammed the Japanese and suffered gunfire across her bridge. Commander Gilmore was badly wounded and ordered *GROWLER* to submerge, thereby saving the ship. Gilmore received the Congressional Medal of Honor for this action, the first awarded to a submariner. *GROWLER* received Navy Unit Commendations for Patrols #1, 2, and 4 under H.W. Gilmore, and for Patrol #10 under T.B. Oakley, Jr. While operating with *HAKE* and *HARDHEAD* in the South China Sea, *GROWLER* was lost with all hands on November 8, 1944 — cause unknown.

GROWLER docking at Hunter's Point Naval Shipyard, February 1, 1944.

U. S. S. GUARDFISH
S. S. 217

U. S. S. GUARDFISH
S. S. 217

GUARDFISH was built at the Electric Boat Company and commissioned on April 8, 1942.

GUARDFISH'S WARTIME PATROLS

NO.	CAPTAIN	DATE	DUR.	BASE	AREA	CLAIMED	CONFIRMED
1	TB KLAKRING	4208	40	PEARL	EMPIRE	6/50000	5/16709
2	TB KLAKRING	4209	59	PEARL	E CHINA SEA	2/15400	2/10400
3	TB KLAKRING	4212	56	PEARL to BRISBANE		3/11500	3/6000
4	TB KLAKRING	4303	52	BRISBANE	SOLOMONS	0	0
5	NG WARD	4305	70	BRISBANE	SOLOMONS	1/4000	1/900
6	NG WARD	4308	70	BRISBANE	BISMARCKS	2/13000	1/5460
7	NG WARD	4312	54	BRISBANE to PEARL		2/11900	2/11500
8	NG WARD	4406	46	PEARL	LUZON STRT	8/58200	4/20400
9	NG WARD	4408	62	PEARL	E CHINA SEA	1/3100	1/873
10	DT HAMMOND	4411	60	PEARL	LUZON STRT	0	0
11	DT HAMMOND	4502	44	PEARL	EMPIRE	0	0
12	DT HAMMOND	4505	49	PEARL	EMPIRE	0	0

GUARDFISH'S VICTORIES

DATE	VESSEL	SIZE	TYPE	CAPTAIN	LOCATION
420724	SEIKAI MARU	03109	PASS-CARGO	TB KLAKRING	KINKISAN
420802	TEIKYU MARU	02332	FREIGHTER	TB KLAKRING	KINKISAN
420804	CHITA MARU	02276	FREIGHTER	TB KLAKRING	MINATO
420804	TENYU MARU	03738	FREIGHTER	TB KLAKRING	MINATO
420804	KAIMEI MARU	05254	FREIGHTER	TB KLAKRING	MINATO
421021	UNKNOWN MARU	04000	FREIGHTER	TB KLAKRING	E CHINA SEA
421021	NICHIHO MARU	06363	FREIGHTER	TB KLAKRING	E CHINA SEA
430112	PATROL BOAT #1	00750	DESTROYER	TB KLAKRING	BISMARCKS
430122	UNKNOWN MARU	04000	FREIGHTER	TB KLAKRING	BISMARCKS
430123	HAKAZI	01300	DESTROYER	TB KLAKRING	BISMARCKS
430613	SUZUYA MARU	00901	FREIGHTER	NG WARD	BISMARCKS
431008	KASHU MARU	05460	FREIGHTER	NG WARD	ANCHORITES
440114	KENYO MARU II	10022	TANKER	NG WARD	PALAUS
440201	UMIKAZI	01580	DESTROYER	NG WARD	TRUK
440716	JINZAN MARU	05215	PASS-CARGO	NG WARD	LUZON
440716	MANTAI MARU	05863	FREIGHTER	NG WARD	LUZON
440717	HIYAMA MARU II	02838	FREIGHTER	NG WARD	LUZON
440719	TEIRYU MARU	06550	FREIGHTER	NG WARD	LUZON
440825	MIYAKAWA M. #2	00873	FREIGHTER	NG WARD	SEA OF JAPAN

GUARDFISH received Presidential Unit Citations for Patrols #1 and 2 under T.B. Klakring, and for Patrol #8 under N.G. Ward. She also ranked 8th in number of vessels sunk and 13th in tonnage. *GUARDFISH* mistakenly sank the *U.S.S. EXTRACTOR*, a Navy salvage vessel, the only such error during World War II.

This builder's photograph was taken at Electric Boat Company, Groton, Connecticut, April 15, 1942.

GUARDFISH was decommissioned on May 25, 1946, stricken from the lists and sunk as a target in October 1961.

U. S. S. GRUNION
S. S. 216

GRUNION was built at the Electric Boat Company and commissioned on April 11, 1942.

★

GRUNION'S WARTIME PATROL

NO.	CAPTAIN	DATE	DUR.	BASE	AREA	CLAIMED	CONFIRMED
1	ML ABELE	4206	00	PEARL	ALASKA	3/4500	2/600

GRUNION'S VICTORIES

DATE	VESSEL	SIZE	TYPE	CAPTAIN	LOCATION
420715	SUBCHASER #25	00300	SUBCHASER	ML ABELE	off KISKA
420715	SUBCHASER #27	00300	SUBCHASER	ML ABELE	off KISKA

GRUNION arrived in Pearl from the States on June 20, 1942. She was given ten days of pre-patrol training and immediately assigned to the Aleutians. Given an area just north of Kiska, she reported being attacked by a Japanese destroyer on July 15. On the same day, she reported sinking two subchasers and damaging a third. On July 19, she and *S-32*, *TRITON*, and *TUNA* were to patrol the approaches to Kiska and pick off any Japanese fleeing an air raid scheduled for the 22nd. The raid was cancelled, but *GRUNION* reported attacking enemy ships off Sirius Point and being depth charged for her trouble. On the 30th, she reported heavy anti-sub forces in her area and was ordered into Kiska to refuel and re-arm. That was her last transmission. Her fate remains a mystery.

GRUNION in a builder's photograph taken March 20, 1942, at Electric Boat Company, Groton, Connecticut.

U. S. S. GUNNEL
S. S. 253

GUNNEL was built at the Electric Boat company and commissioned on August 20, 1942.

★ ★ ★ ★ ★
GUNNEL'S WARTIME PATROLS

NO.	CAPTAIN	DATE	DUR.	BASE	AREA	CLAIMED	CONFIRMED
1	JS McCAIN	4210	36	SCOTLAND	N AFRICA	0	0
2	JS McCA1N	4306	31	PEARL	E CHINA SEA	3/15600	2/13300
3	JS McCAIN	4311	51	PEARL	EMPIRE	1/9500	1/4086
4	JS McCAIN	4402	60	PEARL	to FREMANTLE	0	0
5	JS McCAIN	4405	63	FREMANTLE	S CHINA SEA	0	0
6	GE O'NEIL	4407	54	FREMANTLE	MANILA	0	0
7	GE O'NEIL	4410	65	FREMANTLE	to PEARL	3/14600	3/6795
8	GE O'NEIL	4506	41	PEARL	EMPIRE	0	0

GUNNEL'S VICTORIES

DATE	VESSEL	SIZE	TYPE	CAPTAIN	LOCATION
430615	KOYO MARU	06435	FREIGHTER	JS McCAIN	E CHINA SEA
430619	TOKIWA MARU	06971	FREIGHTER	JS McCAIN	E CHINA SEA
431204	HIYOSHI MARU	04046	PASS-CARGO	JS McCAIN	KYUSHU
441108	SAGI	00595	PT BOAT	GE O'NEIL	LINGAYEN
441117	SHUNTEN MARU	05623	PASS-CARGO	GE O'NEIL	PARASEL ISL
441117	HIYODORI	00595	PT BOAT	GE O'NEIL	PARASEL ISL

GUNNEL first served in the European Theater during the invasion of North Africa. She then returned to the States to have her cranky diesels replaced before reporting to Pacific waters. At the end of 1944, she and two other boats returned to the States for major overhauls and did not see further action until the following June.

GUNNEL at Mare Island Navy Ship Yard, October 31, 1943.

GUNNEL was decommissioned on May 18, 1946, stricken from the lists and sold for scrap in 1959.

U. S. S. GURNARD
S. S. 254

GURNARD was built at the Electric Boat Company and commissioned on September 18, 1942.

★ ★ ★ ★ ★ ★
GURNARD'S WARTIME PATROLS

NO.	CAPTAIN	DATE	DUR.	BASE	AREA	CLAIMED	CONFIRMED
1	CH ANDREWS	4212	30	SCOTLAND	EUROPE	0	0
2	CH ANDREWS	4306	43	PEARL	PALAU	3/15600	1/2000
3	CH ANDREWS	4309	52	PEARL	E CHINA SEA	2/18000	2/11000
4	CH ANDREWS	4311	40	PEARL	EMPIRE	2/11000	3/14000
5	CH ANDREWS	4404	56	PEARL	to FREMANTLE	4/26900	3/19700
6	CH ANDREWS	4407	59	FREMANTLE	CELEBES	0	0
7	ND GAGE	4410	38	FREMANTLE	S CHINA SEA	1/5000	1/6900
8	ND GAGE	4412	51	FREMANTLE	S CHINA SEA	0	0
9	GS SIMMONS	4503	59	FREMANTLE	to PEARL	0	0

GURNARD'S VICTORIES

DATE	VESSEL	SIZE	TYPE	CAPTAIN	LOCATION
430611	TAIKO	00900	FRIGATE	CH ANDREWS	LEYTE
431008	TAIAN MARU	05655	FREIGHTER	CH ANDREWS	LUZON
431008	DAINICHI MARU	05813	PASS-CARGO	CH ANDREWS	LUZON
431224	SEIZAN MARU #2	01898	FREIGHTER	CH ANDREWS	SHIKOKU
431224	TOFUKU MARU	05857	FREIGHTER	CH ANDREWS	SHIKOKU
440506	TENSHINZAN MARU	06886	FREIGHTER	CH ANDREWS	MOLUCCA
440506	TAIJIMA MARU	06995	PASS-CARGO	CH ANDREWS	MOLUCCA
440506	ADEN MARU	05824	PASS-CARGO	CH ANDREWS	MOLUCCA
440524	TATEKAWA MARU	10090	TANKER	CH ANDREWS	TALAUD
441103	TAIMEI MARU	06923	FREIGHTER	ND GAGE	ANAMBAS

GURNARD made her first patrol in the North Sea and Bay of Biscay, and was ordered home to the States to have her balky diesels replaced. She then proceeded to the Pacific Theater where she racked up impressive totals. She received Navy Unit Commendations for Patrols #2, 3, 4, and 5 under C.H. Andrews. C.H. Andrews stood 15th in number of confirmed sinkings among the 77 commanders with five or more.

GURNARD at Mare Island Navy Ship Yard, March 14, 1944.

GURNARD was decommissioned on November 72, 1945, stricken from the lists and sold for scrap in 1961.

U. S. S. HADDO
S. S. 255

HADDO was built at the Electric Boat Company and commissioned on October 9, 1942.

★ ★ ★ ★ ★ ★
HADDO'S WARTIME PATROLS

NO.	CAPTAIN	DATE	DUR.	BASE	AREA	CLAIMED	CONFIRMED
1	WA LENT	4204	21	SCOTLAND	EUROPE	0	0
2	WA LENT	4205	37	SCOTLAND	EUROPE	0	0
3	WA LENT	4207	19	SCOTLAND	EUROPE	0	0
4	J CORBUS	4312	53	PEARL	to FREMANTLE	0	0
5	C NIMITZ, Jr	4401	54	FREMANTLE	MAKASSAR	0	0
6	C NIMITZ, Jr	4405	59	FREMANTLE	CELEBES	0	0
7	C NIMITZ, Jr	4407	52	FREMANTLE	S CHINA SEA	5.5/17100	5/14460
8	FC LYNCH	4410	60	FREMANTLE	to PEARL	3/9000	1/860
9	FC LYNCH	4505	46	PEARL	E CHINA SEA	6/18600	3/6126
10	FC LYNCH	4508	31	PEARL	EMPIRE	0	0

HADDO'S VICTORIES

DATE	VESSEL	SIZE	TYPE	CAPTAIN	LOCATION
440721	KINRYO MARU	04390	PASS-CARGO	C NIMITZ, Jr	MINDORO
440721	NORFOLK MARU	06576	PASS-CARGO	C NIMITZ, Jr	MINDORO
440722	SADO	00860	FRIGATE	C NIMITZ, Jr	MINDORO
440723	ASAKAZE	01270	DESTROYER	C NIMITZ, Jr	LUZON
440821	KATSURIKI	01540	SURVEY VES	C NIMITZ, Jr	PALAWAN
451109	HISHI MARU #2	00856	TANKER	FC LYNCH	SULU SEA
450701	COAST DEF #72	00800	FRIGATE	FC LYNCH	YELLOW SEA
450701	TAIUN MARU	02200	FREIGHTER	FC LYNCH	YELLOW SEA
450701	KONRI MARU	03106	FREIGHTER	FC LYNCH	YELLOW SEA

HADDO made her first patrols out of Lockneath, Scotland, but was returned to the States when it became apparent she was not being used to best advantage. *HADDO* received a Navy Unit Commendation for Patrol #7 under C.W. Nimitz, Jr., and was one of the twelve boats selected to be present at the Japanese surrender in Tokyo Bay.

HADDO at Mare Island Navy Ship Yard, April 10, 1945.

HADDO was decommissioned on Feburary 16, 1946, stricken from the lists and sold for scrap in 1961.

U. S. S. HADDOCK
S. S. 231

HADDOCK was built at the Portsmouth Navy Yard and commissioned on March 14, 1942.

★ ★ ★ ★ ★ ★ ★ ★ ★ ★ ★

HADDOCK'S WARTIME PATROLS

NO.	CAPTAIN	DATE	DUR.	BASE	AREA	CLAIMED	CONFIRMED
1	AH TAYLOR	4207	52	PEARL	E CHINA SEA	3/24300	2/6200
2	AH TAYLOR	4210	54	PEARL	E CHINA SEA	3/24000	2/8500
3	AH TAYLOR	4212	51	PEARL	EMPIRE	2/13300	1/4000
4	RM DAVENPORT	4303	39	PEARL	PALAU	1/11900	2/9200
5	RM DAVENPORT	4306	41	PEARL	PALAU	1/10900	1/5500
6	RM DAVENPORT	4309	27	PEARL	TRUK	3/39000	0
7	RM DAVENPORT	4310	27	PEARL	TRUK	5/32600	0
8	JP ROACH	4312	53	PEARL	MARIANAS	0	0
9	JP ROACH	4403	62	PEARL	EMPIRE	1/1000	0
10	JP ROACH	4410	60	PEARL	LUZON STR	0	0
11	WH BROCKMAN	4501	51	PEARL	EMPIRE	0	0
12	AR STROW	4504	42	PEARL	EMPIRE	0	0
13	AR STROW	4506	51	PEARL	EMPIRE	0	0

HADDOCK'S VICTORIES

DATE	VESSEL	SIZE	TYPE	CAPTAIN	LOCATION
420822	UNKNOWN MARU	04000	TRANSPORT	AH TAYLOR	E CHINA SEA
420826	TEISHUN MARU	02251	FREIGHTER	AH TAYLOR	E CHINA SEA
421103	TEKKAI MARU	01925	FREIGHTER	AH TAYLOR	YELLOW SEA
421111	VENICE MARU	06571	PASS-CARGO	AH TAYLOR	YELLOW SEA
430117	UNKNOWN MARU	04000	FREIGHTER	AH TAYLOR	HONSHU
430403	ARIMA MARU	07389	PASS-CARGO	RM DAVENPORT	PALAU
430408	TOYO MARU #3	01916	FREIGHTER	RM DAVENPORT	PALAU
430721	SAIPAN MARU	05533	TRANSPORT	RM DAVENPORT	PHILIPPINE SEA

HADDOCK received Presidential Unit Citations for Patrol #2 under A.H. Taylor, and for Patrols #5, 6, and 7 under R.M. Davenport. She was the first U.S. submarine to go on patrol with the new SJ Radar. She participated in Operation King Two and stood picket for Japanese fleeing the Battle of Leyte Gulf.

Transferring an appendectomy case to a waiting PBY for a flight to the naval hospital on Midway.

HADDOCK was decommissioned on February 12, 1947, stricken from the lists and sold for scrap in 1960.

U. S. S. HAKE
S. S. 256

HAKE was built at the Electric Boat Company and commissioned on October 30, 1942.

★ ★ ★ ★ ★ ★ ★
HAKE'S WARTIME PATROLS

NO.	CAPTAIN	DATE	DUR.	BASE	AREA	CLAIMED	CONFIRMED
1	JC BROACH	4304	23	SCOTLAND	ICELAND	0	0
2	JC BROACH	4305	51	SCOTLAND	N ATLANTIC	0	0
3	JC BROACH	4312	55	PEARL	to FREMANTLE	3/16500	3/19384
4	JC BROACH	4403	42	FREMANTLE	S CHINA SEA	2/20400	1/5174
5	JC BROACH	4405	50	FREMANTLE	CELEBES	3/14500	3/13375
6	FE HAYLOR	4408	50	FREMANTLE	S CHINA SEA	1/1500	0
7	FE HAYLOR	4410	57	FREMANTLE	S CHINA SEA	0	0
8	FE HAYLOR	4501	61	FREMANTLE	to PEARL	0	0
9	FE HAYLOR	4507	49	PEARL	EMPIRE	0	0

HAKE'S VICTORIES

DATE	VESSEL	SIZE	TYPE	CAPTAIN	LOCATION
440112	NIGITSU MARU	09547	TRANSPORT	JC BROACH	FORMOSA STRT
440201	TACOMA MARU	05772	PASS-CARGO	JC BROACH	HALMAHERA
440201	NANKA MARU	04065	FREIGHTER	JC BROACH	HALMAHERA
440327	YAMAMIZU MARU	05174	TANKER	JC BROACH	BORNEO
440608	KAZEGUMO	01900	DESTROYER	JC BROACH	MORO GULF
440617	KINSHU MARU	05591	FREIGHTER	JC BROACH	MINDANAO
440620	HIBI MARU	05874	PASS-CARGO	JC BROACH	MINDANAO

In April 1943, *HAKE* relieved *HADDO* at Roseneath, Scotland and patroled the North Atlantic convoy routes in search of German U-Boats. When it was decided that submarines were not the most efficient way to hunt submarines, *HAKE* was dispatched to the Pacific Theater. She took part in Operation Forager during the Marianas Operation.

HAKE at Mare Island Navy Yard during a re-fit, November 26, 1943.

HAKE was decommissioned on August 13, 1946, stricken from the lists and sold for scrap in 1967.

U. S. S. HALIBUT
S. S. 232

U. S. S. HALIBUT
S. S. 232

HALIBUT was built at the Portsmouth Navy Yard and commissioned on April 10, 1942.

★ ★ ★ ★ ★ ★ ★
HALIBUT'S WARTIME PATROLS

NO.	CAPTAIN	DATE	DUR.	BASE	AREA	CLAIMED	CONFIRMED
1	PH ROSS	4208	45	PEARL	ALASKA	0	0
2	PH ROSS	4210	21	ALASKA	ALASKA	0	0
3	PH ROSS	4211	54	PEARL	EMPIRE	4/30300	3/12400
4	PH ROSS	4302	50	PEARL	PELAU	2/15000	2/13711
5	PH ROSS	4306	49	PEARL	TRUK	0	0
6	IJ GALANTIN	4308	28	PEARL	EMPIRE	2/9700	2/9800
7	IJ GALANTIN	4310	37	PEARL	EMPIRE	1/3500	1/4653
8	IJ GALANTIN	4312	50	PEARL	MARIANAS	0	0
9	IJ GALANTIN	4403	58	PEARL	EMPIRE	2/4800	3/5550
10	IJ GALANTIN	4410	49	PEARL	LUZON STR	1/10000	1/1900

HALIBUT'S VICTORIES

DATE	VESSEL	SIZE	TYPE	CAPTAIN	LOCATION
421212	GYOKUZAN MARU	01970	FREIGHTER	PH ROSS	HONSHU
421216	SHINGO MARU	04740	FREIGHTER	PH ROSS	HONSHU
421216	GENZAN MARU	05708	PASS-CARGO	PH ROSS	HONSHU
430220	SHINKOKU MARU	03991	PASS-CARGO	PH ROSS	N BIKINI
430303	NICHIYU MARU	06817	PASS-CARGO	PH ROSS	NW TRUK
430830	TAIBUN MARU	06581	PASS-CARGO	IJ GALANTIN	JAPAN SEA
430906	SHOGEN MARU	03362	FREIGHTER	IJ GALANTIN	JAPAN SEA
431102	EHIME MARU	04653	FREIGHTER	IJ GALANTIN	W TRUK
440412	TAICHU MARU	03213	PASS-CARGO	IJ GALANTIN	NANSEI SHOTO
440427	GENBU MARU	01872	PASS-CARGO	IJ GALANTIN	NANSEI SHOTO
440427	KAMOME	00450	MINELAYER	IJ GALANTIN	NANSEI SHOTO
441025	AKITSUKI	01900	DESTROYER	IJ GALANTIN	E CHINA SEA

HALIBUT made her first patrols in the inhospitable waters off Alaska. She later participated in Operation King Two in support of the Leyte Gulf Operation. *HALIBUT* received a Navy Unit Commendation for Patrol #10 under I.J. Galantin. She was severely damaged in a prolonged depth charging in Luzon Strait and was deemed a total economic loss.

A Navy photo of *HAILBUT* at Portsmouth Navy Yard, May 20, 1942.

HALIBUT was decommissioned on July 18, 1945 and scrapped.

U. S. S. HARDER
S. S. 257

U. S. S. HARDER
S. S. 257

HARDER was built at the Electric Boat Company and commissioned on December 2, 1942.

★ ★ ★ ★ ★ ★

HARDER'S WARTIME PATROLS

NO.	CAPTAIN	DATE	DUR.	BASE	AREA	CLAIMED	CONFIRMED
1	SD DEALEY	4306	33	PEARL	EMPIRE	3/15400	1/7000
2	SD DEALEY	4308	46	PEARL	EMPIRE	4/25600	5/15272
3	SD DEALEY	4310	31	PEARL	MARIANAS	5/24800	3/15273
4	SD DEALEY	4403	47	PEARL	to FREMANTLE	2/5300	2/9000
5	SD DEALEY	4405	45	FREMANTLE	CELEBES	5/8500	3/6500
6	SD DEALEY	4408	00	FREMANTLE	S CHINA SEA	1.5/3200	2/1760

HARDER'S VICTORIES

DATE	VESSEL	SIZE	TYPE	CAPTAIN	LOCATION
430623	SAGARA MARU	07189	TENDER	SD DEALEY	S ISE WAN
430909	KOYO MARU II	03010	FREIGHTER	SD DEALEY	TOKYO BAY
430911	YOKO MARU	01050	FREIGHTER	SD DEALEY	TOKYO BAY
430919	KACHISAN MARU	00814	FREIGHTER	SD DEALEY	NAGOYA
430923	KOWA MARU	04520	FREIGHTER	SD DEALEY	NAGOYA
430923	DAISHIN MARU	05878	TANKER	SD DEALEY	NAGOYA
431119	UDO MARU	03936	FREIGHTER	SD DEALEY	MARIANAS
431119	HOKKO MARU	05385	FREIGHTER	SD DEALEY	MARIANAS
431120	NIKKO MARU	05949	FREIGHTER	SD DEALEY	MARIANAS
440413	IKAZUCHI	01950	DESTROYER	SD DEALEY	GUAM
440417	MATSUE MARU	07061	FREIGHTER	SD DEALEY	GUAM
440606	MINATSUKI	01500	DESTROYER	SD DEALEY	TARAKAN
440607	HAYANAMI	02100	DESTROYER	SD DEALEY	TARAKAN
440609	TANIKAZI	01900	DESTROYER	SD DEALEY	TARAKAN
440822	MATSUWA	00860	FRIGATE	SD DEALEY	BATAAN
440822	HIBURI	00900	FRIGATE	SD DEALEY	BATAAN

HARDER received Presidential Unit Citations for Patrols #1, 2, 3, and 4 under S.D. Dealey; and was one of only twenty-six boats to sink five or more vessels on any one patrol. She stands 16th of all boats for total confirmed vessels sunk. While operating near the mouth of Manila Bay with *HADDO* and *HAKE*, *HARDER* was lying in wait for a convoy to come out of the harbor. All three boats underwent attack by anti-submarine forces and *HARDER* was lost with all hands during this action. S.D. Dealey was awarded the Medal of Honor posthumously.

HARDER shown at Mare Island Navy Yard during a re-fit, February 19, 1944.

U. S. S. HERRING
S. S. 233

HERRING was built at the Portsmouth Navy Yard and commissioned on May 4, 1942.

★ ★ ★ ★ ★

HERRING'S WARTIME PATROLS

NO.	CAPTAIN	DATE	DUR.	BASE	AREA	CLAIMED	CONFIRMED
1	RW JOHNSON	4210	35	SCOTLAND	BAY BISCAY	1/7000	0
2	RW JOHNSON	4212	58	SCOTLAND	BAY BISCAY	0	0
3	J CORBUS	4303	37	SCOTLAND	BAY BISCAY	1/500	1/517
4	RW JOHNSON	4305	35	SCOTLAND	N ATLANTIC	0	0
5	RW JOHNSON	4307	19	SCOTLAND	N ATLANTIC	0	0
6	RW JOHNSON	4311	54	PEARL	E CHINA SEA	4/30000	2/10000
7	D ZABRISKIE	4402	54	PEARL	EMPIRE	0	0
8	D ZABRISKIE	4405	00	PEARL	POLAR CIRC	3/3800	4/9960

HERRING'S VICTORIES

DATE	VESSEL	SIZE	TYPE	CAPTAIN	LOCATION
430321	U-163	00517	SUBMARINE	J CORBUS	BAY OF BISCAY
431214	HAKOZAKI MARU	03948	PASS-CARGO	RW JOHNSON	HONSHU
440101	NAGOYA MARU	06072	AIRCRF FERRY	RW JOHNSON	E CHINA SEA
440530	ISHIGAKI	00860	FRIGATE	D ZABRISKIE	KURILES
440531	HOKUYU MARU	01590	FREIGHTER	D ZABRISKIE	KURILES
440601	IWAKI MARU	03124	FREIGHTER	D ZABRISKIE	POINT TAGAN
440601	HIBURU MARU	04365	PASS-CARGO	D ZABRISKIE	POINT TAGAN

During Operation Torch, *HERRING* was stationed off Casablanca to conduct recon patrols. On a later patrol, as part of Squadron 50, she sank the German U-Boat *U-163*. While sinking her last two victims, which were ships at anchor, *HERRING* was hit by shore batteries at Matsuwa Island and went down with all hands.

This photograph was taken off Hunter's Point Navy Yard, October 12, 1943.

U. S. S. HOE
S. S. 258

HOE was built at the Electric Boat Company and commissioned on December 16, 1942.

★ ★ ★ ★ ★ ★ ★

HOE'S WARTIME PATROLS

NO.	CAPTAIN	DATE	DUR.	BASE	AREA	CLAIMED	CONFIRMED
1	VB McCREA	4305	45	PEARL	PALAU	1/9500	0
2	VB McCREA	4308	59	PEARL	TRUK	0	0
3	VB McCREA	4401	38	PEARL	to FREMANTLE	4/29000	1/10526
4	VB McCREA	4404	59	FREMANTLE	S CHINA SEA	1/4000	0
5	VB McCREA	4406	55	FREMANTLE	MANILA	0	0
6	VB McCREA	4409	37	FREMANTLE	S CHINA SEA	2/15000	1/2500
7	MP REFO	4411	50	FREMANTLE	S CHINA SEA	0	0
8	MP REFO	4502	46	FREMANTLE	to PEARL	1/2300	1/900

HOE'S VICTORIES

DATE	VESSEL	SIZE	TYPE	CAPTAIN	LOCATION
440225	NISSHO MARU	10526	TANKER	VB McCREA	MINDANAO
441008	KOHOKU MARU	02573	PASS-CARGO	VB McCREA	LINGAYAN
450225	SHONAN	00900	FRIGATE	MP REFO	HAINAH

HOE had an underwater collision with *FLOUNDER* while they were patroling in the vicinity of Pulo Kambir. *HOE* was not seriously damaged, but *FLOUNDER* was forced to return to base for repairs. As far as is known, this was the only underwater submarine collision ever recorded.

A builder's photograph of *HOE* at Electric Boat Company, Groton, Connecticut, December 26, 1942.

HOE was decommissioned on August 7, 1946, stricken from the lists and sold for scrap in 1960.

U. S. S. JACK
S. S. 259

U. S. S. JACK
S. S. 259

JACK was built at the Electric Boat Company and commissioned on January 6, 1943.

★ ★ ★ ★ ★ ★ ★
JACK'S WARTIME PATROLS

NO.	CAPTAIN	DATE	DUR.	BASE	AREA	CLAIMED	CONFIRMED
1	TM DYKERS	4306	40	PEARL	EMPIRE	3/24300	3/16400
2	TM DYKERS	4309	30	PEARL	EMPIRE	0	0
3	TM DYKERS	4401	51	PEARL	to FREMANTLE	7/53500	4/20441
4	TM DYKERS	4404	35	FREMANTLE	MANILA	0	1/5425
5	AE KRAPF	4406	39	FREMANTLE	MANILA	4/25000	3/15748
6	AE KRAPF	4408	48	FREMANTLE	CELEBES	2/8200	2/6287
7	AS FURHMAN	4410	58	FREMANTLE	to PEARL	1/4000	2/12200
8	AS FURHMAN	4504	51	PEARL	EMPIRE	0	0
9	AS FURHMAN	4507	48	PEARL	FORMOSA	0	0

JACK'S VICTORIES

DATE	VESSEL	SIZE	TYPE	CAPTAIN	LOCATION
430626	TOYO MARU #4	04163	PASS-CARGO	TM DYKERS	TOKYO BAY
430626	SHOZAN MARU	05859	FREIGHTER	TM DYKERS	TOKYO BAY
430704	NIKKYU MARU	06529	FREIGHTER	TM DYKERS	TOKYO BAY
440219	KOKUEI MARU	05154	TANKER	TM DYKERS	S CHINA SEA
440219	NANEI MARU	05019	TANKER	TM DYKERS	S CHINA SEA
440219	NICHIRIN MARU	05162	TANKER	TM DYKERS	S CHINA SEA
440219	ICHIYO MARU	05106	TANKER	TM DYKERS	S CHINA SEA
440526	YOSHIDA MARU	05425	PASS-CARGO	TM DYKERS	MANILA
440625	SAN PEDRO MARU	07268	TANKER	AE KRAPF	LINGAYEN
440630	TSURUSHIMA MARU	04645	FREIGHTER	AE KRAPF	CAVITE
440631	MATSUKAWA MARU	03925	FREIGHTER	AE KRAPF	CAVITE
440729	MINESWEEPER #28	00492	MINESWEEPER	AE KRAPF	CELEBES
440829	MEXICO MARU	05785	PASS-CARGO	AE KRAPF	CELEBES
441114	NICHIEI MARU	05396	FREIGHTER	AS FURHMAN	S CHINA SEA
441115	YUZAN MARU #2	06859	FREIGHTER	AS FURHMAN	S CHINA SEA

JACK received Presidential Unit Citations for Patrols #1 and 3 under T.M. Rykers, and for Patrol #5 under A.E. Krapf. She became known as the "Tanker Killer" since she sank four enemy tankers in one day. *JACK* stands 9th in tonnage and is tied for 10th in number of vessels destroyed.

JACK during a re-fit at Mare Island Naval Ship Yard, December 17, 1943.

JACK was decommissioned on June 8, 1946 and in 1958 was transferred to the Greek Navy as the *AMFITRITI.*

U. S. S. KINGFISH
S. S. 234

U. S. S. KINGFISH
S. S. 234

KINGFISH was built at the Portsmouth Navy Yard and commissioned on May 20, 1942.

★ ★ ★ ★ ★ ★ ★ ★ ★
KINGFISH'S WARTIME PATROLS

NO.	CAPTAIN	DATE	DUR.	BASE	AREA	CLAIMED	CONFIRMED
1	VL LOWERANCE	4209	55	PEARL	EMPIRE	2/12000	2/5500
2	VL LOWERANCE	4211	58	PEARL	E CHINA SEA	2/14000	2/10000
3	VL LOWERANCE	4302	52	PEARL	E CHINA SEA	2/13000	1/8000
4	VL LOWERANCE	4307	56	PEARL	to FREMANTLE	0	0
5	VL LOWERANCE	4309	52	FREMANTLE	S CHINA SEA	2/19100	1/3365
6	HL JUKES	4312	42	FREMANTLE	to PEARL	3/23300	3/14571
7	HL JUKES	4402	49	PEARL	MARIANAS	0	0
8	HL JUKES	4405	50	PEARL	BONINS	0	0
9	TE HARPER	4410	46	PEARL	BONINS	2/7500	3/3137
10	TE HARPER	4412	40	PEARL	EMPIRE	2/15500	2/3800
11	TE HARPER	4503	50	PEARL	EMPIRE	0	0
12	TD KEEGAN	4506	58	PEARL	POLAR CIRC	0	0

KINGFISH'S VICTORIES

DATE	VESSEL	SIZE	TYPE	CAPTAIN	LOCATION
421001	YOMEI MARU	02860	FREIGHTER	VL LOWERANCE	KYUSHU
421023	SE1KYO MARU	02608	GUNBOAT	VL LOWERANCE	KYUSHU
421201	HINO MARU #3	04391	PASS-CARGO	VL LOWERANCE	IWO JIMA
421228	CHOYO MARU	05388	FREIGHTER	VL LOWERANCE	FORMOSA
430319	TAKACHIHO MARU	08154	TRANSPORT	VL LOWERANCE	E CHINA SEA
431020	SANA MARU	03365	FREIGHTER	VL LOWERANCE	S CHINA SEA
440103	RYUEI MARU	05144	TANKER	HL JUKES	S CHINA SEA
440103	BOKUEI MARU	05135	TANKER	HL JUKES	S CHINA SEA
440107	FUSHIMI MARU #3	04292	TANKER	HL JUKES	S CHINA SEA
441024	IKUTAGAWA MARU	02220	FREIGHTER	TE HARPER	BONINS
441027	TOKAI MARU #4	00537	FREIGHTER	TE HARPER	BONINS
441027	TRANSPORT #133	01000	LANDNG CRFT	TE HARPER	BONINS
450103	YAEI MARU	01941	FREIGHTER	TE HARPER	SHICHITO
450103	SHIBAZONO MARU	01831	PASS-CARGO	TE HARPER	SHICHITO

KINGFISH made one of the war's first SJ radar attacks when she sank the *CHOYO MARU* using the new device. *KINGFISH* was tied with *GRAYBACK* for 24th place of all U.S. subs for number of vessels sunk with fourteen victories.

KINGFISH, taken at Mare Island Navy Yard, June 5, 1943.

She was decommissioned on March 9, 1946, and sold for scrap in 1960.

U. S. S. LAPON
S. S. 260

LAPON was built at the Electric Boat Company and commissioned on January 23, 1943.

★ ★ ★ ★
LAPON'S WARTIME PATROLS

NO.	CAPTAIN	DATE	DUR.	BASE	AREA	CLAIMED	CONFIRMED
1	OG KIRK	4306	41	PEARL	EMPIRE	0	0
2	LT STONE	4309	39	PEARL	EMPIRE	1/2900	1/2000
3	LT STONE	4402	47	PEARL	to FREMANTLE	4/32700	3/19500
4	LT STONE	4404	42	FREMANTLE	S CHINA SEA	2/15000	2/11253
5	LT STONE	4406	42	FREMANTLE	S CHINA SEA	3/18000	2/6560
6	DG BAER	4409	56	FREMANTLE	S CHINA SEA	4/25600	3/14170
7	DG BAER	4411	56	FREMANTLE	to PEARL	0	0
8	DG BAER	4505	50	PEARL	EMPIRE	0	0

LAPON'S VICTORIES

DATE	VESSEL	SIZE	TYPE	CAPTAIN	LOCATION
431018	TAICHU MARU II	01906	FREIGHTER	LT STONE	SEA OF JAPAN
440308	TOYOKUNI MARU	05792	FREIGHTER	LT STONE	S CHINA SEA
440309	NICHIREI MARU	05396	FREIGHTER	LT STONE	S CHINA SEA
440318	HOKUROKU MARU	08359	PASS-CARGO	LT STONE	S CHINA SEA
440524	WALES MARU	06586	PASS-CARGO	LT STONE	off SAIGON
440524	BIZEN MARU	04667	FREIGHTER	LT STONE	off SAIGON
440718	KYODO MARU #36	01499	PASS-CARGO	LT STONE	S CHINA SEA
440731	TENSHIN MARU	05061	TANKER	LT STONE	S CHINA SEA
440822	SHUN YUAN	01610	FREIGHTER	DG BAER	LUZON
440827	HOKKI MARU	05599	TANKER	DG BAER	LUZON
441010	EJIRI MARU	06968	TANKER	DG BARR	LUZON

LAPON received Navy Unit Commendations for Patrols #3, 4, and 5 under command of L.T. Stone, and for Patrol #6 under command of D.G. Baer. *LAPON* mistakenly fired on *RATON* while both were patroling areas that somehow overlapped. In the only known instance of this happening, the shots were both misses.

LAPON at Mare Island Navy Ship yard during a re-fit, January 11, 1944.

LAPON was decommissioned July 25, 1946, and transferred to the Greek Navy in 1957 as the *POSEIDON*.

U. S. S. MINGO
S. S. 261

MINGO was built at the Electric Boat Company and commissioned on February 12, 1943.

★ ★ ★ ★ ★

MINGO'S WARTIME PATROLS

NO.	CAPTAIN	DATE	DUR.	BASE	AREA	CLAIMED	CONFIRMED
1	RC LYNCH	4306	57	PEARL	PALAU	0	0
2	RC LYNCH	4309	53	PEARL	TRUK	0	0
3	JJ STALEY	4402	73	PEARL	to BRISBANE	0	0
4	JJ STALEY	4406	46	BRISBANE	CELEBES	1/1700	1/2100
5	JR MADISON	4408	46	FREMANTLE	CELEBES	0	0
6	JR MADISON	4411	52	FREMANTLE	S CHINA SEA	1/10000	1/9500
7	JR MADISON	4502	T6	FREMANTLE	to PEARL	0	0

MINGO'S VICTORIES

DATE	VESSEL	SIZE	TYPE	CAPTAIN	LOCATION
440707	TAMANAMI	02100	DESTROYER	JJ STALEY	LUZON
441125	MANILA MARU	09486	PASS-CARGO	JR MADISON	BRUNEI

On August 1, 1943, *MINGO* reconnoitered and bombarded Solol Island for G-2. While doing lifeguard duty in Borneo waters in October 1944, she was in a firefight with enemy small craft, ran aground, and backed off under fire. She rescued some sixteen Liberator airmen from various islands in the area. On her way home, she was mistakenly attacked by a Liberator and suffered a near miss before communication with the plane was established.

MINGO at Mare Island Naval Ship Yard during a re-fit, July 20, 1945.

MINGO was decommissioned on January 27, 1946, and, ironically, was transferred to the Japanese Navy in 1955 as the *KUROSHIO.*

U. S. S. MUSKALUNGE
S. S. 262

U. S. S. MUSKALUNGE
S. S. 262

MUSKALUNGE was built at the Electric Boat Company and commissioned on March 2, 1943.

★ ★ ★ ★ ★
MUSKALUNGE'S WARTIME PATROLS

NO.	CAPTAIN	DATE	DUR.	BASE	AREA	CLAIMED	CONFIRMED
1	WA SAUNDERS	4309	48	PEARL	PALAU	0	0
2	MP RUSSILO	4311	56	PEARL	PALAU	1/8200	1/7163
3	MP RUSSILO	4404	65	PEARL	to FREMANTLE	0	0
4	MP RUSSILO	4408	54	FREMANTLE	INDOCHINA	1/800	0
5	LA LAJUENE	4410	56	FREMANTLE	to PEARL	0	0
6	WH LAWRENCE	4505	52	PEARL	E CHINA SEA	0	0
7	WH LAWRENCE	4507	40	PEARL	POLAR CIRC	0	0

MUSKALUNGE'S VICTORY

DATE	VESSEL	SIZE	TYPE	CAPTAIN	LOCATION
440821	DURBAN MARU	07163	PASS-CARGO	MP RUSSILO	S CHINA SEA

MUSKALUNGE was part of Operation Forager to the Northwest of the Marianas to cut the supply lines to this crucial area during the invasion. She was one of the twelve boats privileged to be in attendance at the signing of the peace agreement in Tokyo Bay.

MUSKALUNGE at Mare Island Navy Ship Yard for a re-fit, April 1, 1945. White lines indicate some of the changes made during the re-fit.

MUSKALUNGE was decommissioned on January 29, 1947, and transferred to the Brazilian Navy in 1957 as the *HUMAITA.*

The U.S.S. SEALION II fired a salvo of torpedoes at the Japanese battleships KONGO and HARUNA. KONGO was hit and eventually sank, but the HARUNA survived. This was the same battleship supposedly sunk by the Army Air Force Captain Colin Kelly in the early days of the war when America desperately needed a hero. In fact, HARUNA was one of only two Japanese battlewagons to survive the war, and neither was serviceable at the time.

U. S. S. PADDLE
S. S. 263

PADDLE was built at the Electric Boat Company and commissioned on March 29, 1943.

★ ★ ★ ★ ★ ★ ★ ★

PADDLE'S WARTIME PATROLS

NO.	CAPTAIN	DATE	DUR.	BASE	AREA	CLAIMED	CONFIRMED
1	RH RICE	4307	54	PEARL	EMPIRE	1/5500	1/5248
2	RH RICE	4310	58	PEARL	MARSHALLS	0	0
3	BH NOWELL	4403	54	PEARL	to FREMANTLE	2/10800	2/9700
4	BH NOWELL	4406	54	FREMANTLE	CELEBES	1/1200	1/1300
5	BH NOWELL	4408	34	FREMANTLE	SULU SEA	1/5000	1.5/5000
6	J FITZ-PATRICK	4410	29	FREMANTLE	CELEBES	2/1100	0
7	J FITZ-PATRICK	4411	53	FREMANTLE	to PEARL	2/10800	.5/1427
8	J FITZ-PATRICK	4505	60	PEARL	E CHINA SEA	0	0

PADDLE'S VICTORIES

DATE	VESSEL	SIZE	TYPE	CAPTAIN	LOCATION
430723	ATAKA MARU	05248	PASS-CARGO	RH RICE	SHIKOKU
440416	MITO MARU	07061	PASS-CARGO	BH NOWELL	MOLUCCA PASG
440416	HIND MARU #1	02671	FREIGHTER	BH NOWELL	MOLUCCA PASG
440706	HOKAZE	01300	DESTROYER	BH NOWELL	TALAUD ISLE
440807	SHINYO MARU #4	02518	FREIGHTER	BH NOWELL	SULU SEA
441208	EIYO MARU #2	05061	TANKER	BH NOWELL	SULU SEA
	(Shared credit with carrier-based aircraft)				
441208	SHOEI MARU	02854	TANKER	J FITZ-PATRICK	S CHINA SEA
	(Shared credit with *HAMMERHEAD*)				

PADDLE did the weather reporting for Operation Galvanic (invasion of Tarawa) and later took part in Operation Forager during the Marianas campaign.

PADDLE at Mare Island Navy Yard during a re-fit, February 13, 1944.

PADDLE was decommissioned on February 1, 1946 and transferred to the Brazilian Navy in 1957 as the *RIACHEULO*.

U. S. S. PARGO
S. S. 264

PARGO was built at the Electric Boat Company and commissioned on April 26, 1943.

★ ★ ★ ★ ★ ★ ★ ★
PARGO'S WARTIME PATROLS

NO.	CAPTAIN	DATE	DUR.	BASE	AREA	CLAIMED	CONFIRMED
1	IC EDDY	4308	49	PEARL	E CHINA SEA	4/17600	0
2	IC EDDY	4310	40	PEARL	MARIANAS	2/17700	2/7810
3	IC EDDY	4403	60	PEARL to FREMANTLE	2/12200	1/758
4	IC EDDY	4406	57	FREMANTLE	CELEBES	1/6600	1/5236
5	DB BELL	4409	34	FREMANTLE	S CHINA SEA	1/4000	2/2200
6	DB BELL	4410	52	FREMANTLE	S CHINA SEA	1/10000	1/5200
7	DB BELL	4501	54	FREMANTLE to PEARL	3/14800	1/1300
8	DB BELL	4507	41	PEARL	SEA OF JAPAN	2/7200	1/5454

PARGO'S VICTORIES

DATE	VESSEL	SIZE	TYPE	CAPTAIN	LOCATION
431129	MANJU MARU	05877	FREIGHTER	IC EDDY	VOLCANO ISL
431130	SHOKO MARU #3	01933	FREIGHTER	IC EDDY	VOLCANO ISL
440504	EIRYU MARU	00758	NET TENDER	IC EDDY	MINDANAO
440628	YAMAGIKU MARU	05236	FREIGHTER	DB BELL	SULU ARCH
440910	HINOKI MARU	00599	NET TENDER	DB BELL	S CHINA SEA
440926	AOTAKA	01600	MINELAYER	DB BELL	S CHINA SEA
441126	YUHO MARU	05226	TANKER	DB BELL	BANDAR
450220	NOKAZE	01300	DESTROYER	DB BELL	SAIGON
450808	RASHIN MARU	05454	PASS-CARGO	DB BELL	SEA OF JAPAN

PARGO was part of the second wolf pack formed by ComSubPac in late 1943, and did her part as shown above. She also sank the last destroyer to be downed by submaries in the war when she collected *NOKAZE* off Saigon. *PARGO* received a Navy Unit Commendation for Patrol #7 under D.B. Bell.

PARGO at Mare Island Navy Yard, May 28, 1945.

PARGO was decommissioned on June 12, 1946, stricken from the lists and sold for scrap in 1961.

U. S. S. PETO
S. S. 265

PETO was built by the Manitowoc Shipbuilding Company and commissioned on November 21, 1943.

★ ★ ★ ★ ★ ★ ★ ★

PETO'S WARTIME PATROLS

NO.	CAPTAIN	DATE	DUR.	BASE	AREA	CLAIMED	CONFIRMED
1	WT NELSON	4304	48	BRISBANE	SOLOMONS	0	0
2	WT NELSON	4306	53	BRISBANE	BISMARCKS	1/2000	0
3	WT NELSON	4309	51	BRISBANE	BISMARCKS	2/10500	2/10000
4	WT NELSON	4311	54	BRISBANE	BISMARCKS	1/8200	1/2345
5	P VAN LEUNEN	4402	57	BRISBANE	to PEARL	1/4400	1/4370
6	P VAN LEUNEN	4404	52	PEARL	LUZON STRT	0	0
7	RH CALDWELL	4410	43	PEARL	E CHINA SEA	4/28000	3/12600
8	RH CALDWELL	4501	67	PEARL	LUZON STRT	0	0
9	RH CALDWELL	4505	44	PEARL	EMPIRE	0	0
10	RH CALDWELL	4507	47	PEARL	EMPIRE	0	0

PETO'S VICTORIES

DATE	VESSEL	SIZE	TYPE	CAPTAIN	LOCATION
431001	TONEI MARU	04930	PASS-CARGO	WT NELSON	PALAU
431001	KINKASAN MARU	04980	FREIGHTER	WT NELSON	PALAU
431201	KONEI MARU	02345	FREIGHTER	WT NELSON	ANCHORITE
440504	KAYO MARU	04368	PASS-CARGO	P VAN LEUNEN	MAPIA
441112	TATSUSAKI MARU	02766	FREIGHTER	RH CALDWELL	YELLOW SEA
441118	AISAKASAN MARU	06923	FREIGHTER	RH CALDWELL	YELLOW SEA
441118	CHINKAI MARU	02827	FREIGHTER	RH CALDWELL	YELLOW SEA

PETO did lifeguard duty off Wewak, New Guinea in September 1943. In December she reconnoitered and landed personnel on Boang Island.

PETO on sea patrol, May 26, 1945.

PETO was decommissioned on June 25, 1946, stricken from the lists and sold for scrap in 1960.

U. S. S. POMPON
S. S. 267

POMPON was built at the Manitowoc Shipbuilding Company
and commissioned on March 17, 1943.

★ ★ ★ ★
POMPON'S WARTIME PATROLS

NO.	CAPTAIN	DATE	DUR.	BASE	AREA	CLAIMED	CONFIRMED
1	EC HAWK	4307	43	BRISBANE	BISMARCKS	1/6600	1/5871
2	EC HAWK	4309	55	FREMANTLE	S CHINA SEA	0	0
3	EC HAWK	4311	60	FREMANTLE	S CHINA SEA	0	0
4	SH GIMBER	4402	50	FREMANTLE to PEARL		0	0
5	SH GIMBER	4405	50	PEARL	EMPIRE	1/2300	1/742
6	SH GIMBER	4407	46	PEARL	POLAR CIRC	1/4300	1/2000
7	SH GIMBER	4501	34	PEARL	YELLOW SEA	0	0
8	JA BOGLEY	4503	52	PEARL	E CHINA SEA	0	0
9	JA BOGLEY	4506	34	PEARL	TRUK	0	0

POMPON'S VICTORIES

DATE	VESSEL	SIZE	TYPE	CAPTAIN	LOCATION
430725	THAMES MARU	05871	FREIGHTER	EC HAWKE	CAROLINES
440530	SHIGA MARU	00742	FREIGHTER	SH GIMBER	KYUSHU
440812	MAYACHI MARU	02159	FREIGHTER	SH GIMBER	SAKHALIN

POMPON operated as part of "Caddy's Caddies," but most of her patroling was done alone.

POMPON at Mare Island Navy Yard, November 18, 1944.

POMPON was decommissioned on May 11, 1946, stricken from the lists and sold for scrap in 1960.

U. S. S. POGY
S. S. 266

U.S.S. POGY
S.S. 266

POGY was built at the Manitowoc Shipbuilding Company
and commissioned on August 27, 1943.

★ ★ ★ ★ ★ ★ ★ ★
POGY'S WARTIME PATROLS

NO.	CAPTAIN	DATE	DUR.	BASE	AREA	CLAIMED	CONFIRMED
1	GH WALES	4304	51	PEARL	EMPIRE	2/9100	2/3300
2	GH WALES	4306	53	PEARL	TRUK	1/15600	1/7500
3	GH WALES	4309	49	PEARL	PALAU	1/6600	1/7000
4	RM METCALF	4311	29	PEARL	PALAU	3/19500	2/9860
5	RM METCALF	4401	54	PEARL	E CHINA SEA	4/22400	5/21150
6	RM METCALF	4404	52	PEARL	EMPIRE	3/12900	3/9000
7	PG MOLTENI	4410	48	PEARL	BONINS	0	0
8	PG MOLTENI	4412	46	PEARL	EMPIRE	0	0
9	JM BOWERS	4503	61	PEARL	EMPIRE	0	0
10	JM BOWERS	4507	47	PEARL	SEA OF JAPAN	2/12500	2/4668

POGY'S VICTORIES

DATE	VESSEL	SIZE	TYPE	CAPTAIN	LOCATION
430501	KEISHIN MARU	01434	GUNBOAT	GH WALES	N HONSHU
430526	TAINAN MARU #6	01989	FREIGHTER	GH WALES	N HONSHU
430801	MOGAMIGAWA M.	07497	AIRC FERRY	GH WALES	CAROLINES
430830	MAEBASHI MARU	07005	PASS-CARGO	GH WALES	PALAU
431207	SOYO MARU	06081	SUB TENDER	RM METCALF	MARIANAS
431213	FUKKAI MARU	03829	PASS-CARGO	RM METCALF	MARIANAS
440210	MINEKAZE	01300	DESTROYER	RM METCALF	BASHI CHANL
440210	MALTA MARU	05500	PASS-CARGO	RM METCALF	BASHI CHANL
440220	TAIJIN MARU	05154	FREIGHTER	RM METCALF	BASHI CHANL
440220	NANYO MARU	03610	FREIGHTER	RM METCALF	BASHI CHANL
440223	HOREI MARU	05588	FREIGHTER	RM METCALF	NANSEI SHOTO
440428	I-183	01630	SUBMARINE	RM METCALF	BUNGO SUIDO
440505	SHIRANE MARU	02825	FREIGHTER	RM METCALF	KYUSHU
440513	ANBO MARU	04523	FREIGHTER	RM METCALF	SHIKOKU
450513	CHIKUZEN MARU	02448	PASS-CARGO	JM BOWERS	SEA OF JAPAN
450705	KOYOHIRASAN M.	02220	FREIGHTER	JM BOWERS	SEA OF JAPAN

POGY received Navy Unit Commendations for Patrol #5 and 6 under R.M. Metcalf. She tied for 9th place with four other boats with sixteen confirmed sinkings, and stood 21st in tonnage with 62,663.

POGY at Hunter's Point Navy Yard, San Francisco, California.

POGY was decommissioned on July 20, 1946, stricken from the lists and sold for scrap in 1959.

U. S. S. PUFFER
S. S. 268

U. S. S. PUFFER
S. S. 268

PUFFER was built at the Manitowoc Shipbuilding Company
and commissioned on April 27, 1943.

★ ★ ★ ★ ★ ★ ★ ★ ★
PUFFER'S WARTIME PATROLS

NO.	CAPTAIN	DATE	DUR.	BASE		AREA	CLAIMED	CONFIRMED
1	MJ JENSEN	4308	54	FREMANTLE		MAKASSAR	1/5300	0
2	FG SELBY	4311	49	FREMANTLE		S CHINA SEA	1/1500	2/7527
3	FG SELBY	4402	61	FREMANTLE		S CHINA SEA	1/15100	1/15100
4	FG SELBY	4404	52	FREMANTLE		MANILA	3/24300	3/7600
5	FG SELBY	4408	48	FREMANTLE	to PEARL		4.5/37700	1.5/7680
6	CR DWYER	4412	30	PEARL		EMPIRE	4/18900	1/800
7	CR DWYER	4502	70	PEARL	to FREMANTLE		0	0
8	CR DWYER	4505	53	FREMANTLE		S CHINA SEA	0	0
9	CR DWYER	4508	14	FREMANTLE		S CHINA SEA	0	0

PUFFER'S VICTORIES

DATE	VESSEL	SIZE	TYPE	CAPTAIN	LOCATION
431220	FUYO	00820	DESTROYER	FG SELBY	MINDORO
440101	RYUYO MARU	06707	FREIGHTER	FG SELBY	SULU SEA
440222	TEIKO MARU	15105	TRANSPORT	FG SELBY	ANAMBAS ISLE
440518	SHINRYU MARU	03181	FREIGHTER	FG SELBY	BRUNEI
440605	ASHIZURI	02166	TANKER	FG SELBY	SULU ARCH
440605	TAKASAKI	02500	TANKER	FG SELBY	SULU ARCH
440812	TEIKON MARU	05113	TANKER	FG SELBY	PALAWAN
440812	SHIMPO MARU	05135	TANKER	FG SELBY	PALAWAN
	(Shared credit with *BLUEFISH*)				
450110	COAST DEF #42	00800	FRIGATE	CR DWYER	E CHINA SEA

PUFFER received a Navy Unit Commendation for Patrol #4 under F.G. Selby. On her first patrol, she endured a 31-hour "going over" by a Chidori-type anti-sub craft, and this experience was analyzed for later use by other crews who might suffer the same experience.

PUFFER at Mare Island Navy Yard during a re-fit, November 10, 1944.

PUFFER was decommissioned on June 28, 1946, stricken from the lists and sold for scrap in 1960.

---

*The first shore bombardment of the Japanese homeland was made by **U.S.S. STEELHEAD** when she shelled a steel mill in the summer of 1943.*

U. S. S. RASHER
S. S. 269

U. S. S. RASHER
S. S. 269

RASHER was built at the Manitowoc Shipbuilding Company
and commissioned on June 8, 1943.

★ ★ ★ ★ ★ ★ ★
RASHER'S WARTIME PATROLS

NO.	CAPTAIN	DATE	DUR.	BASE	AREA	CLAIMED	CONFIRMED
1	ES HUTCHINSON	4309	61	FREMANTLE	CELEBES	4/21300	4/8894
2	WR LAUGHON	4312	36	FREMANTLE	S CHINA SEA	1/7200	1/7251
3	WR LAUGHON	4402	45	FREMANTLE	CELEBES	5/28600	4/20100
4	WR LAUGHON	4404	55	FREMANTLE	CELEBES	4/24400	4/10900
5	HG MUNSON	4407	43	FREMANTLE to PEARL		5/55700	5/53600
6	BE ADAMS, Jr	4501	53	PEARL	E CHINA SEA	0	0
7	CD NACE	4504	44	PEARL	to FREMANTLE	0	0

RASHER'S VICTORIES

DATE	VESSEL	SIZE	TYPE	CAPTAIN	LOCATION
431009	KOGANE MARU	03132	PASS-CARGO	ES HUTCHINSON	MOLUCCAS
431013	KENKOKU MARU	03127	FREIGHTER	ES HUTCHINSON	MOLUCCAS
431031	KORYO MARU	00589	TANKER	ES HUTCHINSON	MAKASSER
431108	TANGO MARU	02046	TANKER	ES HUTCHINSON	CELEBES
440104	KIYO MARU	07251	TANKER	WR LAUGHON	JAVA SEA
440225	TANGO MARU II	06200	FREIGHTER	WR LAUGHON	JAVA SEA
440225	RYUSEI MARU	04798	PASS-CARGO	WR LAUGHON	JAVA SEA
440303	NITTAI MARU	06484	PASS-CARGO	WR LAUGHON	MOLUCCAS
440327	NICHINAN MARU	02750	FREIGHTER	WR LAUGHON	JAVA SEA
440511	CHOI MARU	01074	FREIGHTER	WR LAUGHON	D'URVILLE
440529	ANSHU MARU	02601	GUNBOAT	WR LAUGHON	D'URVILLE
440608	SHIOYA	04000	TANKER	WR LAUGHON	MANADO
440614	KOAN MARU	03183	FREIGHTER	WR LAUGHON	MAKASSER
440718	EISHIN MARU	00542	FREIGHTER	HG MUNSON	S CHINA SEA
440718	TEIYO MARU	09849	TANKER	HG MUNSON	S CHINA SEA
440718	OTAKA	20000	CARRIER	HG MUNSON	S CHINA SEA
440719	TEIA MARU	17537	TRANSPORT	HG MUNSON	S CHINA SEA
440806	SHIROGANESAN	04739	FREIGHTER	HG MUNSON	PALAWAN

RASHER received Presidential Unit Citations for Patrol #1 under E.S. Hutchinson, for Patrols #3 and 4 under W.R. Laughon, and for Patrol #5 under H.G. Munson. She was 2nd in tonnage destroyed with 99,901 tons sunk, and tied for 7th in number of vessels destroyed with eighteen ships. *RASHER's* fifth patrol was second in total tonnage on a single patrol

RASHER off Manitowoc, Wisconsin, June 18, 1943.

RASHER was decommissioned on June 22, 1946, stricken from the lists and sold for scrap in 1971.

U. S. S. RATON
S. S. 270

U. S. S. RATON
S. S. 270

RATON was built at Manitowoc Shipbuilding Company
and commissioned on July 13, 1943.

★ ★ ★ ★ ★ ★
RATON'S WARTIME PATROLS

NO.	CAPTAIN	DATE	DUR.	BASE	AREA	CLAIMED	CONFIRMED
1	JW DAVIS	4311	24	BRISBANE	BISMARCKS	3/18700	3/18000
2	JW DAVIS	4312	45	FREMANTLE	CELEBES	2/18000	1/5578
3	JW DAVIS	4402	45	FREMANTLE	S CHINA SEA	0	0
4	JW DAVIS	4405	46	FREMANTLE	S CHINA SEA	5/7200	2/1660
5	MW SHEA	4407	55	FREMANTLE	MANILA	0	0
6	MW SHEA	4410	55	FREMANTLE to PEARL		8/57200	4/12300
7	MW SHEA	4504	47	PEARL to FREMANTLE		3/14500	3/5758
8	GF GUGLIOTA	4506	32	FREMANTLE	S CHINA SEA	0	0

RATON'S VICTORIES

DATE	VESSEL	SIZE	TYPE	CAPTAIN	LOCATION
431126	ONCE MARU	06667	FREIGHTER	JW DAVIS	MARIANAS
431128	HOKKO MARU II	05347	FREIGHTER	JW DAVIS	MARIANA
431128	YURI MARU	06787	FREIGHTER	JW DAVIS	MARIANAS
431224	MEIWA MARU II	05578	FREIGHTER	JW DAVIS	CELEBES
440524	IKI	00860	FRIGATE	JW DAVIS	SINGAPORE
440606	COAST DEF #15	00800	FRIGATE	JW DAVIS	S CHINA SEA
441018	SHIRANESAN MARU	04739	FREIGHTER	MW SHEA	PALAWAN
441018	TAIKAI MARU	03812	PASS-CARGO	MW SHEA	PALAWAN
441114	UNKAI MARU #3	02841	TANKER	MW SHEA	PALAWAN
441114	KUKASAKI	00989	AUXILIARY	MW SHEA	PALAWAN
450502	TORYU MARU	01992	FREIGHTER	MW SHEA	YELLOW SEA
450512	REKIZAN MARU	01311	FREIGHTER	MW SHEA	YELLOW SEA
450516	EIJU MARU	02453	FREIGHTER	MW SHEA	YELLOW SEA

RATON received Navy Unit Commendations for Patrol #4 under J.W. Davis, and for Patrol #6 under M.W. Shea. *RATON* was mistakenly fired upon by *LAPON* on May 27, 1944, in the only known instance of such an occurance during World War II. Fortunately both shots were misses.

RATON at Manitowoc, Wisconsin, July 17, 1943.

RATON was decommissioned on March 11, 1949, stricken from the lists and sunk as a target in 1969.

———————————

At the height of World War II, the United States Navy had 311 submarines in service. A total of 249 made war patrols in the Pacific.

U. S. S. RAY
S. S. 271

U. S. S. RAY
S. S. 271

RAY was built at the Manitowoc Shipbuilding Company
and commissioned on July 27, 1943.

★ ★ ★ ★ ★ ★ ★
RAY'S WARTIME PATROLS

NO.	CAPTAIN	DATE	DUR.	BASE		AREA	CLAIMED	CONFIRMED
1	BJ HARRAL	4311	24	BRISBANE		BISMARCKS	2/14300	1/2563
2	BJ HARRAL	4312	24	FREMANTLE		CELEBES	2/14300	2/8696
3	BJ HARRAL	4402	50	FREMANTLE		S CHINA SEA	0	0
4	BJ HARRAL	4404	53	FREMANTLE		CELEBES	6/42500	2/11338
5	WT KINSELA	4407	52	FREMANTLE		S CHINA SEA	4/36400	4/20744
6	WT KINSELA	4409	70	FREMANTLE	to PEARL		6.5/35100	3.3/12651
7	WT KINSELA	4504	49	PEARL	to FREMANTLE		0	0
8	WT KINSELA	4507	30	FREMANTLE		E CHINA SEA	0	0

RAY'S VICTORIES

DATE	VESSEL	SIZE	TYPE	CAPTAIN	LOCATION
431126	NIKKAI MARU	02562	GUNBOAT	BJ HARRAL	CAROLINES
431227	KYOKO MARU	05792	TANKER	BJ HARRAL	CELEBES
440101	OKUYO MARU	02904	GUNBOAT	BJ HARRAL	MOLUCCA PSG
440522	TENPEI MARU	06094	PASS-CARGO	BJ HARRAL	MOLUCCA PSG
440618	JANBI MARU	05244	TANKER	WT KINSELA	JAVA SEA
440704	KOSHU MARU	02612	FREIGHTER	WT KINSELA	JAVA SEA
440814	ZUISHO MARU	05289	PASS-CARGO	WT KINSELA	ANAMBAS ISL
440818	NANSEI MARU	05878	TANKER	WT KINSELA	S CHINA SEA
440821	TAKETOYO MARU	06965	PASS-CARGO	WT KINSELA	MINDORO
441012	TOKO MARU	04180	PASS-CARGO	WT KINSELA	MINDORO
441101	HORAI MARU #7	00865	FREIGHTER	WT KINSELA	MINDORO
441104	KAGI MARU	06806	PASS-CARGO	WT KINSELA	MINDORO

(Shared credit with *BREAM* and *GUITARRO*)

441114	COAST DEF #7	00800	FRIGATE	WT KINSELA	S CHINA SEA

RAY received a Navy Unit Commendation for Patrol #6 under W.T. Kinsela. *RAY* teamed with *GUITARRO*, *BREAM*, and *RATON* to expend a total of 23 torpedos against the heavy cruiser *KUMANO* and succeeded in heavily damaging this tough warship. *RAY* ran aground while attempting to finish her off, and *KUMANO* escaped only to be destroyed later by carrier planes.

RAY off Mare Island Navy Ship Yard, March 9, 1945.

RAY was decommissioned on January 12, 1947, stricken from the lists and sold for scrap in 1960.

U. S. S. REDFIN
S. S. 272

REDFIN was built at the Manitowoc Shipbuilding Company
and commissioned on August 31, 1943.

★ ★ ★ ★ ★ ★
REDFIN'S WARTIME PATROLS

NO.	CAPTAIN	DATE	DUR.	BASE	AREA	CLAIMED	CONFIRMED
1	RD KING	4401	45	FREMANTLE	S CHINA SEA	1/700	0
2	MH AUSTIN	4403	44	FREMANTLE	CELEBES	5/30200	3/10300
3	MH AUSTIN	4405	47	FREMANTLE	CELEBES	2/16100	2/8000
4	MH AUSTIN	4408	57	FREMANTLE	CELEBES	1/5100	0
5	MH AUSTIN	4410	68	FREMANTLE to PEARL	1/10000	1/5300
6	CK MILLER	4505	36	PEARL	EMPIRE	0	0
7	CK MILLER	4507	34	PEARL	E CHINA SEA	0	0

REDFIN'S VICTORIES

DATE	VESSEL	SIZE	TYPE	CAPTAIN	LOCATION
440411	AKIGUMO	01900	DESTROYER	MH AUSTIN	CELEBES
440415	SHINYU MARU	04621	PASS-CARGO	MH AUSTIN	CELEBES
440416	YAMAGATA MARU	03807	PASS-CARGO	MH AUSTIN	CELEBES
440611	ASANIGI MARU	05142	TANKER	MH AUSTIN	CELEBES
440624	ASO MARU	03028	PASS-CARGO	MH AUSTIN	SULU SEA
441108	NICHINAN MARU #2	05226	TANKER	MH AUSTIN	PALAWAN

REDFIN rescued the survivors of *FLIER* after she struck a mine in Balabac Strait. Only eight managed to make it to land where they were picked up on August 30, 1944. *REDFIN* was first to spot Ozawa's fleet in Operation Forager prior to the Marianas Battle.

This photograph was taken off Manitowoc, Wisconsin, September 14, 1943.

REDFIN was decommissioned on November 1, 1946, stricken from the lists and sold for scrap in 1971.

U. S. S. ROBALO
S. S. 273

ROBALO was built at the Manitowoc Shipbuilding Company
and commissioned on September 28, 1943.

★ ★

ROBALO'S WARTIME PATROLS

NO.	CAPTAIN	DATE	DUR.	BASE		AREA	CLAIMED	CONFIRMED
1	SH AMBRUSTER	4401	57	PEARL	to	FREMANTLE	0	0
2	MM KIMMEL	4404	51	FREMANTLE		INDOCHINA	1/7500	0
3	MM KIMMEL	4406	00	FREMANTLE		S CHINA SEA	0	0

ROBALO claimed one sinking, but it could not be confirmed.

ROBALO is believed to have struck a mine on July 26, 1944 off Palawan. Four of her crew survived the explosion and swam the two miles to shore where they were captured by Japanese MP's. Still later, they were taken off Palawan by a Japanese destroyer, destination unknown, as the destroyer was itself sunk with all hands.

ROBALO in the Gulf of Panama, November 19, 1943.

————————————

From the start of hostilities until the end of the war, Electric Boat Company of Groton, Connecticut, built sixty-nine boats and Portsmouth Navy Yard, Portsmouth, New Hampshire, built seventy-three. Smaller numbers were constructed by Mare Island Navy Yard, San Francisco, California; Cramp Shipbuilding, Philadelphia, Pennsylvania; and Manitowoc Shipbuilding, Manitowoc, Wisconsin.

U. S. S. ROCK
S. S. 274

ROCK was built at the Manitowoc Shipbuilding Company
and commissioned on October 26, 1943.

★ ★ ★ ★
ROCK'S WARTIME PATROLS

NO.	CAPTAIN	DATE	DUR.	BASE		AREA	CLAIMED	CONFIRMED
1	JJ FLACHSENHAR	4402	35	PEARL		E CHINA SEA	0	0
2	JJ FLACHSENHAR	4404	55	PEARL		EMPIRE	0	0
3	JJ FLACHSENHAR	4406	52	PEARL	to	FREMANTLE	0	0
4	JJ FLACHSENHAR	4409	61	FREMANTLE		E CHINA SEA	0	1/834
5	JJ FLACHSENHAR	4412	63	FREMANTLE		S CHINA SEA	0	0
6	RA KEATING, Jr	4503	58	FREMANTLE	to	PEARL	1/600	0

ROCK'S VICTORY

DATE	VESSEL	SIZE	TYPE	CAPTAIN	LOCATION
441026	TAKASAGO MARU #3	00834	TANKER	JJ FLACHSENHAR	S CHINA SEA

ROCK took part in Operation King Two during the Leyte Gulf battles and helped patrol the "Convoy College" area. This was the sea lane area between the Philippines and Japan. *ROCK* was ordered to destroy the stranded *DARTER* and expended ten torpedos in the attempt. All exploded against the reef which held *DARTER* fast. *NAUTILUS* finally had to finish the job with her 6-inch deck guns.

ROCK off Manitowoc, Wisconsin, November 13, 1943.

ROCK was decommissioned on May 1, 1945, stricken from the lists and sunk as a target in 1969.

U. S. S. RUNNER
S. S. 275

RUNNER was built at the Portsmouth Navy Yard
and commissioned on July 30, 1942.

★

RUNNER'S WARTIME PATROLS

NO.	CAPTAIN	DATE	DUR.	BASE	AREA	CLAIMED	CONFIRMED
1	FW FENNO	4301	48	PEARL	PALAU	3/19800	0
2	FW FENNO	4304	35	PEARL	E CHINA SEA	0	0
3	JH BOURLAND	4305	00	PEARL	EMPIRE	0	2/6274

RUNNER'S VICTORIES

DATE	VESSEL	SIZE	TYPE	CAPTAIN	LOCATION
430611	SEINAN MARU II	01338	FREIGHTER	JH BOURLAND	SEA OF JAPAN
430626	SNINRYU MARU	04936	PASS-CARGO	JH BOURLAND	KURILES

RUNNER was assigned to lay mines in the approaches to Hong Kong and sowed thirty-two in that area while under the command of F.W. Fenno. She left Midway after topping off on May 28, 1943, and headed for the Kuriles. After scoring her two victories there, she was not heard from again. Postwar records do not indicate an attack by anti-sub forces, and it is presumed she struck a mine and went down with all hands.

Photograph taken at Portsmouth Navy Yard, Portsmouth, New Hampshire, October 16, 1942.

United States Navy submariners suffered a casualty rate of twenty-two percent during World War II. The German U-Boat service casualty rate was seventy-four percent.

U. S. S. SAWFISH
S. S. 276

SAWFISH was built at the Portsmouth Navy Yard and commissioned on August 26, 1942.

★ ★ ★ ★ ★ ★ ★ ★
SAWFISH'S WARTIME PATROLS

NO.	CAPTAIN	DATE	DUR.	BASE	AREA	CLAIMED	CONFIRMED
1	ET SANDS	4301	53	PEARL	EMPIRE	3/13500	0
2	ET SANDS	4304	53	PEARL	EMPIRE	0	1/3000
3	ET SANDS	4306	41	PEARL	E CHINA SEA	3/25600	1/720
4	ET SANDS	4309	36	PEARL	EMPIRE	0	0
S	ET SANDS	4311	48	PEARL	BONINS	1/6000	1/3267
6	AB BANISTER	4404	49	PEARL	EMPIRE	1/5100	0
7	AB BANISTER	4406	55	PEARL	LUZON STRT	1/1900	1/2200
8	AB BANISTER	4409	58	PEARL	LUZON STRT	2/17900	2/13400
9	DH PUGH	4412	47	PEARL	LUZON STRT	0	0
10	DH PUGH	4503	47	PEARL	FORMOSA	0	0

SAWFISH'S VICTORIES

DATE	VESSEL	SIZE	TYPE	CAPTAIN	LOCATION
430505	HAKKAI MARU	02921	FREIGHTER	ET SANDS	SHIKOKU
430727	HIRASHIMA	00720	MINELAYER	ET SANDS	BCNINS
431208	SANSEI MARU	03267	PASS-CARGO	ET SANDS	BONINS
440726	I-29	02212	SUBMARINE	AB BANISTER	LUZON
441009	TACHIBANA MARU	06521	TANKER	AB BANISTER	S CHINA SEA
441023	KIMIKAWA MARU	06863	SPL TENDER	AB BANISTER	S CHINA SEA

SAWFISH was part of Operation King Two which severed the supply line from Japan to the Philippines during the Battle of Leyte Gulf. She led "Banister's Beagles" during wolf pack operations in the "Convoy College" area, along with *DRUM* and *ICEFISH*.

SAWFISH at Hunter's Point Naval Drydock, San Francisco, California, February 29, 1944.

SAWFISH was decommissioned on June 20, 1946, stricken from the lists and sold for scrap in 1960.

U. S. S. SCAMP
S. S. 277

SCAMP was built at the Portsmouth Navy Yard and commissioned on September 18, 1942.

★ ★ ★ ★ ★ ★ ★
SCAMP'S WARTIME PATROLS

NO.	CAPTAIN	DATE	DUR.	BASE	AREA	CLAIMED	CONFIRMED
1	WG EBERT	4303	26	PEARL	EMPIRE	0	0
2	WG EBERT	4304	46	PEARL	to BRISBANE	1/15600	1/7000
3	WG EBERT	4306	47	BRISBANE	BISMARCKS	1/2300	1/2000
4	WG EBERT	4309	30	BRISBANE	BISMARCKS	2/14600	1/8600
5	WG EBERT	4310	35	BRISBANE	BISMARCKS	1/6500	1/6400
6	WG EBERT	4312	52	BRISBANE	BISMARCKS	1/10000	1/10000
7	JC HLNGSWRTH	4403	51	BRISBANE	BISMARCKS	0	0
8	JC HLNGSWRTH	4410	00	PEARL	EMPIRE	0	0

SCAMP'S VICTORIES

DATE	VESSEL	SIZE	TYPE	CAPTAIN	LOCATION
430528	KAMAKAWA MARU	06853	TENDER	WG EBERT	MUSSAU
430727	I-24	02180	SUBMARINE	WG EBERT	ADMIRALTIES
430818	KASNSAI MARU	08614	PASS-CARGO	WG EBERT	ANCHORITE ISL
431110	TOKYO MARU	06486	PASS-CARGO	WG EBERT	CAROLINES
440114	NIPPON MARU	09975	TANKER	WG EBERT	PALAUS

SCAMP carried an illustrious passenger on her maiden trip as Admiral Lockwood rode her up to Midway from Pearl. Of her first nine shots on this patrol, five prematured. On April 7, 1944, *SCAMP* underwent such a drubbing south of Davao Gulf that she had to be drydocked for extensive repair. On her last patrol, she was ordered to stand lifeguard duty on the eastern approaches to Tokyo Bay. Her acknowledgment of this order was the last communication received from her. Post-war records indicate than an anti-sub attack was carried out by Japanese patrol planes in her assigned area and she went down with all hands. Name abreviated above is J.C. Hollingsworth.

SCAMP by Portsmouth Navy Yard, Portsmouth, New Hampshire, January 11, 1943.

U. S. S. SCORPION
S. S. 278

SCORPION was built at the Portsmouth Navy Yard
and commissioned on October 1, 1942.

★ ★ ★

SCORPION'S WARTIME PATROLS

NO.	CAPTAIN	DATE	DUR.	BASE	AREA	CLAIMED	CONFIRMED
1	WN WYLIE	4303	33	PEARL	EMPIRE	3/13100	2/8300
2	WN WYLIE	4305	48	PEARL	E CHINA SEA	0	2/10000
3	MG SCHMIDT	4310	53	PEARL	MARIANAS	0	0
4	MG SCHMIDT	4401	00	PEARL	E CHINA SEA	0	0

SCORPION'S VICTORIES

DATE	VESSEL	SIZE	TYPE	CAPTAIN	LOCATION
430420	MEIJI MARU	01934	GUNBOAT	WN WYLIE	SHIKOKU
430407	YUZAN MARU #4	06380	PASS-CARGO	WN WYLIE	SHIKOKU
430703	ANZAN MARU II	03890	FREIGHTER	WN WYLIE	YELLOW SEA
430703	KOKURYU MARU II	03890	PASS-CARGO	WN WYLIE	YELLOW SEA

SCORPION was first assigned to mine Empire water off Honshu. Later she engaged in running gun battles with various patrol craft and sampans. During one of these, her executive officer, LCDR Raymond was killed. On her fourth patrol, one of her crew suffered a broken arm and she was ordered to rendezvous with *HERRING* who was homeward bound. The transfer could not be accomplished due to foul weather. She continued on her mission, but was not heard from again, the possible victim of a mine.

Photograph taken at Portsmouth Naval Shipyard, Portsmouth, New Hampshire, December 10, 1042.

In World War II, 233 United States submarines were awarded 1229 battle stars.

U.S.S. SHAD
S.S. 235

SHAD was built at the Portsmouth Navy Yard and commissioned on June 12, 1942.

★ ★ ★ ★ ★ ★

SHAD'S WARTIME PATROLS

NO.	CAPTAIN	DATE	DUR.	BASE	AREA	CLAIMED	CONFIRMED
1	EJ McGREGOR	4209	35	SCOTLAND	N AFRICA	0	0
2	EJ McGREGOR	4212	44	SCOTLAND	EUROPE	2/600	0
3	EJ McGREGOR	4303	37	SCOTLAND	EUROPE	0	0
4	RF PRYCE	4305	43	SCOTLAND	EUROPE	0	0
5	EJ McGREGOR	4307	19	SCOTLAND	EUROPE	0	0
6	EJ McGREGOR	4309	58	PEARL	E CHINA SEA	1.5/13400	.5/4500
7	LV JULIHN	4408	50	PEARL	EMPIRE	3/6900	1/900
8	LV JULIHN	4410	63	PEARL	E CHINA SEA	0	0
9	LV JULIHN	4501	57	PEARL	S CHINA SEA	0	0
10	DL MELHOP	4505	45	PEARL	E CHINA SEA	3/13500	2/5309
11	DL MELHOP	4507	41	PEARL	MARCUS ISL	0	0

SHAD'S VICTORIES

DATE	VESSEL	SIZE	TYPE	CAPTAIN	LOCATION
431027	FUJI MARU	09138	TRANSPORT	EJ McGREGOR	E CHINA SEA
	(Shared credit with *GRAYBACK*)				
440919	IOSHIMA	00900	FRIGATE	LV JULIHN	SHIKOKU
450517	CHOSAN MARU	03939	FREIGHTER	DL MELHOP	YELLOW SEA
450607	AZUSU MARU	01370	FREIGHTER	DL MELHOP	YELLOW SEA

SHAD took part in the invasion of North Africa—Operation Torch—and later operated out of Roseneath, Scotland into the Bay of Biscay. She sank a 700-ton ore barge and damaged a 1700-ton destroyer escort. She was then directed to the Pacific Theater. *SHAD* was in the first American wolf-pack of the war when she teamed with *CERO* and *GRAYBACK* for a foray into the East China Sea

SHAD at Mare Island Navy Yard, San Francisco, California, March 2, 1944.

SHAD was decommissioned on June 15, 1947, stricken from the lists and sold for scrap in 1960.

U. S. S. SILVERSIDES
S. S. 236

U.S.S. SILVERSIDES
S.S. 236

SILVERSIDES was built at the Mare Island Navy Yard and commissioned on December 15, 1941.

★ ★ ★ ★ ★ ★
★ ★ ★ ★ ★ ★

SILVERSIDE'S WARTIME PATROLS

NO.	CAPTAIN	DATE	DUR	BASE	AREA	CLAIMED	CONFRMED
1	CC BURLINGAME	4204	52	PEARL	EMPIRE	4/25600	1/4000
2	CC BURLINGAME	4207	56	PEARL	EMPIRE	3/15000	2/9000
3	CC BURLINGAME	4210	54	PEARL	to BRISBANE	2/10800	0
4	CC BURLINGAME	4212	46	BRISBANE	to PEARL	1/10000	4/27798
5	CC BURLINGAME	4305	44	PEARL	to BRISBANE	1/10000	1/52000
6	JS COYE	4307	53	BRISBANE	BISMARCKS	0	0
7	JS COYE	4310	36	BRISBANE	to PEARL	4/22100	4/15000
8	JS COYE	4312	42	PEARL	PALAU	3/18500	3/7192
9	JS COYE	4402	52	PEARL	to FREMANTLE	2/7500	1/1900
10	JS COYE	4404	47	FREMANTLE	to PEARL	5/23600	6/14141
11	JS COYE	4409	60	PEARL	FORMOSA	0	0
12	SC NICHOLS	4412	50	PEARL	E CHINA SEA	0	1/4556
13	SC NICHOLS	4503	50	PEARL	EMPIRE	1/1200	0
14	SC NICHOLS	4505	59	PEARL	EMPIRE	0	0

SILVERSIDE'S VICTORIES

DATE	VESSEL	SIZE	TYPE	CAPTAIN	LOCATION
420517	UNKNOWN MARU	04000	FREIGHTER	CC BURLINGAME	SHIKOKU
420728	UNKNOWN MARU	04000	FREIGHTER	CC BURLINGAME	SHIKOKU
420808	NIKKEI MARU	05811	PASS-CARGO	CC BURLINGAME	SHIKOKU
430118	TOEI MARU	10023	TANKER	CC BURLINGAME	CAROLINES
430120	SOMEDONO MARU	05154	PASS-CARGO	CC BURLINGAME	CAROLINES
430120	SURABAYA MARU	04391	FREIGHTER	CC BURLINGAME	CAROLINES
430120	MEIU MARU	08230	FREIGHTER	CC BURLINGAME	CAROLINES
430611	HIDE MARU	05256	FREIGHTER	CC BURLINGAME	CAROLINES
431018	TAIRIN MARU II	01915	FREIGHTER	JS COYE	NININGO ISL
431024	TENNAN MARU	05407	FREIGHTER	JS COYE	NININGO ISL
431024	KAZAN MARU	01893	FREIGHTER	JS COYE	NININGO ISL
431024	JOHORE MARU	06182	PASS-CARGO	JS COYE	NININGO ISL
431229	TENPOSAN MARU	01970	FREIGHTER	JS COYE	YAP
431229	SHISHISEI MARU	01911	FREIGHTER	JS COYE	YAP
431229	RYUTO MARU	03311	FREIGHTER	JS COYE	YAP
440316	KOFUKO MARU	01920	FREIGHTER	JS COYE	YAP
440510	OKINAWA MARU	02254	FREIGHTER	JS COYE	PALAU
440510	MIKAGE MARU	04319	FREIGHTER	JS COYE	YAP
440510	CHOAN MARU	02631	GUNBOAT	JS COYE	YAP
440520	SHOSSEI MARU	00998	GUNBOAT	JS COYE	GUAM
440529	SHOKEN MARU	01949	FREIGHTER	JS COYE	MARIANAS
440529	HORAIZAN MARU	01999	FREIGHTER	JS COYE	MARIANAS
450125	MAYAY MARU	04556	FREIGHTER	SC NICHOLS	KYUSHU

With 23 confirmed sinkings, *SILVERSIDES* ranks 3rd, behind *TAUTOG* (26) and *TANG* (24). She is 5th in total tonnage with 90,080 tons. She also received Presidential Unit Citations for Patrols #4 and 5 under C.C. Burlingame and for Patrols #7 and 10 under J.J. Coye. A wartime appendectomy was performed aboard her.

SILVERSIDES shown at Mare Island Navy Yard, San Francisco, August 21, 1944.

SILVERSIDES was decommissioned on April 17, 1946, and is now a historic ship exhibit in Muskegon, Michigan.

U. S. S. SNOOK
S. S. 279

U. S. S. SNOOK
S. S. 279

SNOOK was built at the Portsmouth Navy Yard and commissioned on October 24, 1942.

★ ★ ★ ★ ★ ★ ★
SNOOK'S WARTIME PATROLS

NO.	CAPTAIN	DATE	DUR.	BASE	AREA	CLAIMED	CONFIRMED
1	CO TRIEBEL	4304	42	PEARL	E CHINA SEA	3/12000	3/8600
2	CO TRIEBEL	4306	40	PEARL	E CHINA SEA	1/17600	2/11000
3	CO TRIEBEL	4308	52	PEARL	E CHINA SEA	2/12400	2/10000
4	CO TRIEBEL	4310	38	PEARL	MARIANAS	2/14500	2/8440
5	CO TRIEBEL	4401	60	PEARL	E CHINA SEA	5/26800	5/21046
6	GH BROWNE	4406	51	PEARL	EMPIRE	0	0
7	GH BROWNE	4409	63	PEARL	LUZON STRT	3/22500	3/16600
8	JF WALLING	4412	54	PEARL	POLAR CIRC	0	0
9	JF WALLING	4503	00	PEARL	LUZON STRT	0	0

SNOOK'S VICTORIES

DATE	VESSEL	SIZE	TYPE	CAPTAIN	LOCATION
430505	KINKO MARU	01268	FREIGHTER	CO TRIEBEL	YELLOW SEA
430505	DAIFUKU MARU	03194	FREIGHTER	CO TRIEBEL	YELLOW SEA
430507	TOSEI MARU #4	04363	FREIGHTER	CO TRIEBEL	YELLOW SEA
430704	KOKI MARU	05290	FREIGHTER	CO TRIEBEL	E CHINA SEA
430704	LIVERPOOL MARU	05865	FREIGHTER	CO TRIEBEL	E CHINA SEA
430913	YAMATO MARU	09656	TRANSPORT	CO TRIEBEL	E CHINA SEA
430922	KATSURAHAMA M.	00715	FREIGHTER	CO TRIEBEL	E CHINA SEA
431129	YAMAFUKU MARU	04928	PASS-CARGO	CO TRIEBEL	E CHINA SEA
431129	SHIGANOURA MARU	03512	FREIGHTER	CO TRIEBEL	E CHINA SEA
440123	MAGANE MARU	03120	GUNBOAT	CO TRIEBEL	BONINS
440208	LIMA MARU	06989	FREIGHTER	CO TRIEBEL	KYUSHU
440214	NITTOKU MARU	03591	FREIGHTER	CO TRIEBEL	KYUSHU
440215	HOSHI MARU #2	00875	FREIGHTER	CO TRIEBEL	KYUSHU
440223	KOYO MARU #4	05471	PASS-CARGO	CO TRIEBEL	BONINS
441023	SHINSEI MARU #1	05863	PASS-CARGO	GH BROWNE	LUZON
441024	KIKUSUI MARU	03887	TANKER	GH BROWNE	LUZON
441024	ARISAN MARU	06886	FREIGHTER	GH BROWNE	LUZON

SNOOK was tied for 8th place in number of vessels sunk, and stood 10th in enemy tonnage destroyed. She was leaving on her ninth patrol with *BURRFISH* and *BANG* when she was forced to return to Guam for emergency repairs. She departed Guam on March 28, 1945, and was not heard from again. She may have been sunk by a Japanese submarine who was, in turn, sunk before reporting it.

SNOOK at Portsmouth Navy Yard, Portsmouth, New Hampshire, January 11, 1943.

U.S.S. STEELHEAD
S.S. 280

STEELHEAD was built at Portsmouth Navy Yard
and commissioned on December 7, 1942.

★ ★ ★ ★ ★ ★

STEELHEAD'S WARTIME PATROLS

NO.	CAPTAIN	DATE	DUR.	BASE	AREA	CLAIMED	CONFIRMED
1	DL WHELCHEL	4304	49	PEARL	EMPIRE	0	0
2	DL WHELCHEL	4306	47	PEARL	TRUK	1/4800	0
3	DL WHELCHEL	4309	72	PEARL	PALAU	0	.5/8000
4	DL WEHLCHEL	4312	61	PEARL	EMPIRE	1/9000	1/6795
5	DL WEHLCHEL	4403	62	PEARL	E CHINA SEA	0	0
6	DL WEHLCHEL	4406	60	PEARL	LUZON STRT	2/14000	2.5/20000
7	RB BYRNES	4505	T4	PEARL	EMPIRE	0	0

STEELHEAD'S VICTORIES

DATE	VESSEL	SIZE	TYPE	CAPTAIN	LOCATION
430106	KAZAHAYA	08000	TANKER	DL WHELCHEL	CAROLINES
	(Shared credit with *TINOSA*)				
440110	YAMABIKO MARU	06795	SALVG VSL	DL WHELCHEL	KYUSHU
440731	DAKAR MARU	07169	FREIGHTER	DL WHELCHEL	LUZON
440731	FUSO MARU	08195	TRANSPORT	DL WHELCHEL	LUZON
440731	YOSHINO MARU	08990	TRANSPORT	DL WHELCHEL	LUZON
	(Shared credit with *PARCHE*)				

STEELHEAD planted mines off Hokkaido, the last to be used by the U.S. Navy in the war. She then surfaced near shore and shelled a steel plant and metalurgical laboratory at Muroron.

A postwar photograph, probably at Mare Island Navy Yard, San Francisco, California.

STEELHEAD was decommissioned on March 29, 1946, stricken from the lists and sold for scrap in 1960.

U. S. S. TULLIBEE
S. S. 284

TULLIBEE was built at the Mare Island Navy Yard
and commissioned on February 15, 1943.

★ ★ ★

TULLIBEE'S WARTIME PATROLS

NO.	CAPTAIN	DATE	DUR.	BASE	AREA	CLAIMED	CONFIRMED
1	C BRINDUPKE	4307	50	PEARL	TRUK	1/7000	1/4000
2	C BRINDUPKE	4309	52	PEARL	E CHINA SEA	1/6000	1/5886
3	C BRINDUPKE	4312	58	PEARL	MARIANAS	1/2500	1/549
4	C BRINDUPKE	4403	00	PEARL	PALAU	0	0

TULLIBEE'S VICTORIES

DATE	VESSEL	SIZE	TYPE	CAPTAIN	LOCATION
430722	KAISHO MARU II	04164	PASS-CARGO	C BRINDUPKE	CAROLINES
431015	CHICAGO MARU	05866	PASS-CARGO	C BRINDUPKE	FORMOSA
440131	HIRO MARU	00549	TENDER	C BRINDUPKE	GUAM

TULLIBEE was struck by one of her own torpedos while attacking a convoy in a blinding rainstorm. The fate of the *TULLIBEE* was not known until the end of the war when, C.W. Kuykendall, the only survivor was released from a Japanese prisoner of war camp.

TULLIBEE at Mare Island Navy Yard, San Francisco, California, April 2, 1943.

United States Submarines fired a total of 14,748 torpedoes during World War II.

U. S. S. SUNFISH
S. S. 281

U. S. S. SUNFISH
S. S. 281

SUNFISH was built at the Mare Island Navy Yard
and commissioned on July 15, 1942.

★ ★ ★ ★ ★ ★ ★ ★ ★
SUNFISH'S WARTIME PATROLS

NO.	CAPTAIN	DATE	DUR.	BASE	AREA	CLAIMED	CONFIRMED
1	RW PETERSON	4211	53	PEARL	EMPIRE	0	0
2	RW PETERSON	4302	58	PEARL	E CHINA SEA	2/12200	1/3200
3	RW PETERSON	4304	57	PEARL	PALAU	0	0
4	RW PETERSON	4307	60	PEARL	E CHINA SEA	3/29100	2/5479
5	RW PETERSON	4310	59	PEARL	E CHINA SEA	0	0
6	EE SHELBY	4401	53	PEARL	MARIANAS	2/30400	2/9400
7	EE SHELBY	4406	40	PEARL	POLAR CIRC	4/18500	2/8800
8	EE SHELBY	4408	38	PEARL	E CHINA SEA	4/33500	2/11100
9	EE SHELBY	4410	56	PEARL	E CHINA SEA	4/23800	3/16200
10	EE SHELBY	4501	37	PEARL	E CHINA SEA	0	0
11	JW REED	4503	29	PEARL	EMPIRE	4/13200	4/5461

SUNFISH'S VICTORIES

DATE	VESSEL	SIZE	TYPE	CAPTAIN	LOCATION
430313	KOSEI MARU	03262	FREIGHTER	RW PETERSON	E CHINA SEA
430713	EDO MARU	01299	GUNBOAT	RW PETERSON	PHILIPPINE SEA
430904	KOZAN MARU	04180	PASS-CARGO	RW PETERSON	LUZON
440223	SHINYUBARI MARU	05354	FREIGHTER	EE SHELBY	GUAM
440223	KUNISHIMA MARU	04083	FREIGHTER	EE SHELBY	GUAM
440705	SHINMEI MARU	02577	PASS-CARGO	EE SHELBY	KIRULES
440709	TAIHEI MARU	06284	FREIGHTER	EE SHELBY	KIRULES
440910	CHIHAYA MARU	04701	TANKER	EE SHELBY	E CHINA SEA
440913	ETASHIMA MARU	06435	FREIGHTER	EE SHELBY	E CHINA SEA
441117	EDOGAWA MARU	06968	FREIGHTER	EE SHELBY	E CHINA SEA
441118	SIESHO MARU	05463	PASS-CARGO	EE SHELBY	E CHINA SEA
441130	DARIEN MARU	03748	TRANSPORT	EE SHELBY	YELLOW SEA
450416	MANRYU MARU	01620	FREIGHTER	JW REED	SEA OF JAPAN
450416	COAST DEF #73	00800	FRIGATE	JW REED	SEA OF JAPAN
450419	KAIHO MARU	01093	FREIGHTER	JW REED	SEA OF JAPAN
450419	TAISEI MARU	01948	FREIGHTER	JW REED	SEA OF JAPAN

SUNFISH received Navy Unit Commendations for Patrol #9 under E.S. Shelby, and for Patrol #11 under J.W. Reed. She stood 24th in tonnage of all U.S. boats, and was tied for 9th in number of vessels destroyed.

A builder's photograph taken September 21, 1942.

SUNFISH was decommissioned on December 26, 1945, stricken from the lists and sold for scrap in 1960.

U. S. S. TINOSA
S. S. 283

U. S. S. TINOSA
S. S. 283

TINOSA was built at the Mare Island Navy Yard
and commissioned on January 15, 1943.

★ ★ ★ ★ ★ ★ ★ ★ ★
TINOSA'S WARTIME PATROLS

NO.	CAPTAIN	DATE	DUR.	BASE	AREA	CLAIMED	CONFIRMED
1	LR DASPIT	4305	47	PEARL	EMPIRE	0	0
2	LR DASPIT	4307	27	PEARL	TRUK	0	0
3	LR DASPIT	4309	23	PEARL	PALAU	1/10500	.5/4000
4	LR DASPIT	4310	49	PEARL	to FREMANTLE	4/18500	4/18000
5	DF WEISS	4401	55	FREMANTLE	to PEARL	3/16900	4/15600
6	DF WEISS	4403	46	PEARL	LUZON STRT	4/31200	2/12900
7	DF WEISS	4406	54	PEARL	E CHINA SEA	2/19000	2/10700
8	RC LATHAM	4412	56	PEARL	EMPIRE	0	0
9	RC LATHAM	4503	30	PEARL	E CHINA SEA	0	0
10	RC LATHAM	4504	19	PEARL	TRUK	0	0
11	RC LATHAM	4505	37	PEARL	SEA OF JAPAN	4/12100	4/6701

TINOSA'S VICTORIES

DATE	VESSEL	SIZE	TYPE	CAPTAIN	LOCATION
431006	KAZAHAYA	08000	TANKER	LR DASPIT	CAROLINES
	(Shared credit with *STEELHEAD*)				
431122	KISO MARU	04071	FREIGHTER	LR DASPIT	PALAU
431122	YAMATO MARU II	04379	FREIGHTER	LR DASPIT	PALAU
431126	SHINI MARU	03811	FREIGHTER	LR DASPIT	PALAU
431203	AZUMA MARU	06646	PASS-CARGO	LR DASPIT	PALAU
440122	KODHIN MARU	05485	PASS-CARGO	DF WEISS	BRUNEI
440122	SEINAN MARU	05401	FREIGHTER	DF WEISS	BRUNEI
440215	ODATSUKI MARU	01988	FREIGHTER	DF WEISS	SULU SEA
440216	CHOJO MARU	02610	TRANSPORT	DF WEISS	SULU SEA
440504	TAIBU MARU	06440	FREIGHTER	DF WEISS	S CHINA SEA
440504	TOYOHI MARU	06436	FREIGHTER	DF WEISS	S CHINA SEA
440703	KONSAN MARU	02733	PASS-CARGO	DF WEISS	E CHINA SEA
440703	KAMA MARU	07954	PASS-CARGO	DF WEISS	E CHINA SEA
450609	WAKATAMA MARU	02211	FREIGHTER	RC LATHAM	HONSHU
450612	KEITO MARU	00880	FREIGHTER	RC LATHAM	HONSHU
450620	KAISEI MARU	00884	FREIGHTER	RC LATHAM	TSUSHIMA STRT
450620	TAITO MARU II	02726	FREIGHTER	RC LATHAM	TSUSHIMA STRT

TINOSA received Presidential Unit Citations for Patrol #4 under L.R. Daspit, and for Patrols #5 and 6 under D.F. Weiss. She tied for 9th place in number of vessels sunk and stood 19th in total tonnage destroyed.

TINOSA at Mare Island Navy Yard, San Francisco, California, March 5, 1943.

TINOSA was decommissioned on January 23, 1947, and scuttled in November 1960.

U. S. S. TRIGGER
S. S. 237

U. S. S. TRIGGER
S. S. 237

TRIGGER was built at the Mare Island Navy Yard
and commissioned on January 31, 1942.

★ ★ ★ ★ ★
★ ★ ★ ★ ★ ★

TRIGGER'S WARTIME PATROLS

NO.	CAPTAIN	DATE	DUR.	BASE	AREA	CLAIMED	CONFIRMED
00	JH LEWIS	4205	15	PEARL	MIDWAY	0	0
1	JH LEWIS	4206	51	PEARL	ALASKA	0	0
2	RS BENSON	4209	46	PEARL	EMPIRE	1/5000	1/5900
3	RS BENSON	4212	51	PEARL	EMPIRE	4/23700	2/6500
4	RS BENSON	4302	56	PEARL	PALAU	0	1/3000
5	RS BENSON	4304	53	PEARL	EMPIRE	1/8200	1/2000
6	RE DORNIN	4309	29	PEARL	E CHINA SEA	5/40000	4/27095
7	RE DORNIN	4310	49	PEARL	E CHINA SEA	6/44700	4/15114
8	RE DORNIN	4401	55	PEARL	TRUK	2/11800	2/12443
9	F HARLFINGER	4403	58	PEARL	PALAU	5/33200	1/11700
10	F HARLFINGER	4409	49	PEARL	EMPIRE	.3/3300	.3/3333
11	F HARLFINGER	4412	37	PEARL	EMPIRE	0	0
12	DR CONNOLE	4503	00	PEARL	EMPIRE	1/4000	2/2576

TRIGGER'S VICTORIES

DATE	VESSEL	SIZE	TYPE	CAPTAIN	LOCATION
421017	HOLLAND MARU	05869	FREIGHTER	RS BENSON	SW KYUSHU
421222	TEIFUKU MARU	05198	FREIGHTER	RS BENSON	SHIKOKU
430110	OKIKAZI	01300	DESTROYER	RS BENSON	E HONSHU
430315	MOMAHA MARU	03103	FREIGHTER	RS BENSON	MARIANAS
430601	NOBORIKAWA M.	02182	FREIGHTER	RS BENSON	E HONSHU
430918	YOWA MARU	06435	FREIGHTER	RE DORNIN	E CHINA SEA
430921	SHIRIYA MARU	06500	TANKER	RE DORNIN	E CHINA SEA
430921	SHOYO MARU	07498	TANKER	RE DORNIN	E CHINA SEA
430921	ARGUN MARU	06662	FREIGHTER	RE DORNIN	E CHINA SEA
431102	YAWATA MARU	01852	FREIGHTER	RE DORNIN	RYUKUS
431102	DELAGOA MARU	07148	PASS-CARGO	RE DORNIN	RYUKUS
431113	NACHISAN MARU	04443	PASS-CARGO	RE DORNIN	E CHINA SEA
431121	EIZAN MARU II	01681	FREIGHTER	RE DORNIN	YELLOW SEA
440131	NASAMI	00443	MINELAYER	RE DORNIN	CAROLINES
440131	YASUKUNI MARU	11933	TENDER	RE DORNIN	CAROLINES
440427	MIIKE MARU	11739	PASS-CARGO	F HARLFINGER	PALAU
441030	TAKANE MARU	10021	TANKER	F HARLFINGER	KYUSHU

(Shared credit with *SALMON* and *STERLET*)

DATE	VESSEL	SIZE	TYPE	CAPTAIN	LOCATION
450318	TSUKUSHI MARU #3	01012	FREIGHTER	DR CONNOLE	E CHINA SEA
450327	ODATE	01564	REPAIR SHIP	DR CONNOLE	E CHINA SEA

TRIGGER received Presidential Unit Citations for Patrol #5 under R.S. Benson, and for Patrols #6 and 7 under R.E. Dornin. *TRIGGER* was tied for 7th place in number of vessels sunk and stood 7th in total tonnage destroyed. On her twelfth patrol she failed to respond to messages and was presumed lost in the Nansei Shoto area on or about March 28, 1945.

TRIGGER undergoing re-fit at Hunter's Point Navy Yard, San Francisco, California, August 28, 1944. The encircled numbers on the photograph indicate changes made during a refit.

U. S. S. TUNNY
S. S. 282

TUNNY was built at the Mare Island Navy Yard and commissioned on September 1, 1942.

★ ★ ★ ★ ★ ★ ★ ★

TUNNY'S WARTIME PATROLS

NO.	CAPTAIN	DATE	DUR.	BASE		AREA	CLAIMED	CONFIRMED
1	JA SCOTT	4301	43	PEARL		E CHINA SEA	2/16700	1/5300
2	JA SCOTT	4303	36	PEARL		TRUK	2.5/18700	2.5/17000
3	JA SCOTT	4305	50	PEARL		MARIANAS	1/3100	1/2000
4	JA SCOTT	4308	34	PEARL		PALAU	0	0
5	JA SCOTT	4402	44	PEARL	to	BRISBANE	1/2100	7/2200
6	JA SCOTT	4404	66	BRISBANE	to	PEARL	1/5200	1/5000
7	GR PIERCE	4408	44	PEARL		S CHINA SEA	0	0
8	GR PIERCE	4502	52	PEARL		EMPIRE	0	0
9	GR PIERCE	4505	49	PEARL		SEA OF JAPAN	0	0

TUNNY'S VICTORIES

DATE	VESSEL	SIZE	TYPE	CAPTAIN	LOCATION
430208	KUSUYAMA MARU	05306	FREIGHTER	JA SCOTT	LUZON
430328	SUWA MARU	10672	TRANSPORT	JA SCOTT	WAKE
	(Shared credit with *FINBACK* and *SEADRAGON*)				
430402	TOYO MARU #2	04163	FREIGHTER	JA SCOTT	CAROLINES
430407	KOSEI MARU II	08237	PASS-CARGO	JA SCOTT	CAROLINES
430628	SHOTOKU MARU	01964	GUNBOAT	JA SCOTT	MARIANAS
440323	I-42	02212	SUBMARINE	JA SCOTT	PALAU
440517	NICHIWA MARU	04955	FREIGHTER	JA SCOTT	GUAM

TUNNY received Presidential Unit Citations for Patrols #2 and 5. While serving in the wolf pack "Ed's Eradicators" *TUNNY* was damaged by an aircraft bomb and forced to leave the pack for repairs. It was an American bomb dropped in error by confused carrier pilots.

TUNNY at Hunter's Point Naval Drydocks, San Francisco, California, January 21, 1944.

TUNNY was decommissioned on December 13, 1946, stricken from the lists and sunk as a target June 9, 1970.

U. S. S. WHALE
S. S. 239

WHALE was built at the Mare Island Navy Yard and commissioned on June 1, 1942.

★ ★ ★ ★ ★
★ ★ ★ ★ ★ ★

WHALE'S WARTIME PATROLS

NO.	CAPTAIN	DATE	DUR.	BASE	AREA	CLAIMED	CONFIRMED
1	JB AZER	4210	32	PEARL	EMPIRE	1/9400	0
2	JB AZER	4301	30	PEARL	TRUK	2/19300	3/19000
3	AC BURROWS	4302	42	PEARL	MARIANAS	4/33500	1/6500
4	AC BURROWS	4305	47	PEARL	EMPIRE	2/13000	1/3500
5	AC BURROWS	4307	46	PEARL	E CHINA SEA	1/10000	1/7140
6	AC BURROWS	4312	44	PEARL	BONINS	2/14000	1.5/8322
7	JB GRADY	4403	57	PEARL	E CHINA SEA	1/5000	1/5400
8	JB GRADY	4405	50	PEARL	EMPIRE	0	0
9	JB GRADY	4408	68	PEARL	PHILPIN SEA	1/10000	1/10200
10	JB GRADY	4412	54	PEARL	EMPIRE	0	0
11	FH CARDE	4506	68	PEARL	EMPIRE	0	0

WHALE'S VICTORIES

DATE	VESSEL	SIZE	TYPE	CAPTAIN	LOCATION
430113	IWASHIRO MARU	03550	FREIGHTER	JB AZER	KWAJALEIN
430117	HEIYO MARU	09815	PASS-CARGO	JB AZER	CAROLINES
430127	SHOAN MARU	05624	PASS-CARGO	JB AZER	CAROLINES
430323	KENYO MARU	06486	FREIGHTER	AC BURROWS	MARIANAS
430526	SHOEI MARU #4	03580	FREIGHTER	AC BURROWS	GUAM
430808	NARUTO MARU	07149	ARC FERRY	AC BURROWS	PHILIPN SEA
440116	DENMARK MARU	05870	FREIGHTER	AC BURROWS	PHILIPN SEA
440117	TARUSHIMA MARU	04865	FREIGHTER	AC BURROWS	PHILIPN SEA
	(Shared credit with *SEAWOLF*)				
440409	HONAN MARU #3	05401	FREIGHTER	JB GRADY	TSUSHIMA
441006	AKANE MARU	10241	TANKER	JB GRADY	S CHINA SEA

WHALE was in the first group of boats sent to mine enemy waters. It has never been determined just how many Marus went down as a result of this operation. She served as guide ship and did lifeguard duty during Operation Galvanic against Wake Island.

WHALE undergoing re-fit at Mare Island Navy Yard, San Francisco, California, April 21, 1945.

WHALE was decommissioned on June 1, 1946, stricken from the lists and sold for scrap in 1960.

U. S. S. WAHOO
S. S. 238

U.S.S. WAHOO
S.S. 238

WAHOO was built at the Mare Island Navy Yard
and commissioned on May 15, 1942.

★ ★ ★ ★ ★ ★
WAHOO'S WARTIME PATROLS

NO.	CAPTAIN	DATE	DUR.	BASE	AREA	CLAIMED	CONFIRMED
1	MG KENNEDY	4208	55	PEARL	TRUK	1/6500	0
2	MG KENNEDY	4211	23	PEARL to BRISBANE		2/7600	1/5400
3	DW MORTON	4301	23	BRISBANE to PEARL		5/31900	3/11300
4	DW MORTON	4302	42	PEARL	EMPIRE	8/36700	9/20000
5	DW MORTON	4304	26	PEARL	EMPIRE	3/24700	3/10500
6	DW MORTON	4308	27	PEARL	EMPIRE	0	0
7	DW MORTON	4309	00	PEARL	EMPIRE	1/7100	4/13000

WAHOO'S VICTORIES

DATE	VESSEL	SIZE	TYPE	CAPTAIN	LOCATION
421210	KAMOI MARU	05355	FREIGHTER	MG KENNEDY	CAROLINES
430126	UNKNOWN MARU	04000	FREIGHTER	DW MORTON	N NEW GUINA
430126	BUYO MARU	05447	TRANSPORT	DW MORTON	N NEW GUINA
430126	FUKUEI MARU #2	01901	FREIGHTER	DW MORTON	N NEW GUINA
430319	ZOGEN MARU	01428	FREIGHTER	DW MORTON	YELLOW SEA
430319	KOWA MARU II	03217	TRANSPORT	DW MORTON	YELLOW SEA
430321	NITTSU MARU	02183	FREIGHTER	DW MORTON	YELLOW SEA
430321	HOZAN MARU	02260	FREIGHTER	DW MORTON	YELLOW SEA
430323	UNKNOWN MARU	02427	FREIGHTER	DW MORTON	YELLOW SEA
430324	TAKAOSAN MARU	02076	FREIGHTER	DW MORTON	YELLOW SEA
430325	SATUKI MARU	00827	FREIGHTER	DW MORTON	YELLOW SEA
430325	UNKNOWN MARU	02556	FREIGHTER	DW MORTON	YELLOW SEA
430329	YAMABOTO MARU	02556	FREIGHTER	DW MORTON	YELLOW SEA
430507	TAMON MARU #5	05260	PASS-CARGO	DW MORTON	HONSHU
430509	TAKAO MARU	03204	PASS-CARGO	DW MORTON	HONSHU
430509	JINMU MARU	01912	FREIGHTER	DW MORTON	HONSHU
430929	MASAKI MARU #2	01238	FREIGHTER	DW MORTON	HONSHU
431005	KONRON MARU	07908	TRANSPORT	DW MORTON	TSUSHIMA
431006	UNKNOWN MARU	01288	PASS-CARGO	DW MORTON	TSUSHIMA
431009	KANKO MARU	02995	FREIGHTER	DW MORTON	TSUSHIMA

WAHOO received a Presidential Unit Citation for Patrol #3. She was tied for 5th in number of vessels sunk and stood 23rd in total enemy tonnage destroyed. "Mush" Morton is perhaps the best remembered of World War II skippers. He stands 3rd in confirmed sinkings and had the 2nd best single patrol. He went down with his command when *WAHOO* was bombed in La Perouse Strait on October 11, 1943.

WAHOO at Mare Island Naval Yard, San Francisco, California, July 14, 1943.

BALAO CLASS

BALAO Class boats were virtual copies of the *GATO* Class. The *BALAO* was built with several improvement, such as a slightly thicker hull plating. A few additional design changes allowed a more rapid fabrication of the boat itself and some increase of structural strength to allow slightly increased operational depth. The performance and armament remained the same as the *GATO* Class. When it was decided to freeze the design, all boats after #285 were designated *BALAO* Class and 132 boats of this design were built during the war at the Electric Boat Company of Groton, Connecticut, the Porstmouth Navy Yard in Portsmouth, New Hampshire, and the Mare Island Navy Yard in the San Francisco Bay Area, Cramp Shipbuilding at Philadelphia, and Manitowoc Shipbuilding at Manitowoc, Wisconsin.

U. S. S. BALAO
S. S. 285

U. S. S. BALAO
S. S. 285

BALAO was built at the Portsmouth Navy Yard
and commissioned on February 4, 1943.

★ ★ ★ ★ ★ ★ ★ ★ ★

BALAO'S WARTIME PATROLS

NO.	CAPTAIN	DATE	DUR.	BASE	AREA	CLAIMED	CONFIRMED
1	RH CRANE	4307	51	BRISBANE	BISMARCKS	0	0
2	RH CRANE	4310	43	BRISBANE	BISMARCKS	0	0
3	CC COLE	4312	38	BRISBANE	BISMARCKS	0	0
4	CC COLE	4402	43	BRISBANE to	PEARL	4/20300	3/15300
5	M RMRZDLANO	4404	48	PEARL	PALAU	0	0
6	M RMRZDLANO	4407	48	PEARL	PALAU	0	0
7	M RMRZDLANO	4412	42	PEARL	E CHINA SEA	2/11200	1/5200
8	RK WORTHNGTON	4502	40	PEARL	E CHINA SEA	3/20300	2/11293
9	RK WORTHNGTON	4505	35	PEARL	EMPIRE	0	0
10	RK WORTHNGTON	4507	47	PEARL	EMPIRE	0	0

BALAO'S VICTORIES

DATE	VESSEL	SIZE	TYPE	CAPTAIN		LOCATION
440223	NIKKI MARU	05857	PASS-CARGO	CC COLE	off	NEW GUINEA
440228	SHOHO MARU	02723	FREIGHTER	CC COLE	nr	PALAU
440228	AKIURA MARU	06803	PASS-CARGO	CC COLE	nr	PALAU
450108	DAIGO MARU	05244	FREIGHTER	M RMRZDLANO		YELLOW SEA
450319	HAKOZAKI MARU II	10413	TRANSPORT	R WORTHNGTON		YELLOW SEA
450326	SHINTO MARU #1	00880	FREIGHTER	R WORTHNGTON		YELLOW SEA

BALAO suffered from a shortage of targets in her later patrols (as did all U.S. boats), but sank the *HAKOZOKI MARU*, the last large Japanese merchantman to fall victim to U.S. Submarines. The abbreviation above is for M. Ramiriz De Arellano..

BALAO off Mare Island, California.

BALAO was decommissioned on August 20, 1946, stricken from the lists and sunk as a target in 1959.

―――――――――――

*After eighteen months of torpedo failures which went uncorrected, in June 1943,
Admiral Chester Nimitz advised all submarines and destroyers to de-activate
the magnetic exploders and set them for impact hits.*

U. S. S. APOGON
S. S. 308

APOGON was built at the Portsmouth Navy Yard
and commissioned on July 16, 1943.

★ ★ ★ ★ ★ ★
APOGON'S WARTIME PATROLS

NO.	CAPTAIN	DATE	DUR.	BASE	AREA	CLAIMED	COMFIRMED
1	WP SCHOENI	4311	45	PEARL	TRUK	1/3000	1/3000
2	WP SCHOENI	4401	55	PEARL	MARIANAS	2/24000	0
3	WP SCHOENI	4404	49	PEARL	EMPIRE	0	0
4	WP SCHOENI	4406	37	PEARL	LUZON STRT	0	0
5	AC HOUSE	4409	46	PEARL	POLAR CIR	1/6300	1/2000
6	AC HOUSE	4411	46	PEARL	POLAR CIR	0	0
7	AC HOUSE	4505	48	PEARL	POLAR CIR	4/12700	1/2614

APOGON'S VICTORIES

DATE	VESSEL	SIZE	TYPE	CAPTAIN	LOCATION
431218	DAIDO MARU	02962	GUNBOAT	WP SCHOENI	SULU SEA
440927	HACHIROGATA	01999	FREIGHTER	AC HOUSE	CAROLINES
450618	HAKAUAI MARU	02614	TRANSPORT	AC HOUSE	SAKHALIN

APOGON took part in Operation Galvanic in the Gilberts, standing watch over the Japanese base at Truk. She also attended Hailstone doing patrol and lifeguard duty for carrier air strikes. Much of her duty took her north where she helped harry the junks and trawlers that made up the Japanese fishing fleet, thus adding to the food shortage which plagued Japan during the last days of the war.

A postwar *APOGON* entering an undisclosed harbor.

APOGON was decommissioned on October 1, 1945, and used as a target at the Bikini Atoll atom bomb tests.

U. S. S. ARCHERFISH
S. S. 311

ARCHERFISH was built at the Portsmouth Navy Yard
and commissioned on September 4, 1943.

★ ★ ★ ★ ★ ★ ★
ARCHERFISH'S WARTIME PATROLS

NO.	CAPTAIN	DATE	DUR.	BASE	AREA	CLAIMED	CONFIRMED
1	GW KEHL	4312	53	PEARL	E CHINA SEA	1/9000	0
2	GWKEHL	4403	42	PEARL	PALAU	0	0
3	WH WRIGHT	4405	48	PEARL	BONINS	1/1400	1/800
4	WH WRIGHT	4408	53	PEARL	EMPIRE	0	0
5	JF ENRIGHT	4410	43	PEARL	EMPIRE	1/28000	1/59000
6	JF ENRIGHT	4501	49	PEARL	E CHINA SEA	1/1100	0
7	JF ENRIGHT	4507	59	PEARL	EMPIRE	0	0

ARCHERFISH'S VICTORIES

DATE	VESSEL	SIZE	TYPE	CAPTAIN	LOCATION
440628	COAST DEF #24	00800	FRIGATE	WH WRIGHT	KIRULES
441129	SHINANO	59000	CARRIER	JF ENRIGHT	SHIKOKU

ARCHERFISH was one of the boats stationed to intercept fleeing ships from Operation Desecrate when Task Force 58 pounded Northern New Guinea. On her fifth patrol in Empire waters, she encountered *SHINANO*, a battleship hull which had been converted to a carrier, the largest in the world. *SHINANO* was on her way to be fitted out when *ARCHERFISH* fired a spread of six torpedos. Every one was a hit and the largest warship ever sunk by a submarine went down. *ARCHERFISH* was one of the twelve boats honored to be present at the Japanese surrender in Tokyo Bay.

ARCHERFISH at Hunter's point Naval Drydocks, June 5, 1945.

ARCHERFISH was decommissioned on June 12, 1946, stricken from the lists and sunk as a target in 1968.

U. S. S. ASPRO
S. S. 309

ASPRO was built at the Portsmouth Navy Yard and was commissioned on July 31, 1943.

★ ★ ★ ★ ★ ★ ★
ASPRO'S WARTIME PATROLS

NO.	CAPTAIN	DATE	DUR.	BASE	AREA	CLAIMED	CONFIRMED
1	HC STEVENSON	4311	39	PEARL	E CHINA SEA	3/25600	0
2	WA STEVENSON	4402	54	PEARL	TRUK	1/2200	1/2200
3	WA STEVENSON	4404	54	PEARL to FREMANTLE		2/11500	1.5/8650
4	WA STEVENSON	4407	41	FREMANTLE	S CHINA SEA	4/19500	1/2300
5	WA STEVENSON	4409	46	FREMANTLE toPEARL		4/25500	2/1090
6	WA STEVENSON	4412	59	PEARL	LUZON STRT	1/8000	.5/4000
7	JH ASHLEY	4506	49	PEARL	EMPIRE	1/500	0

ASPRO'S VICTORIES

DATE	VESSEL	SIZE	TYPE	CAPTAIN	LOCATION
440215	I-43	02212	SUBMARINE	HC STEVENSON	MARIANAS
440514	MISAN MARU	04500	FREIGHTER	WA STEVENSON	MINDANAO
	(Shared credit with *BOWFIN*)				
440515	JOKUJA MARU	06440	FREIGHTER	WA STEVENSON	MINDANAO
440728	PEKING MARU	02288	TRANSPORT	WA STEVENSON	LUZON
441002	AZUSHISAN MARU	06888	FREIGHTER	WA STEVENSON	LUZON
441007	MACASSAR MARU	04026	PASS-CARGO	WA STEVENSON	LUZON
450103	SHINSU MARU #2	08170	TANKER	WA STEVENSON	S CHINA SEA
	(Shared credit with carrier-based aircraft)				

ASPRO took part in Operation Hailstone in the Truk area while Task Force 58 pounded Truk. She was also on station for Operation King Two during the battle for Leyte. *ASPRO* received Navy Unit Commendations for Patrol #1 under H.C. Stevenson and for Patrol #2 under W.A. Stevenson.

ASPRO at Hunter's Point Navy Yard, San Francisco, California, May 24, 1945.

ASPRO was decommissioned on January 30, 1946, stricken from the lists and sunk as a target in 1963.

U.S.S. ATULE
S.S. 403

ATULE was built at Portsmouth Navy Yard and commissioned on December 21, 1943.

★ ★ ★ ★
ATULE'S WARTIME PATROLS

NO.	CAPTAIN	DATE	DUR.	BASE	AREA	CLAIMED	CONFIRMED
1	JH MAURER	4410	60	PEARL	LUZON STRT	5/26700	4/25691
2	JH MAURER	4501	59	PEARL	E CHINA SEA	1/6700	1/6888
3	JH MAURER	4504	59	PEARL	EMPIRE	0	0
4	JH MAURER	4507	51	PEARL	EMPIRE	1/800	1/800

ATULE'S VICTORIES

DATE	VESSEL	SIZE	TYPE	CAPTAIN	LOCATION
441101	ASAMA MARU	16975	TRANSPORT	JH MAURER	S CHINA SEA
441120	MINESWEEPER #38	00630	MINESWEEPER	JH MAURER	S CHINA SEA
441125	PATROL BOAT #38	00820	FRIGATE	JH MAURER	E CHINA SEA
441125	SANTOS MARU	07266	FREIGHTER	JH MAURER	E CHINA SEA
450124	TAIMAN MARU	06888	FREIGHTER	JH MAURER	off YOKOHAMA
450713	COAST DEF #6	00800	FRIGATE	JH MAURER	off YOKOHAMA

On her first patrol, *ATULE* sank the *ASAMA MARU*, last liner over 15,000 tons to be sunk by U.S. submarines. Less than a month later, she sank an additional three ships for a first patrol total of 25,691 tons. For this performance, *ATULE* received a Navy Unit Commendation.

ATULE was decommissioned on September 8, 1947, stricken from the lists and transferred to the Peruvian Navy in 1974 as the *PACOCHA*.

U. S. S. BANG
S. S. 385

U. S. S. BANG
S. S. 385

BANG was built at the Portsmouth Navy Yard
and commissioned on December 4, 1943.

★ ★ ★ ★ ★ ★
BANG'S WARTIME PATROLS

NO.	CAPTAIN	DATE	DUR.	BASE	AREA	CLAIMED	CONFIRMED
1	AR GALAHER	4403	46	PEARL	LUZON STR.	3/20200	3/10700
2	AR GALAHER	4406	58	PEARL	PHILIPPINE SEA	3/24000	0
3	AR GALAHER	4408	32	PEARL	EMPIRE	5/31400	3/4200
4	AR GALAHER	4410	40	PEARL	FORMOSA	4/18400	2/5200
5	AR GALAHER	4501	50	PEARL	E CHINA SEA	0	0
6	OW BAGBY	4503	55	PEARL	LUZON STR.	0	0

BANG'S VICTORIES

DATE	VESSEL	SIZE	TYPE	CAPTAIN	LOCATION
440429	TAKEGAWA MARU	01930	FREIGHTER	AR GALAHER	off LUZON
440430	NITTATSU MARU	02859	FREIGHTER	AR GALAHER	off LUZON
440504	KINREI MARU	05947	FREIGHTER	AR GALAHER	off HAINAN
440909	TOKIWASAN MARU	01804	FREIGHTER	AR GALAHER	off KYUSHU
440909	SHORYU MARU II	01916	FREIGHTER	AR GALAHER	off KYUSHU
440919	TOSEI MARU #2	00507	TANKER	AR GALAHER	off FORMOSA
441123	SAKAE MARU	02878	FREIGHTER	AR GALAHER	off FORMOSA
441123	AMAKUSA MARU	02340	FREIGHTER	AR GALAHER	off FORMOSA

BANG took part in Operation Forager which covered the landings at Saipan and interrupted re-enforcements destined for that island. As part of "Sandy's Sluggers" and later "Walling's Whalers," she helped make it hot for Japanese shipping transiting "Convoy College" off Luzon and in the Formosa Strait.

A postwar photograph of *BANG*.

BANG was decommissioned on February 12, 1947, and transferred to the Spanish Navy as the *COSME GARCIA* in 1972.

On December 7, 1941, the United States Navy had fifty-one submarines in the Pacific—twenty-nine in Manila and twenty-two at Pearl Harbor. The usual routine was for about a third to be on patrol, a third coming or going, and the last third undergoing re-fit.

U. S. S. BARBEL
S. S. 316

U. S. S. BARBEL
S. S. 316

BARBEL was built at the Electric Boat Company
and was commissioned on April 3, 1944.

★ ★ ★

BARBEL'S WARTIME PATROLS

NO.	CAPTAIN	DATE	DUR.	BASE	AREA	CLAIMED	CONFIRMED
1	RA KEATING, Jr	4407	36	PEARL	EMPIRE	4/32900	3/5170
2	RA KEATING, Jr	4409	40	PEARL	EMPIRE	3/6100	1/1200
3	RA KEATING, Jr	4410	38	PEARL	to FREMANTLE	2/9400	2/8800
4	CL RAGUET	4502	00	FREMANTLE	S CHINA SEA	0	0

BARBEL'S VICTORIES

DATE	VESSEL	SIZE	TYPE	CAPTAIN	LOCATION
440705	MIYAKO MARU	00970	PASS-CARGO	RA KEATING, Jr	NANSEI SHOTO
440709	YAGI MARU	01937	FREIGHTER	RA KEATING, Jr	NANSEI SHOTO
440709	BOKO MARU	02333	FREIGHTER	RA KEATING, Jr	NANSEI SHOTO
440825	BUSHU MARU	01222	FREIGHTER	RA KEATING, Jr	E CHINA SEA
441114	SUGIYAMA MARU	04379	FREIGHTER	RA KEATING, Jr	S CHINA SEA
441114	MISAKI MARU	04422	FREIGHTER	RA KEATING,Jr	S CHINA SEA

On her last patrol, *BARBEL* formed a wolf pack with four other boats and patroled an area in the South China Sea. LCDR C.L. Raguet reported that he was under air attack on February 3, 1944, and would contact the others as soon as he could get clear. No further messages were received, however. Much later, Japanese pilots reported sinking a U.S. sub southwest of Palawan on February 4th. There were no survivors.

BARBEL going down the ways at Electric Boat Company, Groton, Connecticut, November 14, 1943.

From December 7, 1941, through May 30, 1942, six Japanese vessels were sunk by colliding with Japanese mines.

November 1944 was the busiest month for U.S. submariners when a total of 250 war patrols were made.

U. S. S. BARBERO
S. S. 317

BARBERO was built at the Electric Boat Company
and commissioned on April 29, 1944.

★ ★
BARBERO'S WARTIME PATROLS

NO.	CAPTAIN	DATE	DUR.	BASE	AREA	CLAIMED	CONFIRMED
1	IS HARTMAN	4408	55	PEARL	to FREMANTLE	0	0
2	IS HARTMAN	4410	65	FREMANTLE	S CHINA SEA	4/21700	3/9200

BARBERO'S VICTORIES

DATE	VESSEL	SIZE	TYPE	CAPTAIN	LOCATION
441102	KURAMASAN MARU	01995	FREIGHTER	IS HARTMAN	MAKASSAR STR
441108	SHIMOTSU MARU	02854	TANKER	IS HARTMAN	off MINDORO
441225	JUNPO MARU	04277	FREIGHTER	IS HARTMAN	off SINGAPORE

BARBERO was stationed east of San Bernadino Strait in what was known as Stalemate II after the Battle of Leyte Gulf. Her job was to pick off survivors of that action. Homeward bound to Fremantle on December 27, 1944, *BARBERO* was caught by Japanese aircraft and badly damaged near Karamata Strait. She managed to limp home, but had to return to the U.S. for repair and did not make another war patrol.

A postwar *BARBERO* at Mare Island Navy Yard, San Francisco, California, September 24, 1948.

BARBERO was decommissioned on June 30, 1950, and sunk as a target in 1964.

U. S. S. BATFISH
S. S. 310

BATFISH was built at the Portsmouth Navy Yard and commissioned on August 21, 1943.

★ ★ ★ ★ ★ ★ ★ ★ ★

BATFISH'S WARTIME PATROLS

NO.	CAPTAIN	DATE	DUR.	BASE		AREA	CLAIMED	CONFIRMED
1	WR MERRILL	4312	50	PEARL		EMPIRE	2/15700	1/5486
2	WR MERRILL	4402	53	PEARL		EMPIRE	0	0
3	JK FYFE	4405	43	PEARL		EMPIRE	4/9500	1/1000
4	JK FYFE	4408	41	PEARL	to	FREMANTLE	2/2900	1.5/1500
5	JK FYFE	4410	53	FREMANTLE	to	PEARL	2/500	0
6	JK FYFE	4501	61	PEARL		S CHINA SEA	3/4500	3/3262
7	WL SMALL	4506	58	PEARL		EMPIRE	0	0

BATFISH'S VICTORIES

DATE	VESSEL	SIZE	TYPE	CAPTAIN	LOCATION
440120	HIDAKA MARU	05486	FREIGHTER	WR MERRILL	SHIKOKU
440622	NAGARAGWA MARU	00990	PASS-CARGO	JK FYFE	off YOKOHAMA
440723	MINESWEEPER #22	00492	SWEEPER	JK FYFE	PALAU
440722	SAMIDARE	01580	DESTROYER	JK FYFE	PELEWS
	(Shared credit with carrier-based Naval aircraft)				
450209	I-41	02212	SUBMARINE	JK FYFE	LUZON STRAIT
450211	RO-112	00525	SUBMARINE	JK FYFE	LUZON STRAIT
450212	RO-113	00525	SUBMARINE	JK FYFE	LUZON STRAIT

BATFISH took part in Operation King Two during the action at Leyte Gulf and was stationed off northwest Mindanao. *BATFISH* holds the record for enemy submarines, having sunk three within three days on her sixth patrol. *BATFISH* was awarded a Presidential Unit Citation for Patrol #6 under J.K. Fyfe.

An aerial view of *BATFISH* off the Jersey coast, August 21, 1943.

BATFISH was decommissioned on April 6, 1946, and is now a historic ship exhibit at Muskogee, Oklahoma.

U. S. S. BAYA
S. S. 318

BAYA was built at the Electric Boat Company and commissioned on May 20, 1944.

★ ★ ★ ★
BAYA'S WARTIME PATROLS

NO.	CAPTAIN	DATE	DUR.	BASE		AREA	CLAIMED	CONFIRMED
1	AH HOLTZ	4408	56	PEARL	to	FREMANTLE	1/7500	.5/871
2	AH HOLTZ	4411	55	FREMANTLE		S CHINA SEA	1/1100	0
3	BC JARVIS	4502	46	FREMANTLE		S CHINA SEA	3/13500	2/5760
4	BC JARVIS	4505	39	FREMANTLE		S CHINA SEA	3/13000	1/2500
5	BC JARVIS	4506	36	FREMANTLE		S CHINA SEA	1/1700	1/595

BAYA'S VICTORIES

DATE	VESSEL	SIZE	TYPE	CAPTAIN	LOCATION
441007	KINUGASA MARU	08407	PASS-CARGO	AH HOLTZ	PALAWAN
	(Shared credit with *HAWKBILL*)				
450304	PALEMBANG MARU	05236	TANKER	BC JARVIS	off SAIGON
450321	KAINAN MARU	00524	SUB-CHASER	BC JARVIS	S CHINA SEA
450513	YOSEI MARU	02500	TANKER	BC JARVIS	S CHINA SEA
450716	KARI	00595	PT BOAT	BC JARVIS	JAVA SEA

BAYA was nearly pooped by a tidal wave on September 25, 1944, but recovered. The three men washed overboard were picked up. Operation Stalemate saw *BAYA* on picket with twelve other boats during the Palau Invasion. Like most other boats on patrols during the last few months of the war, *BAYA* was plagued by target shortages.

BAYA off the New Jersey coast, June 26, 1944.

BAYA was decommissioned on May 14, 1946, stricken from the lists and scrapped in 1972.

U. S. S. BECUNA
S. S. 319

BECUNA was built at the Electric Boat Company and commissioned on May 27, 1944.

★ ★ ★ ★
BECUNA'S WARTIME PATROLS

NO.	CAPTAIN	DATE	DUR.	BASE		AREA	CLAIMED	CONFIRMED
1	HD STURR	4408	56	PEARL	to	FREMANTLE	2/10000	.5/871
2	HD STURR	4411	53	FREMANTLE		S CHINA SEA	1/1100	0
3	HD STURR	4502	46	FREMANTLE		S CHINA SEA	1/7500	1/1945
4	HD STURR	4505	39	FREMANTLE		S CHINA SEA	0	0
5	HD STURR	4506	36	FREMANTLE		S CHINA SEA	0	0

BECUNA'S VICTORIES

DATE	VESSEL	SIZE	TYPE	CAPTAIN	LOCATION
441009	TOKUWA MARU	01943	TRANSPORT	HD STURR	PALAWAN
	(Shared credit with *HAWKBILL*)				
450222	NICHIYOKU MARU	01945	TANKER	HD STURR	BANDA ARCH

BECUNA, like most U.S. submarines active in late 1944 and 1945 suffered from target shortages. On February 25, 1945, *BECUNA* sighted a small tanker burning and aground in the shallows of Cape Padaran. Authorities estimated this was the last victory of *TAUTOG*, a victory due to a minefield she had planted there in November 1942.

BECUNA was decommissioned on November 7, 1969, and is now a historic ship exhibit at Philadelphia, Pennsylvania.

U. S. S. BERGALL
S. S. 320

BERGALL was built at the Electric Boat Company and was commissioned on June 12, 1944.

★ ★ ★ ★
BERGALL'S WARTIME PATROLS

NO.	CAPTAIN	DATE	DUR.	BASE	AREA	CLAIMED	CONFIRMED
1	JM HYDE	4409	60	PEARL	to FREMANTLE	3/21500	2/14700
2	JM HYDE	4412	21	FREMANTLE	S CHINA SEA	1/12500	0
3	JM HYDE	4501	28	FREMANTLE	S CHINA SEA	1/900	2/974
4	JM HYDE	4503	43	FREMANTLE	S CHINA SEA	0	0
5	JM HYDE	4504	37	FREMANTLE	S CHINA SEA	0	0

BERGALL'S VICTORIES

DATE	VESSEL	SIZE	TYPE	CAPTAIN	LOCATION
441013	SHINSU MARU	04182	FREIGHTER	JM HYDE	off ANDAMAN
441027	NIPPO MARU	10528	TANKER	JM HYDE	N W BORNEO
450127	MINESWEEPER #102	00174	MINESWEEPER	JM HYDE	SUNDA ISLES
450207	COAST DEF #12	00800	FRIGATE	JM HYDE	BANDA ARCH

BERGALL torpedoed the Japanese heavy cruiser **MYOKO** with a spread of all six bow tubes. **MYOKO** broke in two and caught fire, giving the illusion of two ships burning. When **BERGALL** moved in for the kill, an escort cruiser put an 8-inch shell in **BERGALL's** forward torpedo room. **BERGALL** cleared the area but could not submerge and made her way back to base on the surface. **BERGALL** was not credited with a skinking since the forward half of the cruiser was salvaged. **BERGALL** took part in Operation King Two during the action at Leyte Gulf and was stationed in the Palawan Passage. She was awarded a Navy Unit Commendation for Patrol #2 under J.M. Hyde.

The photograph shows **BERGALL** after her postwar conversion under the "Guppy" program July 22, 1952..

BERGALL was decommissioned on October 18, 1958, and transferred to the Turkish Navy as the **TURGUT REIS.**

U. S. S. BESUGO
S. S. 321

BESUGO was built at the Electric Boat Company
and was commissioned on June 19, 1944.

★ ★ ★ ★

BESUGO'S WARTIME PATROLS

NO.	CAPTAIN	DATE	DUR.	BASE	AREA	CLAIMED	CONFIRMED
1	TL WOGAN	4409	39	PEARL	EMPIRE	1/700	0
2	TL WOGAN	4411	23	PEARL	to FREMANTLE	2/8000	1/1000
3	TL WOGAN	4412	53	FREMANTLE	S CHINA SEA	2/11000	2/10800
4	HE MILLER	4503	54	FREMANTLE	S CHINA SEA	3/2700	2/2194
5	HE MILLER	4506	42	FREMANTLE	S CHINA SEA	0	0

BESUGO'S VICTORIES

DATE	VESSEL	SIZE	TYPE	CAPTAIN	LOCATION
441122	TRANSPORT #151	01000	LST	TL WOGAN	ANAMBAS ISL
450106	NICHIEI MARU II	10020	TANKER	TL WOGAN	BAY OF BENGAL
450202	COAST DEF #144	00800	FRIGATE	TL WOGAN	BAY OF BENGAL
450406	MINESWEEPER #12	00630	MINESWEEPER	HE MILLER	MENTAWA ISLE
450423	GERMAN U-183	01564	TYPE IX	HE MILLER	JAVA SEA

BESUGO was first to sight the Japanese carrier force coming out of Bungo Suido for the showdown at Leyte Gulf and managed to damage one of the cruiser escorts. Coming fairly late to the action, *BESUGO* suffered from target shortages. As the Japanese lost ship after ship, quarry became scarce.

BESUGO was decommissioned on March 21, 1958, and transferred to the Italian Navy in 1966 as the *FRANCESCO MOROSINI.*

U. S. S. BILLFISH
S. S. 286

U. S. S. BILLFISH
S. S. 286

BILLFISH was built at Portsmouth Navy Yard
and commissioned on April 20, 1943.

★ ★ ★ ★ ★ ★ ★

BILLFISH'S WARTIME PATROLS

NO.	CAPTAIN	DATE	DUR.	BASE	AREA	CLAIMED	CONFIRMED
1	FC LUCAS	4308	59	FREMANTLE	S CHINA SEA	0	0
2	FC LUCAS	4311	53	FREMANTLE	S CHINA SEA	0	0
3	VC TURNER	4401	66	FREMANTLE	INDOCHINA	1/1000	0
4	VC TURNER	4404	57	FREMANTLE to PEARL		1/8500	0
5	VC TURNER	4407	65	PEARL	EMPIRE	0	0
6	VC TURNER	4410	53	PEARL	EMPIRE	0	0
7	LC FARLEY	4504	54	PEARL	EMPIRE	2/7800	2/2311
8	LC FARLEY	4507	44	PEARL	E CHINA SEA	2/5200	1/1091

BILLFISH'S VICTORIES

DATE	VESSEL	SIZE	TYPE	CAPTAIN	LOCATION
450526	KOTOBUKI MARU #7	00991	FREIGHTER	LC FARLEY	YELLOW SEA
450604	TAIU MARU	02220	FREIGHTER	LC FARLEY	YELLOW SEA
450705	KORI MARU	01091	FREIGHTER	LC FARLEY	YELLOW SEA

BILLFISH operated with *BOWFIN* on their first patrol, and damaged two ships for 11,900 tons. No sinking credit was given, however. Later patrols from Pearl proved only slightly more productive. *BILLFISH* made one of the last periscope attacks of the war as she went practically inside Darien Harbor to register her last kill.

BILLFISH at Portsmouth Naval Shipyard, Portsmouth, New Hampshire, 1943.

BILLFISH was decommissioned on November 1, 1946, stricken from the lists and sold for scrap in 1971.

───────────

There were several double launchings during World War II, but only one triple.
*At that one, **PIRANHA, POMFRET,** and **STERLET** were launched at*
Portsmouth Naval Shipyard, Portsmouth, New Hampshire, on October 27, 1943.

U. S. S. BLACKFIN
S. S. 322

BLACKFIN was built at the Electric Boat Company
and commissioned on July 4, 1944.

★ ★ ★

BLACKFIN'S WARTIME PATROLS

NO.	CAPTAIN	DATE	DUR.	BASE	AREA	CLAIMED	CONFIRMED
1	GH LAIRD	4409	60	PEARL	to FREMANTLE	2/4000	1/2700
2	WL KITCH	4501	45	FREMANTLE	S CHINA SEA	1/1500	1/1580
3	WL KITCH	4503	36	FREMANTLE	S CHINA SEA	0	0
4	WL KITCH	4504	31	FREMANTLE to PEARL		0	0
5	WL KITCH	4507	37	PEARL	E CHINA SEA	0	0

BLACKFIN'S VICTORIES

DATE	VESSEL	SIZE	TYPE	CAPTAIN	LOCATION
441101	UNKAI MARU	2745	FREIGHTER	GH LAIRD	off F LUBANG ISL.
450124	SHIGURE	1580	DESTROYER	WL KITCH	off KOTA BAHARU

BLACKFIN operated in support of Operation King Two with thirteen other boats and stood picket against the retreating survivors of the Battle of Leyte Gulf. On her second patrol she formed a wolf pack with *TUNA*, *GABILAN*, *PERCH*, and *BARBEL* in an area buzzing with enemy aircraft. During this operation, *BARBEL* was lost with all hands.

BLACKFIN is at anchor with a liberty party leaving in the small boat.

BLACKFIN was decommissioned on November 19, 1948, stricken from the lists in 1959 when she was sold for scrap.

U. S. S. BLENNY
S. S. 324

BLENNY was built at the Electric Boat Company and commissioned on July 27, 1944.

★ ★ ★ ★

BLENNY'S WARTIME PATROLS

NO.	CAPTAIN	DATE	DUR.	BASE	AREA	CLAIMED	CONFIRMED
1	WH HAZZARD	4411	62	PEARL	to FREMANTLE	2/11100	2/4956
2	WH HAZZARD	4502	49	FREMANTLE	S CHINA SEA	4/25500	4/12611
3	WH HAZZARD	4505	55	FREMANTLE	S CHINA SEA	1/800	1/525
4	WH HAZZARD	4507	40	FREMANTLE	S CHINA SEA	1/5700	0

BLENNY'S VICTORIES

DATE	VESSEL	SIZE	TYPE	CAPTAIN	LOCATION
441214	COAST DEF #28	00800	FRIGATE	WH HAZZARD	off LUZON
441223	KENZUI MARU	04156	FREIGHTER	WH HAZZARD	SW LUZON
450226	AMATO MARU	10238	TANKER	WH HAZZARD	ANDAMAN ISLE
450320	YAMAKUNI MARU II	00500	FREIGHTER	WH HAZZARD	off SAIGON
450320	NANSHIN MARU #21	00834	TANKER	WH HAZZARD	off SAIGON
450320	HOSEN MARU	01039	FREIGHTER	WH HAZZARD	off SAIGON
450530	HOKOKU MARU	00520	FREIGHTER	WH HAZZARD	MENTAWI ISLE

Targets worthy of a torpedo became very scarce during the last few months of the war so *BLENNY* mopped up the Malay Coast with her deck guns. Hazzard was careful to see that the native crews were unharmed and their possessions were saved. She even ran out of ammunition and had to be resupplied from other U.S. subs in the area. She sank a total of 63 vessels (a record for the war). Total tonnage was only 5,700 tons for the small craft, however.

BLENNY off the New Jersey coast, August 21, 1944.

BLENNY was decommissioned on November 7, 1969, stricken from the lists and scrapped in 1973.

U. S. S. BLOWER
S. S. 325

BLOWER was built at the Electric Boat Company
and commissioned on August 10, 1944.

BLOWER'S WARTIME PATROL

NO.	CAPTAIN	DATE	DUR.	BASE	AREA	CLAIMED	CONFIRMED
1	JH CAMPBELL	4501	60	PEARL	to FREMANTLE	0	0
2	JH CAMPBELL	4505	41	FREMANTLE	S CHINA SEA	0	0
3	NP WATKINS	4506	35	FREMANTLE	S CHINA SEA	0	0

BLOWER did not claim, nor was she credited with any confirmed victories.

BLOWER did spot a Japanese submarine (*I-351*) and managed to direct **BLUEFISH** into an attack position where her skipper, G.W. Forbes, sank it. **BLOWER** did not claim any credit however.

BLOWER at Mare Island Navy Yard, San Francisco, California, September 17, 1946.

BLOWER was decommissioned on November 16, 1950, and transferred to the Turkish Navy as the **DUMLUPINAR**.

U. S. S. BLUEBACK
S. S. 326

BLUEBACK was built at the Electric Boat Company and commissioned on August 28, 1944.

★ ★

BLUEBACK'S WARTIME PATROLS

NO.	CAPTAIN	DATE	DUR.	BASE	AREA	CLAIMED	CONFIRMED
1	MK CLEMENSON	4412	61	PEARL to	FREMANTLE	0	0
2	MK CLEMENSON	4503	44	FREMANTLE	S CHINA SEA	0	0
3	MK CLEMENSON	4504	62	FREMANTLE	JAVA SEA	1/1100	1/300

BLUEBACK'S VICTORY

DATE	VESSEL	SIZE	TYPE	CAPTAIN	LOCATION
450127	SUBCHASER #2	00300	SUBCHASER	MK CLEMENSON	SUNDA STRAIT

BLUEBACK narrowly missed the Japanese cruiser *ASHIGARA* which, at that time, was the only enemy warship left between Singapore and the Java Sea. Teaming up with the *CHUBB*, they attempted an ambush near Djakarta, but both boats missed the opportunity to shoot.

Photograph taken from the deck of the *BLOWER* in 1945 by Lieutenant Herb Hansen.

BLUEBACK was decommissioned on May 23, 1948, and transferred to the Turkish Navy that same year as the *IKINCI INONU*.

U. S. S. BOARFISH
S. S. 327

BOARFISH was built at the Electric Boat Company
and commissioned on September 21, 1944.

★

BOARFISH'S WARTIME PATROLS

NO.	CAPTAIN	DATE	DUR.	BASE	AREA	CLAIMED	CONFIRMED
1	RL GROSS	4412	52	PEARL	to FREMANTLE	1.5/9800	1.5/10445
2	RL GROSS	4503	42	FREMANTLE	S CHINA SEA	0	0
3	EC BLONTS	4504	23	FREMANTLE	JAVA SEA	0	0
4	EC BLONTS	4507	36	FREMANTLE	S CHINA SEA	0	0

BOARFISH'S VICTORIES

DATE	VESSEL	SIZE	TYPE	CAPTAIN	LOCATION
450131	ENKI MARU	06968	FREIGHTER	RL GROSS	off DA NANG
450131	TAIETSU MARU	06890	FREIGHTER	RL GROSS	off DA NANG

(Shared credit with land-based Army aircraft)

BOARFISH landed a "commando" party on the coast of Indochina near Hue. When the party blew up a section of railroad track, they received credit for derailing or damaging a train. As targets became scarce, many U.S. subs cruised the surface like destroyers and shot anything they could find.

A postwar photograph of *BOARFISH*. Note the twin deck guns.

BOARFISH was decommissioned on May 23, 1948, and transferred that year to the Turkish Navy as the *SAKAYARA.*

U. S. S. BRILL
S. S. 330

BRILL was built at the Electric Boat Company
and commissioned on October 26, 1944.

★
BRILL'S WARTIME PATROLS

NO.	CAPTAIN	DATE	DUR.	BASE	AREA	CLAIMED	CONFIRMED
1	HB DODGE	4501	62	PEARL	to FREMANTLE	0	0
2	HB DODGE	4505	41	FREMANTLE	S CHINA SEA	0	0
3	HB DODGE	4507	37	FREMANTLE	S CHINA SEA	0	0

BRILL did not claim any victories, nor was she credited with any.

BRILL made only three patrols, having come to the action in the last few months of the war.

BRILL shown running trials, probably in the Thames River near Groton, Connecticut.

BRILL was decommissioned on May 23, 1948, and transferred to the Turkish Navy as the *BIRINCI INONU*.

———————————

The United States Navy lost a total of fifty-two boats during World War II; eight were from unknown causes.

*The Japanese submarine **I-203** was equipped with H.O.R. engines. It was hoped they had as many problems with them as the United States Navy did.*

U. S. S. BOWFIN
S. S. 287

U. S. S. BOWFIN
S. S. 287

BOWFIN was built at the Portsmouth Navy Yard
and commissioned on May 1, 1943.

★ ★ ★ ★ ★ ★ ★

BOWFIN'S WARTIME PATROLS

NO.	CAPTAIN	DATE	DUR.	BASE	AREA	CLAIMED	CONFIRMED
1	JH WILLINGHAM	4308	57	FREMANTLE	S CHINA SEA	3/23900	1/8120
2	WT GRIFFITH	4311	39	FREMANTLE	S CHINA SEA	9/70900	5/26458
3	WT GRIFFITH	4401	28	FREMANTLE	MAKASSAR	3/12600	1/4408
4	WT GRIFFITH	4402	33	FREMANTLE	CELEBES	3/21000	3/15000
5	J CORBUS	4404	58	FREMANTLE to PEARL		1/6500	.5/2250
6	J CORBUS	4407	59	PEARL	EMPIRE	9/26700	1/6754
7	AK TYREE	4501	56	PEARL	EMPIRE	2/2700	1/750
8	AK TYREE	4504	23	PEARL	EMPIRE	2/9300	2/3599
9	AK TYREE	4505	37	PEARL	SEA OF JAPAN	2/6300	2/2785

BOWFIN'S VICTORIES

DATE	VESSEL	SIZE	TYPE	CAPTAIN	LOCATION
430825	KIRISHIMA MARU	08120	PASS-CARGO	JH WILLINGHAM	S CHINA SEA
431126	OGURASAN MARU	05069	TANKER	WT GRIFFITH	S CHINA SEA
431126	TAINAN MARU	05407	FREIGHTER	WT GRIFFITH	S CHINA SEA
431127	VON VOLLENHOVN	00691	FREIGHTER	WT GRIFFITH	S CHINA SEA
431128	SYDNEY MARU	25425	PASS-CARGO	WT GRIFFITH	S CHINA SEA
431128	TONAN MARU	09866	TANKER	WT GRIFFITH	S CHINA SEA
440117	SHOYU MARU	04408	FREIGHTER	WT GRIFFITH	CAPE ENGANO
440310	TSUKUKAWA MARU	04470	FREIGHTER	WT GRIFFITH	E CHINA SEA
440324	SHINKYO MARU	05139	FREIGHTER	WT GRIFFITH	SULU ARCH
440324	BENGAL MARU	05399	FREIGHTER	WT GRIFFITH	SULU ARCH
440517	BISAN MARU	04500	FREIGHTER	JH CORBUS	off SAMAR
	(Shared credit with *ASPRO*)				
440722	TSUSHIMA MARU	06754	PASS-CARGO	JH CORBUS	RYUKUS
450217	COAST DEF #56	00750	FRIGATE	JH CORBUS	SHIKOKU
450501	CHOWA MARU	02719	PASS-CARGO	AK TYREE	off YOKAHAMA
450508	DAITO MARU #3	00880	FREIGHTER	AK TYREE	off YOKAHAMA
450611	SHINYO MARU #3	01898	PASS-CARGO	AK TYREE	SEA OF JAPAN
450613	AIKIURA MARU	00887	FREIGHTER	AK TYREE	SEA OF JAPAN

BOWFIN received a Presidential Unit Citation for Patrol #2, and a Navy Unit Commendation for Patrol #6. She tied for 9th in number of vessels sunk, and stood 17th in total tonnage.

BOWFIN at Mare Island Naval Yard, San Francisco, California, November 24, 1944.

BOWFIN was decommissioned on February 12, 1947, and is now a historic ship memorial exhibit at Pearl Harbor.

U. S. S. BUGARA
S. S. 331

BUGARA was built at the Electric Boat Company and commissioned on November 15, 1944.

★ ★ ★

BUGARA'S WARTIME PATROLS

NO.	CAPTAIN	DATE	DUR.	BASE	AREA	CLAIMED	CONFIRMED
1	AF SCHADE	4502	54	PEARL to	FREMANTLE	0	0
2	AF SCHADE	4504	40	FREMANTLE	S CHINA SEA	0	0
3	AF SCHADE	4507	34	FREMANTLE	S CHINA SEA	0	0

BUGARA did not claim any victories, nor was she credited with any.

BUGARA did, however, make war on many small craft when torpedo-worthy vessels became scarce. She sank twelve junks, twenty-four schooners, sixteen coasters, three sea-trucks, a Trengganu and a naval auxiliary. Since non of these vessels were within the 500-ton limit, she received no credit.

BUGARA was decommissioned on October 1, 1970, and was claimed by an accident in 1971.

---

*During the Battle of Midway, **U.S.S. TROUT** rescued two sailors from the sunken heavy cruiser **MIKUMA**. They became the first Japanese Navy prisoners of war of World War II.*

A total of eighty-eight Navy Unit Commendations were awarded to thirty-nine different boats during World War II.

U. S. S. BULLHEAD
S. S. 332

BULLHEAD was built at the Electric Boat Company
and commissioned on December 4, 1944.

★ ★

BULLHEAD'S WARTIME PATROLS

NO.	CAPTAIN	DATE	DUR.	BASE	AREA	CLAIMED	CONFIRMED
1	WT GRIFFITH	4503	37	PEARL	to FREMANTLE	0	0
2	WT GRIFFITH	4504	43	FREMANTLE	S CHINA SEA	2/1800	0
3	ER HOLT	4507	00	FREMANTLE	S CHINA SEA	0	0

BULLHEAD claimed two small craft during her second patrol, but these were not allowed since they could not be confirmed.

BULLHEAD has the distinction of being the only U.S. submarine to have carried a war correspondent during a war patrol. Martin Sheridan, of the *Boston Globe* had received permission from Admiral Nimitz to make the trip. During this patrol, BULLHEAD was nearly sunk by an American B-24. When Admiral King in Washington learned of this, he forbad any future trips by war correspondents on submarine war patrols.

The BULLHEAD crew gives food to people on a Chinese junk encountered on her first patrol, April 1945.

On BULLHEAD's third patrol, a Japanese Army plane caught her in Lombok Strait on August 6, 1945 and made two direct hits. She went down with all hands.

U. S. S. BUMPER
S. S. 333

BUMPER was built at the Electric Boat Company
and commissioned on December 9, 1944.

★

BUMPER'S WARTIME PATROLS

NO.	CAPTAIN	DATE	DUR.	BASE	AREA	CLAIMED	CONFIRMED
1	JW WILLIAMS	4504	53	PEARL	to FREMANTLE	0	0
2	JW WILLIAMS	4507	34	FREMANTLE	S CHINA SEA	2/2500	1/1189

BUMPER'S VICTORY

DATE	VESSEL	SIZE	TYPE	CAPTAIN	LOCATION
450720	KYOEI MARU #3	01189	TANKER	JW WILLIAMS	GULF OF SIAM

BUMPER made only two patrols. Her only victory came just 26 days before the war ended, which, in itself, is remarkable considering the severe target shortage.

BUMPER was decommissioned on November 16, 1950, and transferred to the Turkish Navy in 1950 as the *CANNAKALE*.

———————————

During World War II, United States submarines sank a total of 1,178 Japanese merchant vessels, totaling 5,053,491 gross registered tons.

U. S. S. BURRFISH
S. S. 312

BURRFISH was built at the Portsmouth Navy Yard and commissioned on September 13, 1943.

★ ★ ★ ★
BURRFISH'S WARTIME PATROLS

NO.	CAPTAIN	DATE	DUR.	BASE	AREA	CLAIMED	CONFIRMED
1	WB PERKINS	4402	50	PEARL	TRUK	0	0
2	WB PERKINS	4404	52	PEARL	EMPIRE	1/5000	1/5900
3	WB PERKINS	4407	46	PEARL	PALAU	0	0
4	WB PERKINS	4409	69	PEARL	EMPIRE	1/7600	0
5	MH LYTEL	4501	48	PEARL	EMPIRE	0	0
6	MH LYTEL	4503	49	PEARL	FORMOSA STR	0	0

BURRFISH'S VICTORY

DATE	VESSEL	SIZE	TYPE	CAPTAIN	LOCATION
4440507	ROSSBACK	05894	TANKER	WB PERKINS	KYUSHU

BURRFISH took part in Operation Hailstone, and covered the escape routes for Japanese warships fleeing the first major strike against Truk. She also landed a scouting party on Peleliu and on Yap where two of her crew were lost. As part of "Burt's Brooms" she helped sweep a path from Saipan toward Japan to ease the way for Halsey's carriers.

Commissioning ceremony aboard *BURRFISH*, September 14, 1943, Captain Clifford H. Roper in charge.

BURRFISH was decommissioned on October 10, 1946, and transferred to the Canadian Navy in 1962 as the *GRISLE*.

U. S. S. CABEZON
S. S. 334

U. S. S. CABEZON
S. S. 334

CABEZON was built at the Electric Boat Company
and commissioned on December 31, 1944.

★

CABEZON'S WARTIME PATROL

NO.	CAPTAIN	DATE	DUR.	BASE	AREA	CLAIMED	CONFIRMED
1	GW LATHRUP	4505	46	PEARL	POLAR CIRCLE	1/4000	1/2631

CABEZON'S VICTORY

DATE	VESSEL	SIZE	TYPE	CAPTAIN	LOCATION
450619	ZAOSAN MARU	02631	FREIGHTER	GW LAUTRUP	NE ETORUFU

CABEZON made only one patrol just two months before the war's end and that to the Polar Circle. Her job was to harrass the Japanese fishing fleet and deprive the homeland of that source of food. Although they were becoming extremely rare, she did manage to sink a mid-sized freighter.

CABEZON moving down the ways at Electric Boat Company, Groton, Connecticut, August 27, 1944.

CABEZON was decommissioned on October 24, 1953, stricken from the lists and sold for scrap in 1971.

The Italian Navy had more operational submarines when Italy entered the war in June of 1940 than any other maritime power except the Soviet Union. With 115 boats, she had more than twice as many as Germany had, 56, when Germany entered the war. The Italians apparently had trouble making up their minds about design as they had twenty-seven different classes of boats. Seventeen boats is the most they had of any class and most classes ranged from one or two to eight. In the 39 months they were in the war, they made 1553 war patrols, sank 11 enemy warships and 70,000 GRT of enemy merchant shipping, at a cost to them of 59 boats lost in action and another 9 to various other causes, i.e., accidents, foundering, etc.

The part the Italian submarine force played during World War II is usually given short shrift by most historians. Few realize the Italian Submarine Service executed forty-four successful transits of the Straits of Gibraltar during hostilities. One boat was lost on her homeward voyage. She, **GLAUCO**, was sunk nearly 250 miles west of the actual strait.

U. S. S. CABRILLA
S. S. 288

CABRILLA was built at the Portsmouth Navy Yard and commissioned on May 24, 1943.

★ ★ ★ ★ ★ ★

CABRILLA'S WARTIME PATROLS

NO.	CAPTAIN	DATE	DUR.	BASE		AREA	CLAIMED	CONFIRMED
1	DT HAMMOND	4308	54	PEARL	to	FREMANTLE	0	0
2	DT HAMMOND	4312	52	FREMANTLE		S CHINA SEA	1/4100	1/2700
3	WC THOMPSON	4401	56	FREMANTLE		SUNDA STRT	0	0
4	WC THOMPSON	4405	34	FREMANTLE		CELEBES	1/8500	1/8360
5	WC THOMPSON	4407	47	FREMANTLE		S CHINA SEA	4/27900	1/3145
6	WC THOMPSON	4409	43	FREMANTLE	to	PEARL	5/29900	4/24557
7	HC LAUERMAN	4503	48	PEARL	to	FREMANTLE	0	0
8	HC LAUERMAN	4506	58	PEARL	to	FREMANTLE	0	0

CABRILLA'S VICTORIES

DATE	VESSEL	SIZE	TYPE	CAPTAIN	LOCATION
440104	TAMON MARU #8	02705	FREIGHTER	DT HAMMOND	S CHINA SEA
440526	SANYO MARU	08360	TENDER	WC THOMPSON	MOLUCCA PASG
440717	MAYA MARU	03145	PASS-CARGO	WC THOMPSON	SULU SEA
441001	ZYIYO MARU	07385	TANKER	WC THOMPSON	LUZON
441001	KYOKUHO MARU	10059	TANKER	WC THOMPSON	LUZON
441006	YAMAMIZU MARU #2	05154	FREIGHTER	WC THOMPSON	LUZON
441007	SHINYO MARU #8	01959	FREIGHTER	WC THOMPSON	LUZON

CABRILLA made several missions to the Philippines with men, money and supplies for the underground fighters there. *CABRILLA* stands 25th of all the boats in amount of tonnage sunk on one patrol with 24,557 tons on her sixth patrol.

A builder's photograph taken at Portsmouth Naval Shipyard, Portsmouth, New Hampshire, June 14, 1943.

CABRILLA was decommissioned on July 7, 1946, stricken from the lists and sold for scrap in 1972.

U. S. S. CAIMAN
S. S. 323

CAIMAN was built at the Electric Boat Company
and commissioned on July 17, 1944.

★ ★
CAIMAN'S WARTIME PATROLS

NO.	CAPTAIN	DATE	DUR.	BASE	AREA	CLAIMED	CONFIRMED
1	FC LUCAS	4411	62	PEARL	to FREMANTLE	0	0
2	WL FEY, Jr	4502	48	FREMANTLE	S CHINA SEA	0	0
3	WL FEY, Jr	4505	62	FREMANTLE	S CHINA SEA	0	0
4	WL FEY, Jr	4507	28	FREMANTLE	S CHINA SEA	0	0

CAIMAN did not claim any victories, nor was she credited with any.

This photograph was taken while *CAIMAN* was being tracked by a naval airship.

CAIMAN was decommissioned on June 30, 1972, stricken from the lists and scrapped.

U. S. S. CAPELIN
S. S. 289

CAPELIN was built at the Portsmouth Navy Yard
and commissioned on May 24, 1943.

★

CAPELIN'S WARTIME PATROLS

NO.	CAPTAIN	DATE	DUR.	BASE	AREA	CLAIMED	CONFIRMED
1	EE MARSHALL	4310	00	FREMANTLE	MAKASSAR	2/7400	1/3000

CAPELIN'S VICTORY

DATE	VESSEL	SIZE	TYPE	CAPTAIN	LOCATION
431111	KUNITAMA MARU	03127	FREIGHTER	EE MARSHALL	MOLUKKAS

After her victory of **KUNITAMA MARU, CAPELIN** put in at Port Darwin for a few minor repairs.
She resumed her patrol and was later declared overdue in the Halmahera area. Whether an operational
accident, a minefield explosion or Japanese depth charges caused her loss is not clear. She went down
with all hands.

A builder's photograph taken at Portsmouth Navy Yard, Portsmouth, New Hampshire, June 28, 1943.

---

*A total of eight United States submarines made fourteen or more war patrols in the Pacific
during World War II.*

U. S. S. CAPITAINE
S. S. 336

CAPITAINE was built at the Electric Boat Company
and commissioned on January 26, 1945.

★

CAPITAINE'S WARTIME PATROLS

NO.	CAPTAIN	DATE	DUR.	BASE	AREA	CLAIMED	CONFIRMED
1	ES FREDRIC	4505	62	FREMANTLE	S CHINA SEA	0	0
2	ES FREDRIC	4508	14	FREMANTLE to	S CHINA SEA	0	0

CAPITAINE did not claim, nor was it credited with, any victories.

A postwar photograph of *CAPITAINE* with a helicopter near her stern, July 15, 1949.

CAPITAINE was decommissioned on February 10, 1950, and transferred to the Italian Navy as the *ALFREDO CAPPELLINI* in 1966.

Harry C. Stevenson was commander of *U.S.S. ASPRO* during her first patrol. In February 1944, his brother, William A. Stevenson, relieved him and commanded *ASPRO* on her next five patrols.

U. S. S. CARBONERO
S. S. 337

CARBONERO was built at the Electric Boat Company
and commissioned on February 7, 1945.

★
CARBONERO'S WARTIME PATROLS

NO.	CAPTAIN	DATE	DUR.	BASE	AREA	CLAIMED	CONFIRMED
1	CL MURPHY	4505	42	FREMANTLE	S CHINA SEA	0	0
2	CL MURPHY	4508	15	PEARL	to FREMANTLE	0	0

CARBONERO did not claim, nor was credited with, any victories

CARBONERO was decommissioned on December 1, 1970, stricken from the lists and sold for scrap.

U.S.S. ALBACORE holds the record for Japanese warships sunk. She collected a Fleet Carrier, a Light Cruiser, two Destroyers, two Gunboats, a Frigate, and a Sub-Chaser.

U. S. S. CARP
S. S. 338
CARP was built at the Electric Boat Company
and commissioned on February 28, 1945.

★

CARP'S WARTIME PATROL

NO.	CAPTAIN	DATE	DUR.	BASE	AREA	CLAIMED	CONFRMED
1	JL HUNICUT	4506	54	PEARL	EMPIRE	0	0

CARP did not claim any victories, nor were any credited to her.

An aerial view of ***CARP*** taken in Panama Bay, April 28, 1945.

CARP was decommissioned on March 18, 1968, stricken from the lists and sold for scrap in 1971.

———————————

More than 150 German U-Boats were scuttled at the dock by their crews in Northern Germany when the surrender was announced the first week in May 1945. An additional 102 boats were towed out into the deepest part of the Atlantic and scuttled by the Royal Navy in what was known as "Operation Deadlight." It was thought that this was done to avoid sharing this war booty with the Soviets.

U. S. S. CATFISH
S. S. 339

CATFISH was built at the Electric Boat Company
and commissioned on March 19, 1945.

★

CATFISH'S WARTIME PATROL

NO.	CAPTAIN	DATE	DUR.	BASE	AREA	CLAIMED	CONFRMED
1	WA OVERTON	4507	40	PEARL	EMPIRE	0	0

CATFISH did not claim any victories, nor were any credited to her.

CATFISH at Mare Island Navy Yard, San Francisco, California, June 9, 1947.

CATFISH was decommissioned on July 1, 1971, and transferred to the Argentine Navy as the *SANTA FE*.

---

*Commander Roy M. Davenport earned five Navy Crosses for his patrols on **U.S.S. HAD-DOCK** and **U.S.S. TREPANG**, more than any other commander. Except for those who earned Congressional Medals, he was the most decorated submariner of World War II.*

U. S. S. CHARR
S. S. 328

CHARR was built at the Electric Boat Company
and commissioned on September 23, 1944.

★

CHARR'S WARTIME PATROLS

NO.	CAPTAIN	DATE	DUR.	BASE		AREA	CLAIMED	CONFIRMED
1	FD BOYLE	4412	63	PEARL	to	FREMANTLE	0	0
2	FD BOYLE	4503	51	FREMANTLE		S CHINA SEA	2/5700	0.5/2850
3	FD BOYLE	4506	42	FREMANTLE		S CHINA SEA	0	0

CHARR'S VICTORY

DATE	VESSEL	SIZE	TYPE	CAPTAIN	LOCATION
450407	ISUZU	5700	LT CRUISER	FD BOYLE	BIMA BAY

On her first patrol, *CHARR* was placed in the fifteen-boat trap-line set up by Admiral Fife to get the *ISE* and *HYUGA*. The Japanese battleship-carrier and heavy cruiser had been pressed into service carrying oil in drums from Singapore to the Empire. Somehow, these two fast warships and their escorts managed to elude the entire line, although several of the boats got off long shots. Codebreaking allowed Fife to set another trap the first week in April for the light cruiser *ISUZU* which was being used as a troop ferry. After one missed attempt, the Japanese warship sought shelter in Bima Bay while *CHARR, BESUGO* and *GABILAN* lay outside waiting. *GABILAN* got the first hit and escorts drove her down. Boyle brought *CHARR* in closer where he could see that *ISUZU* was damaged but still making way. He fired six torpedos, three of which were hits, but had to go deep when escorts found him. The cruiser sank.

CHARR was decommissioned on June 28, 1969, stricken from the lists and scrapped in 1971.

U. S. S. CHUB
S. S. 329

CHUB was built at the Electric Boat Company and commissioned on October 21, 1944.

★ ★ ★
CHUB'S WARTIME PATROLS

NO.	CAPTAIN	DATE	DUR.	BASE	AREA	CLAIMED	CONFIRMED
1	CD RHYMES	4502	64	PEARL to	FREMANTLE	0	0
2	CD RHYMES	4504	38	FREMANTLE	JAVA SEA	3/2400	1/492
3	CD RHYMES	4507	33	FREMANTLE	S CHINA SEA	1/1500	0

CHUB'S VICTORY

DATE	VESSEL	SIZE	TYPE	CAPTAIN	LOCATION
450545	MINESWEEPER #34	00492	MINESWEEPER	CD RHYMES	JAVA SEA

CHUB came late to the action and, like similar boats, suffered from target shortages as Marus and warships worthy of the name had largely been erased. Japan began the war with over six million tons of merchant shipping and finished with less than one million tons.

CHUB going down the ways at Electric Boat Company, Groton, Connecticut, June 18, 1944.

CHUB was decommissioned on May 23, 1948, transferred to the Turkish Navy in 1948 as the *GUR*.

U. S. S. CISCO
S. S. 290

CISCO was built at the Portsmouth Navy Yard
and commissioned on May 10, 1943.

CISCO'S WARTIME PATROL

NO.	CAPTAIN	DATE	DUR.	BASE	AREA	CLAIMED	CONFIRMED
1	JW COE	4309	00	FREMANTLE	S CHINA SEA	0	0

CISCO did not claim any victories, nor was she credited with any.

A builder's photograph of *CISCO* at Portsmouth Naval Shipyards, Portsmouth, New Hampshire, June 14, 1943.

CISCO was lost on her first patrol, the victim of a well-coordinated sea and air attack in the middle of the Sulu Sea. She went down with all hands on September 28, 1943.

During 1944, twenty-three older submarines were taken out of combat status and sent stateside for use as training boats. Two Gato-class boats were also retired because of severe battle damage and returned stateside for extensive repairs.

U. S. S. CREVALLE
S. S. 291

U. S. S. CREVALLE
S. S. 291
CREVALLE was built at the Portsmouth Navy Yard
and commissioned on June 24, 1943.

★ ★ ★ ★
CREVALLE'S WARTIME PATROLS

NO.	CAPTAIN	DATE	DUR.	BASE	AREA	CLAIMED	CONFIRMED
1	HG MUNSON	4310	49	FREMANTLE	MANILA	4/29800	1/6783
2	HG MUNSON	4312	60	FREMANTLE	S CHINA SEA	3/19900	1/2552
3	HG MUNSON	4404	54	FREMANTLE	S CHINA SEA	2/26400	2/17771
4	FD WALKER	4406	50	FREMANTLE	S CHINA SEA	3.5/28000	2.5/10950
5	FD WALKER	4409	20	FREMANTLE	JAVA SEA	0	0
6	EH STEINMETZ	4503	46	PEARL	E CHINA SEA	1/1300	0
7	EH STEINMETZ	4505	38	PEARL	SEA OF JAPAN	4/8500	3/6643

CREVALLE'S VICTORIES

DATE	VESSEL	SIZE	TYPE	CAPTAIN	LOCATION
431115	KYOKKU MARU	06783	PASS-CARGO	HG MUNSON	off CAVITE
440126	BUSHO	02552	GUNBOAT	HG MUNSON	S CHINA SEA
440425	KASHIWA MARU II	00976	TENDER	FD WALKER	SULU SEA
440506	NISSHIN MARU	16801	TANKER	FD WALKER	SULU SEA
440726	AKI MARU	11409	PASS-CARGO	FD WALKER	S CHINA SEA
440726	TOSAN MARU	08666	PASS-CARGO	FD WALKER	S CHINA SEA
	(Shared credit with *FLASHER*)				
440728	HAKUBASAN MARU	06650	PASS-CARGO	FD WALKER	S CHINA SEA
450609	HOKUTO MARU	02215	FREIGHTER	EH STEINMETZ	SEA OF JAPAN
450610	KAIKI MARU	02217	FREIGHTER	EH STEINMETZ	SEA OF JAPAN
450611	HAKUSAN MARU	02211	FREIGHTER	EH STEINMETZ	SEA OF JAPAN

CREVALLE sank the largest tanker and merchant vessel to be downed by a U.S. submarine when she torpedoed the *NISSHIN MARU*. She also delivered arms and supplies to guerilla bands in the Philippines.

A builder's photograph at Portsmouth Navy Yard, Portsmouth, New Hampshire, July 10, 1943.

CREVALLE was decommissioned on August 20, 1946, stricken from the lists and sold for scrap in 1971.

U.S.S. DENTUDA
S.S. 335

DENTUDA was built at the Electric Boat Company
and commissioned on December 30, 1944.

★

		DENTUDA'S WARTIME PATROL				
NO.	CAPTAIN	DATE	DUR.	BASE	AREA	CLAIMED	CONFIRMED
1	JS McCAIN	4505	58	PEARL	E CHINA SEA	1/4000	0

DENTUDA came late to the action and, like many of her sisters, was plagued by target shortages. She claimed one vessel sunk but it was not confirmed nor credited.

DENTUDA was decommissioned on December 11, 1946, stricken from the lists and sold for scrap in 1969.

———————————

The Japanese Navy used seventeen classes of combat boats and six classes of transport submarines during World War II. This does not include the eight classes of midget one- and two-man boats or the suicide boats classed as Kaitens.

U. S. S. DEVILFISH
S. S. 292

DEVILFISH was built at the Cramp Shipbuilding Company
and commissioned on September 1, 1944.

★ ★ ★
DEVILFISH'S WARTIME PATROLS

NO.	CAPTAIN	DATE	DUR.	BASE	AREA	CLAIMED	CONFIRMED
1	EC STEPHAN	4412	41	PEARL	EMPIRE	0	0
2	SS MANN, Jr	4503	21	PEARL	EMPIRE	0	0
3	SS MANN, Jr	4505	47	PEARL	EMPIRE	0	0
4	SS MANN, Jr	4508	20	PEARL	EMPIRE	0	0

DEVILFISH did not claim any victories, nor was she credited with any.

While cruising enroute to her area on her second patrol, *DEVILFISH* spotted an enemy plane making a run at her from astern. She crash dived and as she passed 50 feet, she heard what seemed like a small explosion. Water came in from an 8-inch hole near the SJ mast. She was forced to surface to effect repairs and discovered that a Kamikaze had crashed her upper works just as she submerged. Both periscopes were put out of action, as were her radar attennas. She was given credit for a Japanese plane destroyed and her crew received the Combat Insignia for this action, even though the cost to the boat far exceeded the cost of the plane.

DEVILFISH was decommissioned on September 30, 1946, stricken from the lists and sunk has a target in 1969.

U. S. S. DRAGONET
S. S. 293

U. S. S. DRAGONET
S. S. 293

DRAGONET was built at the Cramp Shipbuilding Company
and commissioned on March 6, 1944.

★ ★

DRAGONET'S WARTIME PATROLS

NO.	CAPTAIN	DATE	DUR.	BASE	AREA	CLAIMED	CONFIRMED
1	JH LEWIS	4411	49	PEARL	POLAR CIRC	0	0
2	JH LEWIS	4504	50	PEARL	E CHINA SEA	0	0
3	GG HINMAN	4507	50	PEARL	EMPIRE	0	0

DRAGONET did not claim, nor was she credited with, any victories.

After making several false starts on her first patrol, and being forced to return for yet another series of repairs, she became known around the base as the "Reluctant Dragonet." This was understandable to most submariners since she was a "Cramp Boat," and these boats had a less than enviable reputation among the underwater sailors.

She redeemed herself, however, off the Kirules, when she was forced down by aircraft and hit bottom rather solidly which damaged and flooded her forward torpedo room. She managed to surface again and crept away under the noses of the Japanese at Matsuwa Air Base. If this was not enough, she ran into a typhoon which nearly swamped her and rolled the boat over sixty-three degrees. She made it to Midway in time for Christmas, but a Navy yard overhaul was required to put her back in fighting trim.

DRAGONET undergoing a re-fit at Mare Island Navy Yard, San Francisco, California, March 25, 1945.

DRAGONET was decommissioned on April 16, 1946, stricken from the lists and sunk as a target in 1961.

———————————

The first semi-practical plan for a submarine boat was advanced by the Englishman William Bourne during the reign of Queen Elizabeth I. He published a paper in which he proposed a vessel with ballast tanks whose walls could be moved in and out to admit or expell water, thus changing the buoyancy of the boat and permitting it to sink or rise. There is no record of any such vessel having been built.

U. S. S. ENTEMEDOR
S. S. 340
The *ENTEMEDOR* was built at the Electric Boat Company
and commissioned on April 6, 1945.

ENTEMEDOR'S WARTIME PATROL

NO.	CAPTAIN	DATE	DUR.	BASE	AREA	CLAIMED	CONFIRMED
1	WR SMITH	4507	30	PEARL	EMPIRE	0	0

ENTEMEDOR did not claim, nor was she credited with, any victories.

ENTEMEDOR was not at sea long enough to collect any Marus, even if there had not been an extreme shortage of targets.

Going down the ways at Electric Boat Company, Groton, Connecticut, December 17, 1944.

ENTEMEDOR was decommissioned on December 10, 1948, and transferred to the Turkish Navy as the *PREVEZE* in 1972.

U. S. S. ESCOLAR
S. S. 294

ESCOLAR was built at the Cramp Shipbuilding Company
and commissioned on June 2, 1944.

ESCOLAR'S WARTIME PATROL

NO.	CAPTAIN	DATE	DUR.	BASE	AREA	CLAIMED	CONFIRMED
1	WJ MILLICAN	4409	00	PEARL	E CHINA SEA	0	0

ESCOLAR did not claim, nor was she credited with, any victories.

ESCOLAR left Pearl on her first patrol. After topping off at Midway, she joined *CROAKER* and *PERCH II* to form the wolf pack, "Millican's Marauders." They were scheduled to operate in the Yellow Sea and were in touch every day. On October 17, 1944, *ESCOLAR* gave her position to the other boats and was not heard from again. It is presumed that she struck a mine and went down with all hands since later records did not indicate any anti-submarine activity by Japan in that area.

The photograph is probably from the builder, Cramp Shipbuilding, Philadelphia, Pennsylvania.

U.S.S. STINGRAY (S.S. 186) completed sixteen Pacific War Patrols. This was the record for any United States submarine in World War II.

U. S. S. GOLET
S. S. 361

GOLET was built at the Manitowoc Shipbuilding Company
and commissioned on November 30, 1943.

GOLET'S WARTIME PATROLS

NO.	CAPTAIN	DATE	DUR.	BASE	AREA	CLAIMED	CONFIRMED
1	PH ROSS	4403	46	PEARL	POLAR CIRC	0	0
2	JS CLARK	4405	00	PEARL	POLAR CIRC	0	0

GOLET did not claim, nor was she credited with, any victories.

GOLET topped off at Midway on her second patrol to the area north of Honshu. On July 9, she failed to respond to a message from CINCPAC and was pronounced overdue. On July 26, she was presumed lost. Postwar Japanese records indicate an anti-submarine action in her area in which they report "on the spot of fighting we later discovered corks, raft and so on, and thick pool of oil." It was on June 14, 1944, that she went down with all hands.

GOLET, just prior to her sideways launch into the river at Manitowoc Shipbuilding, Manitowoc, Wisconsin.

U. S. S. GUAVINA
S. S. 362

GUAVINA was built at Manitowoc Shipbuilding Company and commissioned on December 23, 1944.

★ ★ ★ ★ ★
GUAVINA'S WARTIME PATROLS

NO.	CAPTAIN	DATE	DUR.	BASE	AREA	CLAIMED	CONFIRMED
1	C TIEDEMAN	4404	52	PEARL	BONIN	3/19500	1/2300
2	C TIEDEMAN	4406	42	PEARL	BRISBANE	1/5800	1/3000
3	C TIEDEMAN	4408	44	BRISBANE	DAVAO	3/3000	1/1500
4	C TIEDEMAN	4410	60	FREMANTLE	S CHINA SEA	3.5/24800	2/6117
5	R LOCKWOOD	4501	42	FREMANTLE	S CHINA SEA	2/20000	2/15565
6	R LOCKWOOD	4503	48	FREMANTLE	S CHINA SEA	0	0

GUAVINA'S VICTORIES

DATE	VESSEL	SIZE	TYPE	CAPTAIN	LOCATION
440426	NOSHIRO MARU	02333	FREIGHTER	C TIEDEMAN	VOLCANO ISL
440704	TAMA MARU	03052	PASS-CARGO	C TIEDEMAN	PALAU
440915	TRANSPORT #3	01500	LANDING CRFT	C TIEDEMAN	SULU ARCH
441121	GYOSAN MARU	05698	FREIGHTER	C TIEDEMAN	PALAWAN
	(Shared credit with *FLOUNDER*)				
441122	DAWA MARU	01916	FREIGHTER	C TIEDEMAN	PALAWAN
450207	TAIGYO MARU	06892	FREIGHTER	R LOCKWOOD	MALAY
450220	EIYO MARU	08673	TANKER	R LOCKWOOD	MALAY

GUAVINA was an average boat. She did six patrols, which is half what some boats did and twice as many as others. Her tonnage was 24,366, which was less than 79 boats, but more than 109.

GUAVINA just after her sideways launch at Manitowoc Shipbuilding, Manitowoc, Wisconsin.

GUAVINA was decommissioned on March 27, 1959, and sunk as a target in 1969.

U. S. S. GUITARRO
S. S. 363

U. S. S. GUITARRO
S. S. 363

GUITARRO was built at Manitowoc Shipbuilding Company
and commissioned on January 26, 1944.

★ ★ ★ ★

GUITARRO'S WARTIME PATROLS

NO.	CAPTAIN	DATE	DUR.	BASE	AREA	CLAIMED	CONFIRMED
1	ED HASKINS	4405	51	PEARL	to FREMANTLE	3/21300	2/3100
2	ED HASKINS	4407	48	FREMANTLE	S CHINA SEA	5/11800	4/11200
3	ED HASLINS	4410	38	FREMANTLE	S CHINA SEA	3.5/28200	2.3/10999
4	TB DABNEY	4412	83	FREMANTLE	S CHINA SEA	0	0
5	TB DABNEY	4505	61	FREMANTLE	S CHINA SEA	0	0

GUITARRO'S VICTORIES

DATE	VESSEL	SIZE	TYPE	CAPTAIN	LOCATION
440530	SHISEN MARU	02201	FREIGHTER	ED HASKINS	FORMOSA
440602	AWAJI	00900	FRIGATE	ED HASKINS	BASHI CHANL
440707	KUSAKAKI	00900	FRIGATE	ED HASKINS	off MANILA
440710	SHINEI MARU	05135	FREIGHTER	ED HASKINS	LINGAYEN
440721	UGA MARU	04433	PASS-CARGO	ED HASKINS	CAPE CALAVITE
440722	NANSHIN MARU #15	00834	TANKER	ED HASKINS	MINDORO
441031	KOMEI MARU	02857	FREIGHTER	ED HASKINS	off LUZON
441031	PACIFIC MARU	05872	PASS-CARGO	ED HASKINS	off LUZON
441104	KAGU MARU	06806	PASS-CARGO	ED HASKINS	off LUZON

(Shared credit with *RAY* and *BREAM*)

GUITARRO took part in Operation King Two, along with thirteen other SubSoWesPac boats, and formed the main picket line from Luzon to Northern Borneo.

GUITARRO was decommissioned in 1954, and transferred to the Turkish Navy.

The Imperial Japanese Navy had a total of 64 submarines on December 7, 1941. During the course of the war they built 126 new submarines. Twenty-five of these were designed specifically as transport subs to service the isolated garrisons in the Pacific islands and bases under siege by the Allies.

U. S. S. HACKLEBACK
S. S. 295

HACKLEBACK was built at the Cramp Shipbuilding Company
and commissioned on November 7, 1944.

HACKLEBACK'S WARTIME PATROLS

NO.	CAPTAIN	DATE	DUR.	BASE	AREA	CLAIMED	CONFIRMED
1	FE JANNEY	4503	51	PEARL	EMPIRE	0	0
2	FE JANNEY	4505	49	PEARL	EMPIRE	0	0

HACKLEBACK did not claim, nor was she credited with, any victories.

HACKLEBACK and *THREADFIN* were on picket in the Bungo Suido with the last large units of the Japanese Navy sortied in April 1945 during the Okinawa Invasion. They reported this movement and the force which included the giant battlewagon *YAMATO* was attacked and sent to the bottom by the airmen of Mitchers'(??? 's) Task Force.

HACKLEBACK in Panama Bay, January 13, 1945.

HACKLEBACK was decommissioned on March 20, 1946, stricken from the lists and sold for scrap in 1968.

In 1653, a Frenchman named de Son, working in Holland, built a twin-hulled submersible vessel powered by an oversized clockwork. The motor proved to be too weak to move the contraption and the idea was abandoned.

U. S. S. HAMMERHEAD
S. S. 364

HAMMERHEAD was built at Manitowoc Shipbuilding and commissioned on March 3, 1944.

★ ★ ★ ★ ★ ★ ★
HAMMERHEAD'S WARTIME PATROLS

NO.	CAPTAIN	DATE	DUR.	BASE	AREA	CLAIMED	CONFIRMED
1	JC MARTIN	4406	65	PEARL	to FREMANTLE	1/8700	0
2	JC MARTIN	4409	54	FREMANTLE	S CHINA SEA	6/41500	5/25178
3	JC MARTIN	4411	52	FREMANTLE	S CHINA SEA	1/5000	0.5/1427
4	GH LAIRD	4502	22	FREMANTLE	S CHINA SEA	1/800	1/900
5	FM SMITH	4503	28	FREMANTLE	S CHINA SEA	1/1800	1/1000
6	FM SMITH	4505	25	FREMANTLE	S CHINA SEA	2/8500	2/6823
7	FM SMITH	4506	60	FREMANTLE	S CHINA SEA	1/1100	2/1734

HAMMERHEAD'S VICTORIES

DATE	VESSEL	SIZE	TYPE	CAPTAIN	LOCATION
441001	KOKUSEI MARU	05396	FREIGHTER	JC MARTIN	NW BORNEO
441001	HIGANE MARU	05320	FREIGHTER	JC MARTIN	NW BORNEO
441001	HIYORI MARU	05320	FREIGHTER	JC MARTIN	NW BORNEO
441020	UGO MARU	03684	PASS-CARGO	JC MARTIN	NW BORNEO
441020	OYO MARU	05458	PASS-CARGO	JC MARTIN	NW BORNEO
441208	SHOEI MARU	02854	TANKER	JC MARTIN	NW BORNEO
	(Shared credit with *PADDLE*)				
450223	YAKU	00900	FRIGATE	FM SMITH	PHAN RANG
450329	COAST DEF #84	01000	FRIGATE	FM SMITH	PHAN RANG
450506	KENREI MARU #4	00850	TANKER	FM SMITH	GULF THAILND
450515	TOTTORI MARU	05973	PASS-CARGO	FM SMITH	GULF THAILND
450710	SAKURA MARU	00900	FREIGHTER	FM SMITH	GULF THAILND
450710	NUNMER MARU #5	00834	TANKER	FM SMITH	GULF THAILND

HAMMERHEAD received a Navy Unit Commendation for Patrol #2 under J.C. Martin.

A builder photograph of *HAMMERHEAD* off Manitowoc Shipbuilding, Manitowoc, Wisconsin, March 15, 1944.

HAMMERHEAD was decommissioned on February 9, 1946, and transferred to the Turkish Navy as the *CERBE* in 1954.

U. S. S. HARDHEAD
S. S. 365

HARDHEAD was built at the Manitowoc Shipbuilding Company
and was commissioned on April 18, 1944.

★ ★ ★ ★ ★ ★

HARDHEAD'S WARTIME PATROLS

NO.	CAPTAIN	DATE	DUR.	BASE	AREA	CLAIMED	CONFIRMED
1	F McMASTER	4407	33	PEARL	to FREMANTLE	1/5200	1/5700
2	FA GREENUP	4410	45	FREMANTLE	S CHINA SEA	2/9800	2/6100
3	FA GREENUP	4412	53	FREMANTLE	S CHINA SEA	1/2500	1/834
4	FA GREENUP	4503	56	FREMANTLE	S CHINA SEA	1/10300	1/6886
5	FA GREENUP	4506	33	FREMANTLE	S CHINA SEA	2/2500	3/500
6	JL HAINES	4507	24	FREMANTLE	S CHINA SEA	1/1800	1/200

HARDHEAD'S VICTORIES

DATE	VESSEL	SIZE	TYPE	CAPTAIN	LOCATION
440718	NATORI	05700	CRUISER	F McMASTERS	MINDANAO
441108	MANEI MARU	05226	TANKER	FW GREENUP	PALAWAN
441125	COAST DEF #38	00800	FRIGATE	FW GREENUP	PALAWAN
450202	NANSHIN MARU #19	00834	TANKER	FW GREENUP	GULF OF SIAM
450406	ARACSAN MARU	06886	FREIGHTER	FW GREENUP	GULF OF SIAM
450623	SHUTTLE BT #833	00200	AUXILIARY	FW GREENUP	BRUNEI
450623	SUBCHASER #42	00100	SUBCHASER	FW GREENUP	BRUNEI
450623	SUBCHASER #113	00200	SUBCHASER	FW GREENUP	BRUNEI
450723	SUBCHASER #117	00200	SUBCHASER	JL HAINES	SPRATLY IS

HARDHEAD took part in Operation Stalemate for the capture of Palau, Yap, and Ulithi.

A builder's photograph taken off Manitowoc Shipbuilding, Manitowoc, Wisconsin, May 5, 1944.

HARDHEAD was decommissioned on May 10, 1947, and transferred to the Greek Navy in 1972 as
the *PAPANIKOLIS*.

U.S.S. HAWKBILL
S.S. 366

HAWKBILL was built at Manitowoc Shipbuilding Company
and commissioned on March 3, 1944.

★ ★ ★ ★ ★ ★

HAWKBILL'S WARTIME PATROLS

NO.	CAPTAIN	DATE	DUR.	BASE	AREA	CLAIMED	CONFIRMED
1	FW SCANLAND	4408	53	PEARL	to FREMANTLE	2/11500	2/5075
2	FW SCANLAND	4411	50	FREMANTLE	S CHINA SEA	1/1300	1/760
3	FW SCANLAND	4502	58	FREMANTLE	S CHINA SEA	2/12800	3/5596
4	FW SCANLAND	4505	44	FREMANTLE	S CHINA SEA	1/2400	1/1500
5	FW SCANLAND	4507	31	FREMANTLE	S CHINA SEA	1/700	0

HAWKBILL'S VICTORIES

DATE	VESSEL	SIZE	TYPE	CAPTAIN	LOCATION
441007	KINUGASA MARU	08407	PASS-CARGO	FW SCANLAND	S CHINA SEA
	(Shared credit with *BAYA*)				
441009	TOKUWA MARU	01943	FREIGHTER	FW SCANLAND	S CHINA SEA
	(Shared credit with *BECUNA*)				
441215	MOMO	00760	DESTROYER	FW SCANLAND	S CHINA SEA
450214	SUBCHASER #4	00100	SUBCHASER	FW SCANLAND	SPRATLY IS
450214	SUBCHASER #114	00100	SUBCHASER	FW SCANLAND	SPRATLY IS
450220	DAIZEN MARU	05396	FREIGHTER	FW SCANLAND	SINGAPORE
450516	HATSUTAKA	01500	MINELAYER	FW SCANLAND	MALAY

HAWKBILL came to the action late in the war, but made the most of her few opportunities. Her sinking of the minelayer *HATSUTAKA* probably avenged the *LAGARTO*. *HAWKBILL* received Navy Unit Commendations for Patrols #1, 2, and 3 under F.W. Scanland, Jr.

This aerial photograph was taken in the Gulf of Mexico, June 16, 1944.

HAWKBILL was decommissioned on September 30, 1946, and transferred to The Netherlands Navy in 1954 as the *ZEELEEUW*.

U. S. S. ICEFISH
S. S. 367

ICEFISH was built at Manitowoc Shipbuilding Company
and commissioned on June 10, 1944.

★ ★ ★ ★

ICEFISH'S WARTIME PATROLS

NO.	CAPTAIN	DATE	DUR.	BASE	AREA	CLAIMED	CONFIRMED
1	RW PETERSON	4409	61	PEARL	LUZON STR	2/13300	2/8400
2	RW PETERSON	4412	42	PEARL	E CHINA SEA	0	0
3	RW PETERSON	4502	57	PEARL	E CHINA SEA	0	0
4	RW PETERSON	4505	50	PEARL	to FREMANTLE	0	0
5	RW PETERSON	4507	24	FREMANTLE	E CHINA SEA	0	0

ICEFISH'S VICTORIES

DATE	VESSEL	SIZE	TYPE	CAPTAIN	LOCATION
441024	TENSHIN MARU #3	04236	FREIGHTER	RW PETERSON	S CHINA SEA
441026	TAIYO MARU II	04168	FREIGHTER	RW PETERSON	S CHINA SEA

ICEFISH participated in the Operation King Two near the Luzon Strait. She scored her victories while a part of "Banister's Beagles" wolf pack operating in the famed "Convoy College" area.

A builder's photograph taken off Manitowoc Shipbuilding, Manitowoc, Wisconsin, June 23, 1944.

ICEFISH was decommissioned on June 21, 1946, and transferred to The Netherlands Navy in 1953 as the *WALRUS*.

U. S. S. JALLAO
S. S. 368

JALLAO was built at Manitowoc Shipbuilding Company and commissioned on July 8, 1944.

★ ★ ★ ★

JALLAO'S WARTIME PATROLS

NO.	CAPTAIN	DATE	DUR.	BASE	AREA	CLAIMED	CONFIRMED
1	JB ICENHOWER	4410	61	PEARL	LUZON STRAIT	1/5200	1/5711
2	JB ICENHOWER	4501	65	PEARL	E CHINA SEA	0	0
3	JB ICENHOWER	4504	55	PEARL	EMPIRE	0	0
4	JB ICENHOWER	4507	51	PEARL	SEA OF JAPAN	1/4000	1/5795

JALLAO'S VICTORIES

DATE	VESSEL	SIZE	TYPE	CAPTAIN	LOCATION
441025	TAMA	05700	CRUISER	JB ICENHOWER	BATAN ISL
	(Shared credit with carrier-based aircraft)				
450811	TEIHOKU MARU	05795	PASS-CARGO	JB ICENHOWER	SEA OF JAPAN

JALLAO was part of "Clarey's Crushers" wolf pack during the Operation King Two and was stationed in Luzon Strait. Later she took part in Operation Barney which severed Japan's last link with the Asiatic mainland by making the Sea of Japan unusable.

JALLAO, at the moment of her sideways launch into the river at Manitowoc Shipbuilding, Manitowoc, Wisconsin, March 12, 1944.

JALLAO was decommissioned on September 30, 1946, stricken from the lists and transferred to Spain in 1974.

U. S. S. KETE
S. S. 369

KETE was built at the Manitowoc Shipbuilding Company
and commissioned on July 31, 1943.

★

KETE'S WARTIME PATROLS

NO.	CAPTAIN	DATE	DUR.	BASE	AREA	CLAIMED	CONFIRMED
1	RL RUTTER	4410	60	PEARL	EMPIRE	0	0
2	E ACKERMAN	4503	00	PEARL	EMPIRE	3/12000	3/6875

KETE'S VICTORIES

DATE	VESSEL	SIZE	TYPE	CAPTAIN	LOCATION
450310	KEIZAN MARU #3	02116	FREIGHTER	E ACKERMAN	NENSEI SHOTO
450310	SANKA MARU	02495	FREIGHTER	E ACKERMAN	NANSEI SHOTO
450310	DAKAN MARU	02270	FREIGHTER	E ACKERMAN	NANSEI SHOTO

On patrol off Okinawa on January 12, 1945, *KETE* reported contact with another submarine but was unable to identify her. Later she heard prolonged depth charging in the area of the other submarine and probably witnessed by ear the destruction of *SWORDFISH*. After her victories on March 10, 1945, and a probable on March 14, 1945, *KETE* was ordered to return to Pearl via Midway for refueling. That was the last communication with her and she was lost due to unknown causes.

KETE, off Manitowoc Shipbuilding, Manitowoc, Wisconsin, March 15, 1944.

U. S. S. KRAKEN
S. S. 370

KRAKEN was built at Manitowoc Shipbuilding Company
and commissioned on September 8, 1944.

★

KRAKEN'S WARTIME PATROLS

NO.	CAPTAIN	DATE	DUR.	BASE	AREA	CLAIMED	CONFIRMED
1	TH HENRY	4412	64	PEARL	to FREMANTLE	0	0
2	TH HENRY	4503	43	FREMANTLE	S CHINA SEA	0	0
3	TH HENRY	4504	45	FREMANTLE	S CHINA SEA	3/3000	0
4	TH HENRY	4507	23	FREMANTLE	JAVA SEA	0	0

KRAKEN claimed three victories which were never confirmed.

A builder's photograph taken off Manitowoc Shipbuilding, Manitowoc, Wisconsin, September 23, 1944.

KRAKEN was decommissioned on May 9, 1946, and transferred to the Spanish Navy as the *ALMIRANTE GARCIA DE LOS REYS*.

───────────────

Two United States submarines were sunk by their own torpedoes making circular runs.

U. S. S. LAGARTO
S. S. 371

LAGARTO was built by the Manitowoc Shipbuilding Company
and commissioned on October 14, 1944.

★

LAGARTO'S WARTIME PATROLS

NO.	CAPTAIN	DATE	DUR.	BASE	AREA	CLAIMED	CONFIRMED
1	FD LATTA	4501	55	PEARL	to FREMANTLE	1/900	2/1845
2	FD LATTA	4505	00	FREMANTLE	S CHINA SEA	0	0

LAGARTO'S VICTORIES

DATE	VESSEL	SIZE	TYPE	CAPTAIN	LOCATION
450224	TATSUMOMO MARU	00880	FREIGHTER	FD LATTA	BUNGO SUIDO
450224	RO-49	00965	SUBMARINE	FD LATTA	BUNGO SUIDO

LAGARTO was one of the last submarines to be lost in the war. On her maiden patrol she had conducted a diversionary sweep south of Honshu. On her second patrol she was ordered into the Gulf of Siam with *BAYA*. While conducting a co-ordinated attack plan she was discovered by the Japanese minelayer *HATSUTKA*, depth charged in thirty fathoms and sunk.

This photograph of **LAGARTO** is from the McPherson Collection and taken during World War II.

U. S. S. LAMPREY
S. S. 372

LAMPREY was built at the Manitowoc Shipbuilding Company
and commissioned on November 17, 1944.

★ ★ ★ ★

LAMPREY'S WARTIME PATROLS

NO.	CAPTAIN	DATE	DUR.	BASE	AREA	CLAIMED	CONFIRMED
1	WT NELSON	4502	53	PEARL to	FREMANTLE	0	0
2	LB McDONALD	4504	40	FREMANTLE	S CHINA SEA	0	0
3	LB McDONALD	4507	25	FREMANTLE	S CHINA SEA	0	0

LAMPREY claimed no victories, nor was she credited with any.

This aerial photograph was taken in Panama Bay, January 5, 1945.

LAMPREY was decommissioned on June 3, 1946, and transferred to the Argentine Navy in 1960.

—————————————

The German Navy used only eight classes of U-Boats during World War II.

U. S. S. LIONFISH
S. S. 298

LIONFISH was built at Cramp Shipbuilding Company
and commissioned on November 1, 1944.

★

LIONFISH'S WARTIME PATROLS

NO.	CAPTAIN	DATE	DUR.	BASE	AREA	CLAIMED	CONFIRMED
1	ED SPRUANCE	4504.	51	PEARL	E CHINA SEA	0	0
2	BM GANYARD	4506	58	PEARL	EMPIRE	0	0

LIONFISH claimed no victories, nor was she credited with any.

This aerial photograph of *LIONFISH* was taken off Philadelphia before she was completely fitted out.

LIONFISH was decommissioned on January 16, 1946, stricken from the lists in 1971, and is now a historic ship exhibit at Battleship Park in Fall River, Massachusetts.

———————

In late 1943, German U-Boat production rate was just over one boats per day compared to twenty per month for 1942. They could hardly keep up, however, as United States merchant shipbuilding had increased to three ships per day in the Liberty Ship program alone by mid-1942.

U. S. S. LIZARDFISH
S. S. 373

LIZARDFISH was built by the Manitowoc Shipbuilding Company
and commissioned on December 30, 1944.

★
LIZARDFISH'S WARTIME PATROLS

NO.	CAPTAIN	DATE	DUR.	BASE		AREA	CLAIMED	CONFIRMED
1	OM BUTLER	4504	52	PEARL	to	FREMANTLE	0	0
2	OM BUTLER	4506	39	FREMANTLE		S CHINA SEA	0	1/100

LIZARDFISH'S VICTORY

DATE	VESSEL	SIZE	TYPE	CAPTAIN	LOCATION
450707	SUBCHASER #37	00100	SUBCHASER	OM BUTLER	S CHINA SEA

LIZARDFISH did not even put in a claim for her only victory, even though it was a Japanese warship. This was one of the last Japanese warships of torpedo-shooting size to fall victim to U.S. submarines.

A builder's photograph off Manitowoc Shipbuilding, Manitowoc, Wisconsin, January 15, 1945.

LIZARDFISH was decommissioned on June 6, 1946, and transferred to the Italian Navy in 1960 as the *EVANGELISTA TORRICELLI.*

U. S. S. LOGGERHEAD
S. S. 374

LOGGERHEAD was built at Manitowoc Shipbuilding Company
and commissioned on February 9, 1945.

LOGGERHEAD'S WARTIME PATROLS

NO.	CAPTAIN	DATE	DUR.	BASE	AREA	CLAIMED	CONFIRMED
1	RM METCALF	4505	64	PEARL	to FREMANTLE	0	0
2	RM METCALF	4508	9	FREMANTLE	S CHINA SEA	0	0

LOGGERHEAD claimed no victories, nor was she credited with any.

A builder's photograph of *LOGGERHEAD* at rest off Manitowoc Shipbuilding, Manitowoc, Wisconsin.

LOGGERHEAD was decommissioned on October 22, 1945, stricken from the lists and sold for scrap in 1969.

The German U-Boat service totaled 1162 boats between 1939 and 1945.

U. S. S. MACABI
S. S. 375

MACABI was built at Manitowoc Shipbuilding Company
and commissioned on March 29, 1945.

MACABI'S WARTIME PATROL

NO.	CAPTAIN	DATE	DUR.	BASE	AREA	CLAIMED	CONFIRMED
1	AH DROPP	4507	42	PEARL	TRUK	0	0

MACABI claimed no victories, nor was she credited with any.

MACABI, off Manitowoc Shipbuilding, Manitowoc, Wisconsin, April 12, 1945.

MACABI was decommissioned on June 16, 1946, and transferred to the Argentine Navy in 1960 as the *SANTIAGO DEL ESTERO*.

Half of the United States submarines lost during World War II were pre-war boats.

U. S. S. MANTA
S. S. 299

MANTA was built by Cramp Shipbuilding Company
and launched on November 3, 1943.

MANTA'S WARTIME PATROL

NO.	CAPTAIN	DATE	DUR.	BASE	AREA	CLAIMED	CONFRMED
1	EP MADLEY	4505	46	PEARL	POLAR CIRC	0	0

MANTA did not claim any victories, nor were any credited to her.

Captain Clifford H. Roper reads commissioning orders to *MANTA's* officers and crew at Portsmouth
Navy Yard, Portsmouth, New Hampshire, December 18, 1944.

MANTA was decommissioned on June 10, 1946, stricken from the lists and sunk as a target in 1969.

U. S. S. MORAY
S. S. 300

MORAY was built at Cramp Shipbuilding Company and commissioned on January 26, 1945.

★

MORAY'S WARTIME PATROL

NO.	CAPTAIN	DATE	DUR.	BASE	AREA	CLAIMED	CONFIRMED
1	FL BARROWS	4506	52	PEARL	EMPIRE	0	0

MORAY claimed no victories, nor was she credited with any.

MORAY at Cramp Shipbuilding, Philadelphia, Pennsylvania, January 2, 1945.

MORAY was decommissioned on April 12, 1946, stricken from the lists and sunk as a target in 1970.

U. S. S. PAMPANITO
S. S. 383

PAMPANITO was built at the Portsmouth Navy Yard and commissioned on November 6, 1943.

★ ★ ★ ★ ★ ★

PAMPANITO'S WARTIME PATROLS

NO.	CAPTAIN	DATE	DUR.	BASE	AREA	CLAIMED	CONFIRMED
1	PE SUMMERS	4403	54	PEARL	MARIANAS	0	0
2	PE SUMMERS	4406	50	PEARL	EMPIRE	0	0
3	PE SUMMERS	4408	42	PEARL	LUZON STRT	3/23600	2/15600
4	FW FENNO	4410	59	PEARL	to FREMANTLE	1/7500	1/1200
5	PE SUMMERS	4501	20	FREMANTLE	S CHINA SEA	2/12500	2/10488
6	PE SUMMERS	4502	57	FREMANTLE	S CHINA SEA	0	0

PAMPANITO'S VICTORIES

DATE	VESSEL	SIZE	TYPE	CAPTAIN	LOCATION
440912	KACHIDOKI MARU	10509	TRANSPORT	PE SUMMERS	S CHINA SEA
440912	ZUIHO MARU	05135	TANKER	PE SUMMERS	S CHINA SEA
441119	SHINKO MARU #1	01200	FREIGHTER	FW FENNO	S CHINA SEA
450206	ENGEN MARU	06968	FREIGHTER	PE SUMMERS	MALAY PEN
450208	EIFUKU MARU II	03520	PASS-CARGO	PE SUMMERS	MALAY PEN

On September 11-12, 1944, "Ben's Busters," of which *PAMPANITO, GROWLER*, and *SEALION II* were a part, torpedoed and sank seven ships of an Empire-bound convoy. Unknown to the submariners, some of the vessels carried Allied prisoners of war. On the 15th, *PAMPANITO* discovered their plight and called for more help. *GROWLER* had left the area, so *QUEENFISH* and *BARB* were called in to help. They rescued 159 of the desperate, malnourished men, seven of whom died before reaching port.

PAMPANITO during a war-time re-fit.

PAMPANITO was decommissioned on December 15, 1945, stricken from the lists in 1971, and is now a historic ship memorial in San Francisco, California.

U. S. S. PARCHE
S. S. 384

PARCHE was built at the Portsmouth Navy Yard and commissioned on November 20, 1943.

★ ★ ★ ★ ★
PARCHE'S WARTIME PATROLS

NO.	CAPTAIN	DATE	DUR.	BASE	AREA	CLAIMED	CONFIRMED
1	LP RAMAGE	4403	56	PEARL	LUZON STRAIT	3/23900	2/11700
2	LP RAMAGE	4406	59	PEARL	LUZON STRAIT	4/34300	2.5/19200
3	LP RAMAGE	4409	77	PEARL	LUZON STRAIT	0	0
4	WW McCRORY	4412	53	PEARL	EMPIRE	1/2000	1/1000
5	WW McCRORY	4503	42	PEARL	EMPIRE	3/5200	1/615
6	WW McCRORY	4505	59	PEARL	EMPIRE	2/7200	2/3669

PARCHE'S VICTORIES

DATE	VESSEL	SIZE	TYPE	CAPTAIN	LOCATION
440504	TAIYOKU MARU	05244	FREIGHTER	LP RAMAGE	S CHINA SEA
440504	SHORYU MARU	06475	FREIGHTER	LP RAMAGE	S CHINA SEA
440731	KOEI MARU II	10238	TANKER	LP RAMAGE	BASHI CHANL
440731	MANKO MARU	04471	PASS-CARGO	LP RAMAGE	BASHI CHANL
440731	YOSHINO MARU	08990	TRANSPORT	LP RAMAGE	BASHI CHANL
	(Shared credit with *STEELHEAD*)				
450207	OKINOYAMA M. II	00984	FREIGHTER	WW McCRORY	OSUMI ISLES
450409	MINESWEEPER #3	00615	MINESWEEPER	WW McCRORY	SEA OF JAPAN
450621	HIZEN MARU	00946	FREIGHTER	WW McCRORY	SEA OF JAPAN
450626	KAMTSU MARU	02723	GUNBOAT	WW McCRORY	SEA OF JAPAN

PARCHE received Presidential Unit Citations for Patrols #1 and 2 under L.P. Ramage. Commander Ramage received the Congressional Medal of Honor for the night surface action of July 31, 1944, in which he and his packmates, *STEELHEAD* and *HAMMERHEAD* sent 39,000 tons of enemy shipping to the bottom.

A post-war *PARCHE*.

PARCHE was decommissioned on December 11, 1945, stricken from the lists and sold for scrap in 1970.

U. S. S. PERCH II
S. S. 313

PERCH II was built at the Electric Boat Company
and commissioned on January 1, 1944.

★ ★ ★ ★
PERCH II'S WARTIME PATROLS

NO.	CAPTAIN	DATE	DUR.	BASE	AREA	CLAIMED	CONFIRMED
1	BC HILLS	4404	35	PEARL	LUZON STR	0	0
2	BC HILLS	4406	59	PEARL	PHILIPPINE SEA	0	0
3	BC HILLS	4409	48	PEARL	E CHINA SEA	0	0
4	BC HILLS	4412	59	PEARL	to FREMANTLE	0	0
5	BC HILLS	4503	10	FREMANTLE	JAVA SEA	0	0
6	CD McCALL	4505	53	FREMANTLE	to PEARL	0	0
7	CD McCALL	4507	47	PEARL	EMPIRE	0	0

PERCH II did not claim any victories, nor was she credited with any.

PERCH II was decommissioned in 1973, stricken from the lists and sold for scrap.

---

*When Admiral Nimitz assumed command of the Pacific Fleet in December 1941, he raised his flag aboard **U.S.S. Grayling**. When he relinquished command nearly four years later, he lowered his flag aboard **U.S.S. Menhaden**. His choice of vessels is hardly surprising since he spent most of his Navy career as a submariner.*

U. S. S. PILOTFISH
S. S. 386

PILOTFISH was built at Portsmouth Navy Yard
and commissioned on December 16, 1943.

★ ★ ★ ★ ★
PILOTFISH'S WARTIME PATROLS

NO.	CAPTAIN	DATE	DUR.	BASE	AREA	CLAIMED	CONFIRMED
1	RH CLOSE	4405	49	PEARL	MARIANAS	0	0
2	RH CLOSE	4407	49	PEARL	BONINS	0	0
3	AG SCHNABLE	4410	56	PEARL	BONINS	0	0
4	AG SCHNABLE	4501	64	PEARL	E CHINA SEA	0	0
5	AG SCHNABLE	4505	51	PEARL	EMPIRE	0	0
6	AG SCHNABLE	4508	32	PEARL	EMPIRE	0	0

PILOTFISH claimed no victories, nor was she credited with any.

PILOTFISH was decommissioned on August 29, 1946, stricken from the lists and sunk as a target in 1948.

U. S. S. PICUDA
S. S. 382

U. S. S. PICUDA
S. S. 382

PICUDA was built at the Portsmouth Navy Yard
and commissioned on October 16, 1943.

★ ★ ★ ★ ★ ★

PICUDA'S WARTIME PATROLS

NO.	CAPTAIN	DATE	DUR.	BASE	AREA	CLAIMED	CONFIRMED
1	AL RABORN	4402	49	PEARL	TRUK	3/24400	3/10000
2	AL RABORN	4405	54	PEARL	LUZON SRTR	3/13000	1.5/2786
3	GR DONAHUE	4407	66	PEARL	LUZON STRT	5/20000	4/11270
4	ET SHEPARD	4410	35	PEARL	E CHINA SEA	4/35300	3/21600
5	ET SHEPARD	4412	48	PEARL	E CHINA SEA	3/22500	1.3/6448
6	ET SHEPARD	4503	63	PEARL	EMPIRE	0	0

PICUDA'S VICTORIES

DATE	VESSEL	SIZE	TYPE	CAPTAIN	LOCATION
440302	SHINKYO	02672	GUNBOAT	AL RABORN	CAROLINES
440320	HOKO MARU	01504	FREIGHTER	AL RABORN	PALAU
440330	ATLANTIC MARU	05873	FREIGHTER	AL RABORN	CAROLINES
440522	HASHIDATE	01200	GUNBOAT	AL RABORN	S CHINA SEA
440522	TSUKUBA MARU	03172	FREIGHTER	AL RABORN	S CHINA SEA
	(Shared credit with land-based aircraft)				
440825	YUNAGI	01270	DESTROYER	GR DONAHO	LUZON
440825	KOTOKU MARU	01943	FREIGHTER	GR DONAHO	LUZON
440916	TOKUSHIMA MARU	05975	PASS-CARGO	GR DONAHO	LUZON
440921	AWAJI MARU	01948	FREIGHTER	GR DONAHO	LUZON
441117	MAYASAN MARU	09433	PASS-CARGO	ET SHEPARD	E CHINA SEA
441123	SHOJU MARU	06933	FREIGHTER	ET SHEPARD	KYUSHU
441123	FUKUJU MARU	05291	PASS-CARGO	ET SHEPARD	KYUSHU
450108	HIKOSHIMA MARU	02854	TANKER	ET SHEPARD	FORMOSA
	(Shared credit with *BARB* and *QUEENFISH*)				
450129	CLYDE MARU	05497	PASS-CARGO	ET SHEPARD	FORMOSA

PICUDA won Navy Unit Commendations for patrols #1 and 2 under A.L. Rayborn, for Patrol #3 under G.R. Donaho, and for Patrols #4 and 5 under E.T. Shepard.

PICUDA is placed in commission on October 16, 1943. Captain C.H. Roper reads the orders.

PICUDA was decommissioned on September 25, 1946, and transferred to the Spanish Navy in 1972 as the *NARCISO MONTURIOL*.

U. S. S. PINTADO
S. S. 387

PINTADO was built at Portsmouth Navy Yard
and commissioned on January 1, 1944.

★ ★ ★ ★ ★
PINTADO'S WARTIME PATROLS

NO.	CAPTAIN	DATE	DUR.	BASE	AREA	CLAIMED	CONFIRMED
1	BA CLAREY	4405	46	PEARL	MARIANAS	4/31000	3/13200
2	BA CLAREY	4407	54	PEARL	E CHINA SEA	5/46300	2/24633
3	BA CLAREY	4410	74	PEARL to BRISBANE		4/21300	3/5100
4	BA CLAREY	4501	51	BRISBANE to PEARL		0	0
5	R BUDD	4506	41	PEARL	EMPIRE	0	0

PINTADO'S VICTORIES

DATE	VESSEL	SIZE	TYPE	CAPTAIN	LOCATION
440601	TOHO MARU #3	04716	FREIGHTER	BA CLAREY	GUAM
440606	KASHIMASAN MARU	02825	FREIGHTER	BA CLAREY	GUAM
440606	HAVRE MARU	05652	FREIGHTER	BA CLAREY	GUAM
440808	SHONAN MARU II	05401	FREIGHTER	BA CLAREY	E CHINA SEA
440822	SUNAN MARU #2	19262	TANKER	BA CLAREY	E CHINA SEA
441103	AKIKAZI	01300	DESTROYER	BA CLAREY	S CHINA SEA
441213	TRANSPORT #12	01900	LANDG CRAFT	BA CLAREY	S CHINA SEA
441213	TRANSPORT #104	01900	LANDG CRAFT	BA CLAREY	S CHINA SEA

PINTADO received Presidential Unit Citations for Patrols #1, 2, and 3. She sank the *SUNAN MARU,* an ex-whale factory ship which had been converted to a tanker. The *SUNAN MARU* previously had been sunk in shallow water and then salvaged. This was the largest Japanese merchant ship to be sunk in World War II, and the only tanker to be sunk twice.

PINTADO was decommissioned on March 6, 1946, stricken from the lists and sold for scrap in 1969.

U. S. S. PIPEFISH
S. S. 388

PIPEFISH was built at Portsmouth Navy Yard and commissioned on January 22, 1944.

★ ★ ★ ★ ★ ★

PIPEFISH'S WARTIME PATROLS

NO.	CAPTAIN	DATE	DUR	BASE	AREA	CLAIMED	CONFIRMED
1	WN DERAGON	4405	52	PEARL	PHILIPPINE SEA	0	0
2	WN DERAGON	4408	52	PEARL	EMPIRE	1/4000	1/1000
3	WN DERAGON	4410	70	PEARL	LUZON STRAIT	0	1/800
4	WN DERAGON	4501	53	PEARL	EMPIRE	0	0
5	WN DERAGON	4504	47	PEARL	EMPIRE	0	0
6	WN DERAGON	4507	42	PEARL	EMPIRE	0	0

PIPEFISH'S VICTORIES

DATE	VESSEL	SIZE	TYPE	CAPTAIN	LOCATION
440912	HAKUTETSU MARU #7	01018	FREIGHTER	WN DERAGON	SHIKOKU
441203	COAST DEF #64	00800	FRIGATE	WN DERAGON	HAINAN

PIPEFISH was deployed westward of the Marianas during the Battle of the Philippine Sea and helped to interrupt Japanese supplies and troops destined for the Marianas.

PIPEFISH going down the ways at Portsmouth Navy Yard, Portsmouth, New Hampshire, October 12, 1943.

PIPEFISH was decommissioned on March 19, 1946, stricken from the lists and sold for scrap in 1969.

U. S. S. PIPER
S. S. 409

PIPER was built at Portsmouth Navy Yard
and commissioned on August 23, 1944.

★ ★ ★ ★

PIPER'S WARTIME PATROLS

NO.	CAPTAIN	DATE	DUR.	BASE	AREA	CLAIMED	CONFIRMED
1	BF McMAHON	4501	60	PEARL	EMPIRE	1/1200	0
2	BF McMAHON	4504	47	PEARL	POLAR CIRC	1/2000	0
3	EL BEACH	4507	46	PEARL	SEA OF JAPAN	0	0

PIPER claimed two victories, but they were never confirmed.

PIPER became the leader of "Mac's Mops," wolf pack along with *STERLET, POMFRET, TREPANG,* and *BOWFIN*, and conducted sweeps ahead of the carriers during Operation Detachment, the attack on Iwo Jima.

PIPER was decommissioned on June 16, 1967, stricken from the lists and sold for scrap in 1970.

---

*Both George Grider and Richard O'Kane served as Lieutenants aboard the **U.S.S. WAHOO** under "Mush" Morton. Grider then commanded two patrols aboard **U.S.S. FLASHER**, the boat with the highest total tonnage destroyed of all United States submarines. O'Kane commanded all of **U.S.S. TANG's** patrols and was the highest scoring skipper in number of vessels destroyed. O'Kane earned the Medal of Honor for his performance.*

U. S. S. PIRANHA
S. S. 389

PIRANHA was built at Portsmouth Navy Yard and commissioned on February 5, 1944.

★ ★ ★ ★ ★
PIRANHA'S WARTIME PATROLS

NO.	CAPTAIN	DATE	DUR.	BASE	AREA	CLAIMED	CONFIRMED
1	HE RUBLE	4406	52	PEARL	LUZON STRT	2/17400	2/12300
2	HE RUBLE	4408	56	PEARL	PHILIPPINE SEA	0	0
3	HE RUBLE	4411	52	PEARL	E CHINA SEA	0	0
4	DG IRVINE	4502	69	PEARL	LUZON STRT	0	0
5	DG IRVINE	4505	49	PEARL	EMPIRE	3/9800	0

PIRANHA'S VICTORIES

DATE	VESSEL	SIZE	TYPE	CAPTAIN	LOCATION
440712	NICHIRAN MARU	06504	PASS-CARGO	HE RUBLE	LUZON
440716	SEATTLE MARU	05773	PASS-CARGO	HE RUBLE	LUZON

PIRANHA became a member of the "Mickey Finns" wolf pack and operated in the "Convoy College" area.

PIRANHA is tied to the dock at New London, Connecticut, to await the ship breakers, circa 1969.

PIRANHA was decommissioned on May 31, 1946, stricken from the lists and sold for scrap in 1970.

U.S.S. PLAICE
S.S. 390

PLAICE was built at Portsmouth Navy Yard and commissioned on February 12, 1944.

★ ★ ★ ★ ★ ★

PLAICE'S WARTIME PATROLS

NO.	CAPTAIN	DATE	DUR.	BASE	AREA	CLAIMED	CONFIRMED
1	CB STEVENS	4406	52	PEARL	BONINS	4/18900	3/2150
2	CB STEVENS	4408	56	PEARL	EMPIRE	2/10600	1/800
3	CB STEVENS	4411	39	PEARL	E CHINA SEA	0	0
4	CB STEVENS	4501	58	PEARL	LUZON STRT	0	0
5	RS ANDREWS	4504	47	PEARL	POLAR CIRC	0	0
6	RS ANDREWS	4507	35	PEARL	E CHINA SEA	0	0

PLAICE'S VICTORIES

DATE	VESSEL	SIZE	TYPE	CAPTAIN	LOCATION
440630	HYAKUFUKU MARU	00986	GUNBOAT	CB STEVENS	VOLCANO ISLE
440705	KOGI MARU	00857	TENDER	CB STEVENS	VOLCANO ISLE
440718	SUBCHASER #50	00300	SUBCHASER	CB STEVENS	VOLCANO ISLE
440927	COAST DEF #10	00800	FRIGATE	CB STEVENS	RYUKUS

PLAICE was part of "Mac's Moppers" who conducted the sweep ahead of Halsey's carriers for the July attack on the Japanese homeland. Targets were so scarce that the boats were cruising on the surface like destroyers pursuing sampans, dhows, and junks.

PLAICE under way off Oahu, Hawaii on July 1, 1963.

PLAICE was decommissioned on April 30, 1949, and transferred to the Brazilian Navy in 1963 as the **BAHIA**.

U. S. S. POMFRET
S. S. 391

POMFRET was built at Portsmouth Navy Yard and commissioned on February 19, 1944.

★ ★ ★ ★ ★

POMFRET'S WARTIME PATROLS

NO.	CAPTAIN	DATE	DUR.	BASE	AREA	CLAIMED	CONFIRMED
1	FC ACKER	4406	54	PEARL	EMPIRE	0	0
2	FC ACKER	4409	30	PEARL	LUZON STR	1/7500	1/6900
3	JB HESS	4410	45	PEARL	LUZON STR	2/2600	3/14000
4	JB HESS	4501	62	PEARL	EMPIRE	0	0
5	JB HESS	4504	42	PEARL	POLAR CIRC	0	0
6	JB HESS	4507	59	PEARL	E CHINA SEA	0	0

POMFRET'S VICTORIES

DATE	VESSEL	SIZE	TYPE	CAPTAIN	LOCATION
441002	TSUYAMA MARU	06962	PASS-CARGO	FC ACKER	LUZON
441102	ATLAS MARU	07347	PASS-CARGO	JH HESS	LUZON
441102	HAMBURG MARU	05271	PASS-CARGO	JH HESS	LUZON
441125	SHOHO MARU #3	01356	FREIGHTER	JH HESS	LUZON

    POMFRET was part of Operation King Two during the Leyte Gulf action and patrolled the area known as "Convoy College." All of her victories were scored during this time. She joined "Mac's Mops" in their sweeps in advance of Halsey's carriers as he struck at the Japanese homeland in July 1945.

    POMFRET off the New Jersey Coast, April 7, 1944.

    POMFRET was decommissioned on April 30, 1952, and transferred to the Turkish Navy in 1971 as the *ORUC REIS*.

U. S. S. QUEENFISH
S. S. 393

QUEENFISH was built at Portsmouth Navy Yard and commissioned on March 11, 1944.

★ ★ ★ ★ ★
QUEENFISH'S WARTIME PATROLS

NO.	CAPTAIN	DATE	DUR.	BASE	AREA	CLAIMED	CONFIRMED
1	CE LOUGHLIN	4408	59	PEARL	LUZON STRT	6/48800	3/14300
2	CE LOUGHLIN	4410	35	PEARL	E CHINA SEA	4/38500	4/14300
3	CE LOUGHLIN	4412	32	PEARL	E CHINA SEA	1/10100	.3/951
4	CE LOUGHLIN	4502	46	PEARL	FORMOSA STRT	1/12000	1/11600
5	FN SHAMER	4505	69	PEARL	E CHINA SEA	0	0

QUEENFISH'S VICTORIES

DATE	VESSEL	SIZE	TYPE	CAPTAIN	LOCATION
440831	CHIYODA MARU	04700	TANKER	CE LOUGHLIN	LUZON
440909	TOYOOKA MARU	07097	PASS-CARGO	CE LOUGHLIN	LUZON
440909	MANSHU MARU	03054	TRANSPORT	CE LOUGHLIN	LUZON
441108	KEIJO MARU	01051	FREIGHTER	CE LOUGHLIN	RUYKUS
441108	HAKKO MARU #4	01948	FREIGHTER	CE LOUGHLIN	RUYKUS
441109	CHOJUSAN MARU	02131	GUNBOAT	CE LOUGHLIN	RUYKUS
441115	AKITSU MARU	09186	ARC FERRY	CE LOUGLLIN	RUYKUS
450108	HIKOSHIMA MARU	02854	TANKER	CE LOUGHLIN	YELLOW SEA
	(Shared credit with *BARB* and *PICUDA*)				
450401	AWA MARU	11600	PASS-CARGO	CE LOUGHLIN	FORMOSA

QUEENFISH received a Presidential Unit Citation for Patrols #1 and 2. She took part in the rescue of Allied prisoners of war that had been dunked when *NANKAI MARU* and *RAKUYO MARU* were torpedoed by *SEALION II*. *QUEENFISH's* last sinking was the *AWA MARU*, one of Japan's last fast ocean liners. She had been given safe passage by ComSubPac as she was carrying Red Cross supplies to prison camps in Malaya. Through a mixup of signals, and heavy fog which made identification difficult, she was sunk. Loughlin was court martialed and found guilty of negligence in obeying orders.

A builder's photograph taken at Portsmouth Navy Yard, Portsmouth, New Hampshire, April 23, 1944.

QUEENFISH was decommissioned on March 1, 1963, and sunk as a target that same year.

U. S. S. RAZORBACK
S. S. 394

RAZORBACK was built at Portsmouth Navy Yard and commissioned on April 3, 1944.

★ ★ ★ ★ ★

RAZORBACK'S WARTIME PATROLS

NO.	CAPTAIN	DATE	DUR.	BASE	AREA	CLAIMED	CONFIRMED
1	RS BENSON	4408	55	PEARL	PHILIPPINE SEA	0	0
2	CD BROWN	4411	47	PEARL	LUZON STRT	3.5/20800	1.5/4287
3	CD BROWN	4502	53	PEARL	E CHINA SEA	0	0
4	CD BROWN	4505	50	PEARL	EMPIRE	0	0
5	CD BROWN	4507	39	PEARL	POLAR CIRC	0	0

RAZORBACK'S VICTORIES

DATE	VESSEL	SIZE	TYPE	CAPTAIN	LOCATION
441206	KENJO MARU	06933	FREIGHTER	CD BROWN	LUZON
		(Shared credit with *SEGUNDO*)			
441230	KURITAKE	00820	DESTROYER	CD BROWN	LUZON

RAZORBACK took part in Operation Stalemate (Palau Islands) as part of Halsey's zoo line. She was privileged to be in attendance with eleven other subs at the Japanese surrender in Tokyo Bay.

RAZORBACK at Pearl Harbor Naval Shipyard, April 11, 1946.

RAZORBACK was decommissioned on July 15, 1952, and transferred to the Turkish Navy in 1970 as the *MURAT REIS*.

U. S. S. REDFISH
S. S. 395

REDFISH was built at Portsmouth Navy Yard
and commissioned on April 12, 1944.

★ ★

REDFISH'S WARTIME PATROLS

NO.	CAPTAIN	DATE	DUR.	BASE	AREA	CLAIMED	CONFIRMED
1	LD McGREGOR	4407	65	PEARL	LUZON STRT	5/33500	3/21800
2	LD McGREGOR	4410	64	PEARL	E CHINA SEA	3/36100	2/20800

REDFISH'S VICTORIES

DATE	VESSEL	SIZE	TYPE	CAPTAIN	LOCATION
440825	BATOPAHA MARU	05953	FREIGHTER	LD McGREGOR	LUZON
440916	OGURA MARU #2	07311	TANKER	LD McGREGCR	LUZON
440921	MIZUHO MARU	08506	TRANSPORT	LD McGREGOR	LUZON
441123	HOZAN MARU II	02345	TRANSPORT	LD McGREGOR	BASHI CHNL
441219	UNRYU	18500	CARRIER	LD McGREGOR	E CHINA SEA

REDFISH received a Presidential Unit Citation for Patrols #1 and 2 under L.D. McGregor. She was one of only seven boats to collect an aircraft carrier. *REDFISH* was so badly knocked about after her successful attack on carrier *UNRYU*, that she was returned to Portsmouth Navy Yard for repair and did not see further action.

REDFISH was decommissioned on June 27, 1968, and sunk as a target in 1969.

U. S. S. RONQUIL
S. S. 396

RONQUIL was built at Portsmouth Navy Yard
and commissioned on April 22, 1944.

★ ★ ★ ★ ★ ★
RONQUIL'S WARTIME PATROLS

NO.	CAPTAIN	DATE	DUR.	BASE	AREA	CLAIMED	CONFIRMED
1	HS MONROE	4407	39	PEARL	FROMOSA	1/7100	2/10600
2	HS MONROE	4409	57	PEARL	EMPIRE	0	0
3	RB LANDER	4501	43	PEARL	BONINS	1/10000	0
4	RB LANDER	4503	45	PEARL	BONINS	0	0
5	RB LANDER	4505	67	PEARL	E CHINA SEA	1/4000	0

RONQUIL'S VICTORIES

DATE	VESSEL	SIZE	TYPE	CAPTAIN	LOCATION
440824	OSHIDA MARU #3	01338	FREIGHTER	HS MONROE	FORMOSA STRT
440824	FUKUREI MARU	05969	FREIGHTER	HS MONROE	FORMOSA STRT

RONQUIL took part in Operation Hotfoot which was to sweep picket boats and patrol craft out of action prior to Halsey's carrier strike at the Japanese homeland. The operation backfired and only served to alert the defenses, which were immediately beefed up. *RONQUIL* also pulled lifeguard duty for the B-29 strikes against Japan

This photograph is postwar after her "Guppy 11-A" modernization, March 30, 1953.

RONQUIL was decommissioned on May 29, 1952, and was transferred to the Spanish Navy in 1971 as the *ISAAC PERAL*.

U. S. S. SANDLANCE
S. S. 381

SANDLANCE was built at Portsmouth Navy Yard and commissioned on October 9, 1943.

★ ★ ★ ★ ★

SANDLANCE'S WARTIME PATROLS

NO.	CAPTAIN	DATE	DUR.	BASE		AREA	CLAIMED	CONFIRMED
1	ME GARRISON	4402	44	PEARL		POLAR CIRC	5/28300	4/16056
2	ME GARRISON	4404	35	PEARL	to	FREMANTLE	4/22300	5/18328
3	ME GARRISON	4408	45	FREMANTLE	to	PEARL	1/7500	1/3000
4	ME GARRISON	4504	54	PEARL		EMPIRE	1/2000	0
5	JC GLAES	4507	54	PEARL		EMPIRE	0	0

SANDLANCE'S VICTORIES

DATE	VESSEL	SIZE	TYPE	CAPTIN	LOCATION
440228	KAIKO MARU	03568	FREIGHTER	ME GARRISON	KIRULES
440303	AKASHISAN MARU	04541	FREIGHTER	ME GARRISON	KIRULES
440313	TATSUTA	03300	CRUISER	ME GARRISON	KYUSHU
440313	KOKUYO MARU	04667	FREIGHTER	ME GARRISON	KYUSHU
440503	KENAN MARU	03129	FREIGHTER	ME GARRISON	MARIANAS
440511	MITAKESAN MARU	04441	PASS-CARGO	ME GARRISON	MARIANAS
440514	KOHO MARU	04291	FREIGHTER	ME GARRISON	MARIANAS
440517	TAIKOKU MARU	02633	FREIGHTER	ME GARRISON	MARIANAS
440517	FUKKO MARU	03834	PASS-CARGO	ME GARRISON	MARIANAS
440714	TAIKO MARU #4	02984	GUNBOAT	ME GARRISON	FLORES SEA

SANDLANCE received a Presidential Unit Citation for Patrol #3 under M.A. Garrison.

SANDLANCE at Mare Island Navy Ship Yard, San Francisco, California, February 26, 1945.

SANDLANCE was decommissioned on February 14, 1946, and transferred to the Brazilian Navy in 1963 as *RIO GRANDE DO SUL*.

U.S.S. SCABBARDFISH
S.S. 397

SCABBARDFISH was built at Portsmouth Navy Yard
and commissioned on April 29, 1944.

★ ★ ★ ★ ★

SCABBARDFISH'S WARTIME PATROLS

NO.	CAPTAIN	DATE	DUR.	BASE	AREA	CLAIMED	CONFIRMED
1	FA GUNN	4408	56	PEARL	EMPIRE	0	0
2	FA GUNN	4411	47	PEARL	EMPIRE	3/8600	2/2345
3	FA GUNN	4501	52	PEARL	LUZON STRT	0	0
4	FA GUNN	4504	53	PEARL	E CHINA SEA	0	0
5	FA GUNN	4507	51	PEARL	EMPIRE	0	0

SCABBARDFISH'S VICTORIES

DATE	VESSEL	SIZE	TYPE	CAPTAIN	LOCATION
441116	KISARAGI MARU	00875	FREIGHTER	FA GUNN	BONINS
441128	I-365	01470	SUBMARINE	FA GUNN	SHIKOKU

SCABBARDFISH suffered from target shortages as the war wound down in 1945 and Marus became scarcer and scarcer.

An aerial photograph off the New Jersey coast, May 30, 1944.

SCABBARDFISH was decommissioned on January 5, 1948, and transferred to the Greek Navy in 1963 as *TRAINA*.

U. S. S. SEA CAT
S. S. 399

SEA CAT was built at Portsmouth Navy Yard
and commissioned on May 16, 1944.

★ ★ ★

SEA CAT'S WARTIME PATROLS

NO.	CAPTAIN	DATE	DUR.	BASE	AREA	CLAIMED	CONFIRMED
1	RR McGREGOR	4410	58	PEARL	INDOCHINA	1.5/15000	0
2	RH BOWERS	4502	52	PEARL	E CHINA SEA	1/1200	0
3	RH BOWERS	4504	57	PEARL	E CHINA SEA	0	0
4	RH BOWERS	4508	27	PEARL	POLAR CIRC	0	0

SEA CAT claimed two and a half victories, but they were not confirmed.

SEA CAT was one of the twelve boats honored by being present at the surrender of the Japanese in Tokyo Bay.

SEA CAT at Mare Island Navy Yard, San Francisco, California, July 22, 1946.

SEA CAT was decommissioned on December 2, 1968, stricken from the lists and sold for scrap in May 1973.

During the reign of James I of England, Cornelius Van Drebbel, a Dutchman, built an oar propelled craft which apparently submerged and moved under water in the Thames. It was claimed that the King himself witnessed this event and later inspected the boat. No record exists of the King making a trip in it.

U. S. S. SEA DOG
S. S. 401

SEA DOG was built at the Portsmouth Navy Yard
and commissioned on June 3, 1944.

★ ★

SEA DOG'S WARTIME PATROLS

NO.	CAPTAIN	DATE	DUR.	BASE	AREA	CLAIMED	CONFIRMED
1	VL LOWRANCE	4409	53	PEARL	E CHINA SEA	1/4000	2/7400
2	VL LOWRANCE	4411	68	PEARL	LUZON STRT	0	0
3	ET HYDEMAN	4503	47	PEARL	EMPIRE	1/6700	1/6850
4	ET HYDEMAN	4505	39	PEARL	SEA OF JAPAN	6/29500	6/7186

SEA DOG'S VICTORIES

DATE	VESSEL	SIZE	TYPE	CAPTAIN	LOCATION
441022	TOMITSU MARU	02933	GUNBOAT	VL LOWRANCE	RYUKUS
441022	MUROTO	04500	SUPPLY SHIP	VL LOWRANCE	RYUKUS
450416	TOYO MARU	06850	FREIGHTER	ET HYDEMAN	SHIKOKU
450609	SAGAWA MARU	01186	FREIGHTER	ET HYDEMAN	SEA OF JAPAN
450609	SHOYO MARU II	02211	FREIGHTER	ET HYDEMAN	SEA OF JAPAN
450611	KOFUKU MARU	00753	FREIGHTER	ET HYDEMAN	SEA OF JAPAN
450612	SHINSEN MARU	00880	FREIGHTER	ET HYDEMAN	SEA OF JAPAN
450612	KOAN MARU #3	00884	PASS-CARGO	ET HYDEMAN	SEA OF JAPAN
450619	KOKAI MARU	01272	FREIGHTER	ET HYDEMAN	SEA OF JAPAN

SEA DOG was in the line patrolling in support of Operation King Two and detected a large convoy heading south to take part in the Battle of Leyte Gulf. Later, after the Battle of Engano Gulf, she detected, but missed, Ozawa's reating battleships, as did *SILVERSIDES* and *TRIGGER*. *SEA DOG* was flagship of the "Hellcats" during Operation Barney which cleared Tsushima Strait of mines and thereby denied enemy merchant vessels the use of the Sea of Japan

SEA DOG undergoing a refit at Mare Island Naval Shipyard, San Francisco, California, June 11, 1946.

SEA DOG was decommissioned on June 27, 1956, stricken from the lists and scrapped in 1968.

U. S. S. SEA DEVIL
S. S. 400

U. S. S. SEA DEVIL
S. S. 400

SEA DEVIL was built at the Portsmouth Navy Yard
and commissioned on May 24, 1944.

★ ★ ★ ★ ★

SEA DEVIL'S WARTIME PATROLS

NO.	CAPTAIN	DATE	DUR.	BASE	AREA	CLAIMED	CONFIRMED
1	RE STYLES	4409	51	PEARL	EMPIRE	1/1900	1/1000
2	RE STYLES	4411	54	PEARL	EMPIRE	2/17500	2/16300
3	RE STYLES	4502	63	PEARL	E CHINA SEA	6/17600	3/10017
4	CF McGIVERN	4508	25	PEARL	E CHINA SEA	1/2400	1/2211

SEA DEVIL'S VICTORIES

DATE	VESSEL	SIZE	TYPE	CAPTAIN	LOCATION
440915	RO-42	00965	SUBMARINE	RE STYLES	HONSHU
441202	AKIGAWA MARU	06859	FREIGHTER	RE STYLES	SW KYUSHU
441202	HAWAII MARU	09467	PASS-CARGO	RE STYLES	SW KYUSHU
450402	TAIJO MARU	06866	FREIGHTER	RE STYLES	KYUSHU
450402	EDOGAWA MARU II	01972	FREIGHTER	RE STYLES	KYUSHU
450402	NISSHIN MARU #3	01179	FREIGHTER	RE STYLES	KYUSHU
450614	WAKAMIYASSN M.	02211	FREIGHTER	CF McGIVERN	YELLOW SEA

SEA DEVIL received a Navy Unit Commendation for Patrol #3 under R.E. Styles. She damaged the Japanese carrier *JUNYO* so badly that the enemy flat-top remained out of action for the rest of the war, but *SEA DEVIL* did not receive credit for a sinking. Target shortages kept her score down during the last few months of the war.

A bow-on photograph of *SEA DEVIL* taken at Mare Island Navy Yard, San Francisco, California, March 14, 1946.

SEA DEVIL was decommissioned on September 9, 1948, stricken from the lists and sunk as a target in 1964.

———————————

*The last German U-Boat to surrender in World War II was **U-977**, commanded by Lieutenant Heinz Shaeffer, an ardent Nazi out on his first patrol as Captain. At first he refused to believe his country had surrendered. When it became clear to him, he persuaded his crew to sail to Argentina and avoid surrendering. The boat and crew arrived at Buenos Aires on August 17, 1945, were interned and turned over to the United States. By then, Argentina had switched sides and declared war on Germany.*

U.S.S. SEA FOX
S.S. 402

SEA FOX was built at the Portsmouth Navy Yard
and commissioned on June 13, 1944.

★ ★ ★ ★

SEA FOX'S WARTIME PATROLS

NO.	CAPTAIN	DATE	DUR.	BASE	AREA	CLAIMED	CONFIRMED
1	RC KLINKER	4410	49	PEARL	EMPIRE	2/8000	0
2	RC KLINKER	4412	46	PEARL	EMPIRE	0	0
3	RC KLINKER	4503	59	PEARL	E CHINA SEA	0	0
4	RC KLINKER	4506	49	PEARL	EMPIRE	0	0

SEA FOX claimed two victories but they were not confirmed.

SEA FOX was decommissioned on October 15, 1952, and transferred to the Turkish Navy in 1970 as the *BURAK REIS*.

U.S.S. TAUTOG planted a minefield in the Bawean Area of the Java Sea south of Borneo. On April 23, 1944, the Japanese destroyer AMAGIRI hit one of these mines and was sunk. This was the same destroyer that had sliced PT 109 in half on the night of August 1-2, 1943, in the Blackett Strait area. PT 109 was under the command of Lieutenant John F. Kennedy.

U. S. S. SEA OWL
S. S. 405

SEA OWL was built at the Portsmouth Navy Yard
and commissioned on June 13, 1944.

★ ★ ★ ★ ★

SEA OWL'S WARTIME PATROLS

NO.	CAPTAIN	DATE	DUR.	BASE	AREA	CLAIMED	CONFIRMED
1	CL BENNETT	4411	54	PEARL	E CHINA SEA	1/1600	0
2	CL BENNETT	4502	70	PEARL	S CHINA SEA	1/2800	1/889
3	WC HALL, Jr	4505	67	PEARL	EMPIRE	1/2600	1/800

SEA OWL'S VICTORIES

DATE	VESSEL	SIZE	TYPE	CAPTAIN	LOCATION
450417	RO-56	00889	SUBMARINE	CL BENNETT	WAKE ISLAND
450609	COAST DEF #41	00800	FRIGATE	WC HALL, Jr	SW KOREA

SEA OWL came late to the action and suffered from a shortage of targets.

SEA OWL underway off the New Jersey coast, September 9, 1944.

SEA OWL was decommissioned on November 15, 1969, stricken from the lists and scrapped in 1971.

U. S. S. SEA POACHER
S. S. 406

SEA POACHER was built at the Portsmouth Navy Yard
and commissioned on September 4, 1943.

★ ★ ★ ★

SEA POACHER'S WARTIME PATROLS

NO.	CAPTAIN	DATE	DUR.	BASE	AREA	CLAIMED	CONFIRMED
1	FM GAMBACORTA	4411	52	PEARL	E CHINA SEA	0	0
2	FM GAMBACORTA	4502	48	PEARL	FORMOSA STR	0	0
3	CF LEIGH	4504	24	PEARL	POLAR CIRC	1/700	0
4	CF LEIGH	4506	54	PEARL	E CHINA SEA	0	0

SEA POACHER claimed one sinking but it was not confirmed.

SEA POACHER was decommissioned on November 15, 1969, stricken from the lists and transferred to the Peruvian Navy in July 1974 as *PABELLON DE PICA*.

During World War II a total of thirty-three million tons of merchant shipping went to the bottom with twenty-three million tons attributed to submarines. The German and United States navies gained the largest advantage from the employment of the submarine. Submarines from those two navies sank fourteen million tons in the Atlantic and four and eight-tenths million tons in the Pacific.

U. S. S. SEA ROBIN
S. S. 407

SEA ROBIN was built at Portsmouth Navy Yard
and commissioned on October 7, 1944.

★ ★ ★

SEA ROBIN'S WARTIME PATROLS

NO.	CAPTAIN	DATE	DUR.	BASE	AREA	CLAIMED	CONFIRMED
1	PC STIMSON	4412	62	PEARL	to FREMANTLE	1/4000	1/5600
2	PC STIMSON	4502	66	FREMANTLE	to PEARL	5/15900	4/7113
3	PC STIMSON	4506	65	PEARL	E CHINA SEA	4/5600	1/1224

SEA ROBIN'S VICTORIES

DATE	VESSEL	SIZE	TYPE	CAPTAIN	LOCATION
440106	TARAKAN MARU	05135	TANKER	PC STIMSON	HAINAN
450303	SUITEN MARU	00250	FREIGHTER	PC STIMSON	S CHINA SEA
450305	SHOYO MARU #4	00853	FREIGHTER	PC STIMSON	S CHINA SEA
450305	NAGARA MARU	00856	FREIGHTER	PC STIMSON	S CHINA SEA
450305	MANYO MARU	02904	GUNBOAT	PC STIMSON	S CHINA SEA
450710	SAKISHIMA MARU	01224	FREIGHTER	PC STIMSON	E CHINA SEA

SEA ROBIN used a submerged radar attack plan to collect the three-in-one-day score that she racked up on March 5, 1945.

A builder's photograph taken off the Portsmouth Navy Yard, Portsmouth, New Hampshire, September 4, 1944.

SEA ROBIN was decommissioned on October 1, 1970, stricken from the lists and sold for scrap in 1971.

U. S. S. SEAHORSE
S. S. 304

U. S. S. SEAHORSE
S. S. 304

SEAHORSE was built at Mare Island Navy Yard
and commissioned on March 31, 1943.

★ ★ ★ ★ ★ ★ ★ ★ ★
SEAHORSE'S WARTIME PATROLS

NO.	CAPTAIN	DATE	DUR.	BASE		AREA	CLAIMED	CONFIRMED
1	D McGREGOR	4308	55	PEARL		PALAU	0	0
2	SD CUTTER	4310	53	PEARL		E CHINA SEA	6/48700	5/27579
3	SD CUTTER	4401	41	PEARL		PALAU	5/30900	5/20900
4	SD CUTTER	4403	56	PEARL	to	BRISBANE	4/25700	5/19374
5	SD CUTTER	4406	47	BRISBANE	to	PEARL	6/37000	4/11000
6	CW WILKINS	4408	71	PEARL		LUZON STRT	1/1700	1/800
7	HH GREER	4503	46	PEARL		EMPIRE	0	0
8	HH GREER	4507	38	PEARL		EMPIRE	0	0

SEAHORSE'S VICTORIES

DATE	VESSEL	SIZE	TYPE	CAPTAIN	LOCATION
431102	CHIIHAYA MARU	07089	FREIGHTER	SD CUTTER	E CHINA SEA
431102	UME MARU	05859	PASS-CARGO	SD CUTTER	E CHINA SEA
431122	DAISHU MARU	03322	FREIGHTER	SD CUTTER	YELLOW SEA
431126	UNKNOWN MARU	04000	FREIGHTER	SD CUTTER	YELLOW SEA
431127	SAN RAMON MARU	07309	TANKER	SD CUTTER	YELLOW SEA
440116	NIKKO MARU #3	00784	FREIGHTER	SD CUTTER	PALAU
444012	YASAKUNI MARU #3	03025	FREIGHTER	SD CUTTER	FAIS ISLE
440121	IKOMA MARU	03156	FREIGHTER	SD CUTTER	FAIS ISLE
440130	TOKO MARU II	02747	PASS-CARGO	SD CUTTER	MALAKAL
440201	TOEI MARU II	04004	FREIGHTER	SD CUTTER	MALAKAL
440408	ARATAMA MARU	06784	TENDER	SD CUTTER	GUAM
440408	KIZUGAWA MARU	01915	FREIGHTER	SD CUTTER	GUAM
440409	BISAKU MARU	04467	FREIGHTER	SD CUTTER	GUAM
440420	RO-45	00965	SUBMARINE	SD CUTTER	SAIPAN
440427	AKIGAWA MARU #3	05244	FREIGHTER	SD CUTTER	SAIPAN
440627	MAKAN MARU	05135	TANKER	SD CUTTER	FORMOSA
440703	NITTO MARU	02186	FREIGHTER	SD CUTTER	S CHINA SEA
440703	GYOYU MARU	02232	PASS-CARGO	SD CUTTER	S CHINA SEA
440704	KYODO MARU #28	01506	FREIGHTER	SD CUTTER	S CHINA SEA
441006	COAST DEF #21	00800	FRIGATE	CW WILKINS	BASHI CHAN

SEAHORSE received Presidential Unit Citations for Patrols #2, 3, and 4 under S.D. Cutter. She tied for 5th place with *WAHOO* for number of vessels sunk with 20, and ranked 12th in total tonnage destroyed.

SEAHORSE at Mare Island Navy Yard, San Francisco, California, June 16, 1943.

SEAHORSE was decommissioned on March 2, 1946, stricken from the lists and scrapped in 1969.

U. S. S. SEALION II
S. S. 315

SEALION II was built at Electric Boat Company and commissioned on March 8, 1944.

★ ★ ★ ★ ★

SEALION II'S WARTIME PATROLS

NO.	CAPTAIN	DATE	DUR.	BASE	AREA	CLAIMED	CONFIRMED
1	ET REICH	4406	42	PEARL	E CHINA SEA	4/19700	4/7800
2	ET REICH	4408	44	PEARL	LUZON STRT	6/51700	3/19100
3	ET REICH	4410	32	PEARL	E CHINA SEA	1/30000	1/32900
4	CF PUTNAM	4412	43	PEARL	to FREMANTLE	1/15800	1/7000
5	CF PUTNAM	4502	47	FREMANTLE	S CHINA SEA	1/7300	1/1548
6	CF PUTNAM	4505	62	FREMANTLE	S CHINA SEA	0	0

SEALION II'S VICTORIES

DATE	VESSEL	SIZE	TYPE	CAPTAIN	LOCATION
440628	SANSEI MARU II	02686	FREIGHTER	ET REICH	KYUSHU
440106	SETSUZAN MARU	01922	FREIGHTER	ET REICH	E CHINA SEA
440711	TSUKUSHI MARU #2	02411	FREIGHTER	ET REICH	E CHINA SEA
440711	TAIAN MARU #2	01034	FREIGHTER	ET REICH	E CHINA SEA
440831	SHIRATAKA	01345	MINELAYER	ET REICH	LUZON
440912	NANKAI MARU	08416	PASS-CARGO	ET REICH	S CHINA SEA
440912	RAKUYO MARU	09419	PASS-CARGO	ET REICH	S CHINA SEA
441121	KONGO	31000	BATTLESHIP	ET REICH	FORMOSA STRT
441121	URUKAZE	01900	DESTROYER	ET REICH	FORMOSA STRT
441220	MAMIYA	07000	SPLY SHIP	CF PUTNAM	S CHINA SEA
450617	SAMUI	01458	TANKER	CF PUTNAM	MALAY

SEALION II received Presidential Unit Citations for Patrols #2 and 3 under E.T. Reich, and stands 16th in enemy tonnage destroyed. She was in the wolf pack that attacked a convoy containing many Allied prisoners of war, and assisted with their rescue. *SEALION II* sank *KONGO*, one of Japan's first-line battlewagons, and the only one to be downed by a U.S. submarine during World War II.

SEALION II off the New Jersey coast, April 3, 1944.

SEALION II was decommissioned on February 2, 1946, stricken from the lists on March 15, 1977, and sunk as a target in July 1978.

U. S. S. SENNET
S. S. 408

SENNET was built at Portsmouth Navy Yard
and commissioned on August 22, 1944.

★ ★ ★ ★
SENNET'S WARTIME PATROLS

NO.	CAPTAIN	DATE	DUR.	BASE	AREA	CLAIMED	CONFIRMED
1	GE PORTER	4501	25	PEARL	BONINS	1/500	0
2	GE PORTER	4502	30	PEARL	EMPIRE	1/2000	1/720
3	GE PORTER	4504	43	PEARL	EMPIRE	3/8700	2/3901
4	CR CLARK	4507	34	PEARL	SEA OF JAPAN	4/24500	4/13105

SENNET'S VICTORIES

DATE	VESSEL	SIZE	TYPE	CAPTAIN	LOCATION
450216	NARIU	00720	MINELAYER	GE PORTER	KYUSHU
450419	HAGANE MARU	01901	FREIGHTER	GE PORTER	SHIKOKU
450428	HATSUSHIMA	02000	REPAIR SHIP	GE PORTER	SHIKOKU
450728	UNKAI MARU #15	01208	FREIGHTER	CR CLARK	SEA OF JAPAN
450728	HAGAKAWA MARU	02995	FREIGHTER	CR CLARK	SEA OF JAPAN
450728	HAKUEI MARU	02863	TANKER	CR CLARK	SEA OF JAPAN
450730	YUZAN MARU	06039	PASS-CARGO	CR CLARK	SEA OF JAPAN

    SENNET was a part of "Latta's Lances" wolf pack during the sweeps conducted for Operation Detachment—the capture of Iwo Jima. She had her best day in the Emperor's private lake—the Sea of Japan—when she destroyed four vessels in two days. Not a bad performance for this late in the war.

    SENNET was used by the Navy after the war for several missions to Antartica. She was decommissioned on December 2, 1968, stricken from the lists and sold for scrap in 1972.

U. S. S. SEGUNDO
S. S. 398

U. S. S. SEGUNDO
S. S. 398

SEGUNDO was built at Portsmouth Navy Yard
and commissioned on February 5, 1944.

★ ★ ★ ★

SEGUNDO'S WARTIME PATROLS

NO.	CAPTAIN	DATE	DUR.	BASE	AREA	CLAIMED	CONFIRMED
1	JD FULP	4408	60	PEARL	PHILIPPINE SEA	0	0
2	JD FULP	4411	49	PEARL	LUZON STRT	2.5/20200	2/6363
3	JD FULP	4502	54	PEARL	E CHINA SEA	1/4000	1/3087
4	JD FULP	4504	54	PEARL	E CHINA SEA	4/13800	1/1578
5	JD FULP	4508	30	PEARL	POLAR CIRCLE	0	0

SEGUNDO'S VICTORIES

DATE	VESSEL	SIZE	TYPE	CAPTAIN	LOCATION
441206	KENJO MARU	06933	FREIGHTER	JD FULP	W LUZON
	(Shared credit with **RAZORBACK**)				
441206	YASAKUNI MARU II	05794	FREIGHTER	JD FULP	W LUZON
	(Shared credit with carrier-based aircraft)				
450311	SHORI MARU	03087	FREIGHTER	JD FULP	YELLOW SEA
450611	FUKUI MARU #2	01578	FREIGHTER	JD FULP	YELLOW SEA

SEGUNDO came late to the action and suffered target shortages, as did most of the newer boats. She was honored by being chosen as one of the twelve boats present at the Japanese surrender in Tokyo Bay.

This bow-on photograph of **SEGUNDO** was taken at Mare Island Navy Yard, April 24, 1944.

SEGUNDO was decommissioned on August 1, 1970, stricken from the lists and sunk as a target a year later.

U. S. S. SHARK II
S. S. 314

SHARK II was built at Electric Boat Company and commissioned on February 14, 1944.

★

SHARK II'S WARTIME PATROLS

NO.	CAPTAIN	DATE	DUR.	BASE	AREA	CLAIMED	CONFIRMED
1	EN BLAKELY	4405	32	PEARL	MARIANAS	4/32000	4/21672
2	EN BLAKELY	4407	50	PEARL	BONINS	0	0
3	EN BLAKELY	4409	00	PEARL	LUZON STRT	0	0

SHARK II'S VICTORIES

DATE	VESSEL	SIZE	TYPE	CAPTAIN	LOCATION
440602	CHIYO MARU	04700	FREIGHTER	EN BLAKELY	MARIANAS
440604	KATSUKAWA MARU	06886	FREIGHTER	EN BLAKELY	MARIANAS
440605	TAMAHIME MARU	03080	FREIGHTER	EN BLAKELY	MARIANAS
440605	TAKAOKA MARU	07006	PASS-CARGO	EN BLAKELY	MARIANAS

   SHARK II was named for one of the first U.S. boats to be lost in the war. While operating with "Blakes Blasters" in the Marianas, she made four kills in three days. On her third patrol, she was depth charged by Japanese escort vessels and went down with all hands.

   SHARK going down the ways at Electric Boat Company, Groton, Connecticut, October 17, 1943.

U. S. S. SKATE
S. S. 305

SKATE was built at Mare Island Navy Yard and commissioned on April 15, 1943.

★ ★ ★ ★ ★ ★ ★ ★

SKATE'S WARTIME PATROLS

NO.	CAPTAIN	DATE	DUR.	BASE	AREA	CLAIMED	CONFIRMED
1	EB McKINNEY	4309	31	PEARL	WAKE	0	0
2	EB McKINNEY	4311	54	PEARL	TRUK	1/6400	1/6429
3	WP GRUNER	4402	42	PEARL	PALAU	1/7000	1/7000
4	WP GRUNER	4404	50	PEARL	BONINS	0	0
5	WP GRUNER	4406	45	PEARL	POLAR CIRCLE	3/13300	3/4500
6	RB LYNCH	4409	54	PEARL	EMPIRE	1/4000	1/ 3700
7	RB LYNCH	4505	49	PEARL	SEA OF JAPAN	5/8700	4/6398

SKATE'S VICTORIES

DATE	VESSEL	SIZE	TYPE	CAPTAIN	LOCATION
431221	TERUKAWA MARU	06429	FREIGHTER	EB McKINNEY	CAROLINES
440216	AGANO	07000	CRUISER	EB McKINNEY	CAROLINES
440707	UNSUGUMO	01950	DESTROYER	WP GRUNER	KIRULES
440715	MIHO MARU	00515	FREIGHTER	WP GRUNER	KIRULES
440716	NIPPO MARU #5	01942	FREIGHTER	WP GRUNER	KIRULES
440929	EKISAN MARU	03690	FREIGHTER	RB LYNCH	RYUKUS
450610	I-122	01142	SUBMARINE	RB LYNCH	SEA OF JAPAN
450612	YOZAN MARU	01227	FREIGHTER	RB LYNCH	SEA OF JAPAN
450612	KENJO MARU II	03142	FREIGHTER	RB LYNCH	SEA OF JAPAN
450612	ZUIKO MARU	00887	FREIGHTER	RB LYNCH	SEA OF JAPAN

SKATE received Navy Unit Commendations for Patrols #1 and 2 under E.B. McKinney, for Patrol #3 under W.P. Gruner, and for Patrol #7 under R.B. Lynch. She performed the first successful lifeguard operation during an attack on Wake by picking up downed fliers while under enemy fire.

SKATE at Mare Island Navy Yard, July 28, 1943.

SKATE was decommissioned on December 11, 1946, and used as a target during the Bikini atomic bomb tests.

U. S. S. SPADEFISH
S. S. 411

U. S. S. SPADEFISH
S. S. 411

SPADEFISH was built at Mare Island Navy Yard
and commissioned on March 8, 1944.

★ ★ ★ ★
SPADEFISH'S WARTIME PATROLS

NO.	CAPTAIN	DATE	DUR.	BASE	AREA	CLAIMED	CONFRMED
1	G UNDERWOOD	4407	59	PEARL	LUZON STRT	6/40000	6/31500
2	G UNDERWOOD	4410	49	PEARL	E CHINA SEA	4/33200	4/30400
3	G UNDERWOOD	4501	38	PEARL	E CHINA SEA	4/16400	4/13423
4	W GERMHSEN	4503	35	PEARL	E CHINA SEA	1/7000	2/4127
5	W GERMHSEN	4505	39	PEARL	SEA OF JAPAN	6/26100	5/8578

SPADEFISH'S VICTORIES

DATE	VESSEL	SIZE	TYPE	CAPTAIN	LOCATION
440719	TAMATSU MARU	09589	PASS-CARGO	G UNDERWOOD	LUZON
440722	HAKKO MARU #2	10023	TANKER	G UNDERWOOD	LUZON
440908	NICHIMAN MARU	01922	FREIGHTER	G UNDERWOOD	FORMOSA
440908	NICHIAN MARU	06197	FREIGHTER	G UNDERWOOD	FORMOSA
440908	SHINTEN MARU	01254	FREIGHTER	G UNDERWOOD	FORMOSA
440908	SHOKEI MARU	02557	FREIGHTER	G UNDERWOOD	FORMOSA
441114	GYOKUYO MARU	05396	FREIGHTER	G UNDERWOOD	E CHINA SEA
441117	JINYO	21000	AIRC CARRIER	G UNDERWOOD	E CHINA SEA
441118	SUBCHASER #156	00100	SUBCHASER	G UNDERWOOD	E CHINA SEA
441129	DAIBOSHI MR #6	03925	FREIGHTER	G UNDERWOOD	YELLOW SEA
450128	KUME	00900	FRIGATE	G UNDERWOOD	YELLOW SEA
450128	SANUKI MARU	07158	TENDER	G UNDERWOOD	YELLOW SEA
450204	TAIRAI MARU	04273	PASS-CARGO	G UNDERWOOD	YELLOW SEA
450206	SHOHEI MARU II	01092	PASS-CARGO	G UNDERWOOD	YELLOW SEA
450323	DORYO MARU	02274	FREIGHTER	W GERMHSEN	RYUKUS
450409	LEE TUNG	01853	FREIGHTER	W GERMHSEN	YELLOW SEA
450610	DAIGEN MARU #2	01999	PASS-CARGO	W GERMHSEN	HOKKAIDO
450610	UNKAI MARU #8	01293	PASS-CARGO	W GERMHSEN	HOKKAIDO
450610	JINTSU MARU	00994	PASS-CARGO	W GERMHSEN	HOKKAIDO
450614	SEIZAN MARU #4	02018	PASS-CARGO	W GERMHSEN	SEA OF JAPAN
450617	EIJO MARU	02274	FREIGHTER	W GERMHSEN	SEA OF JAPAN

SPADEFISH received Presidential Unit Citations for Patrols #1 and 2 under G.W. Underwood. She tied for 4th in number of vessels sunk and stood 6th in enemy tonnage destroyed; a remarkable record for a boat coming so late to the action. G.W. Underwood took 7th among the top 77 skippers who had five or more confirmed sinkings. The name abbreviated above is W. Germerhausen.

SPADEFISH undergoing trials at Mare Island Navy Yard, San Francisco, California, May 11, 1944.

SPADEFISH was decommissioned on May 3, 1946, and sold for scrap in 1967.

U. S. S. SPIKEFISH
S. S. 404

SPIKEFISH was built at Portsmouth Navy Yard
and commissioned on June 30, 1944.

★ ★ ★
SPIKEFISH'S WARTIME PATROLS

NO.	CAPTAIN	DATE	DUR.	BASE	AREA	CLAIMED	CONFIRMED
1	NJ NICHOLAS	4412	47	PEARL	POLAR CIRCLE	0	0
2	NJ NICHOLAS	4501	51	PEARL	EMPIRE	0	0
3	RR MANAGHAN	4504	52	PEARL	EMPIRE	0	0
4	RR MANAGHAN	4507	54	PEARL	E CHINA SEA	1/1800	1/1660

SPIKEFISH'S VICTORY

DATE	VESSEL	SIZE	TYPE	CAPTAIN	LOCATION
450713	I-373	01660	SUBMARINE	RR MANAGHAN	E CHINA SEA

SPIKEFISH downed the last Japanese submarine to be destroyed in the war.

SPIKEFISH off the Jersey coast, August 22, 1944.

SPIKEFISH was decommissioned on April 2, 1963, and sunk as a target that same year.

U. S. S. SPOT
S. S. 413

SPOT was built at Mare Island Navy Yard
and commissioned on August 3, 1944.

★ ★ ★ ★

SPOT'S WARTIME PATROLS

NO.	CAPTAIN	DATE	DUR.	BASE	AREA	CLAIMED	CONFIRMED
1	WS POST. Jr	4412	55	PEARL	E CHINA SEA	4/11200	0
2	WS POST, Jr	4502	61	PEARL	E CHINA SEA	2/11700	1.5/4592
3	JM SEYMOUR	4506	58	PEARL	EMPIRE	0	0

SPOT'S VICTORIES

DATE	VESSEL	SIZE	TYPE	CAPTAIN	LOCATION
450317	NANKING MARU	03005	PASS-CARGO	WS POST, Jr	FORMOSA
450317	IKOMASAN MARU	03173	PASS-CARGO	WS POST, Jr	FORMOSA

(Shared credit with Navy land-based aircraft)

SPOT fought a surface gun battle with an enemy minelayer and was nearly rammed by that ship in a wild gale. Later on that same patrol, she was attacked by the *U.S.S. CASE*, a destroyer on patrol. Through a mix-up of signals, some fire was directed at *SPOT*, and only after three rounds were fired did they come to recognize each other.

A builder's photograph taken at Mare Island Navy Yard, San Francisco, California, September 22, 1944.

SPOT was decommissioned on June 19, 1946, and transferred to the Chilean Navy in 1962 as the *Al SIMPSON*.

U. S. S. SPRINGER
S. S. 414

SPRINGER was built at Mare Island Navy Yard
and commissioned on October 18, 1944.

★ ★ ★

SPRINGER'S WARTIME PATROLS

NO.	CAPTAIN	DATE	DUR.	BASE	AREA	CLAIMED	CONFIRMED
1	R KEFAUVER	4502	48	PEARL	EMPIRE	1/1500	1/1500
2	R KEFAUVER	4504	28	PEARL	E CHINA SEA	3/4300	3/2400
3	JF BAUER	4506	40	PEARL	EMPIRE	0	0

SPRINGER'S VICTORIES

DATE	VESSEL	SIZE	TYPE	CAPTAIN	LOCATION
450319	TRANSPORT #18	01500	LANDING CRAFT	R KEFAUVER	RYUKYUS
450428	SUBCHASER #17	00440	SUBCHASER	R KEFAUVER	KYUSHU
450502	OJIKA	01000	FRIGATE	R KEFAUVER	YELLOW SEA
450503	COAST DEF #25	01000	FRIGATE	R KEFAUVER	YELLOW SEA

SPRINGER suffered from target shortages, especially larger vessels as the war wound down. Many boats starting this late came up empty.

A builder's photograph taken at Mare Island Navy Yard, San Francisco, California, December 2, 1944.

SPRINGER was decommissioned on January 23, 1961, and transferred to the Chilean Navy in 1961 for spare parts.

U. S. S. STICKLEBACK
S. S. 415
STICKLEBACK was built at Mare Island Navy Yard
and commissioned on March 29, 1945.

STICKLEBACK'S WARTIME PATROL

NO.	CAPTAIN	DATE	DUR.	BASE	AREA	CLAIMED	CONFIRMED
1	HK NAUMAN	4508	34	PEARL	SEA OF JAPAN	0	0

STICKLEBACK claimed no victories, nor was she credited with any

A builder's photograph taken off Mare Island Navy Yard, San Francisco, California, May 25, 1945.

STICKLEBACK was decommissioned on June 26, 1946, and sunk in a collision in 1958 with *U.S.S. SILVERSTEIN..*

Japanese submarines sank a total of 184 Allied Merchantmen during World War II, totaling just under a million tons. They also collected two carriers, two cruisers, ten destroyers, and several submarines, escort vessels and minor auxiliaries. Their losses were 129 boats. At the time of surrender, about fifty boats remained, most of those were unserviceable.

U. S. S. STERLET
S. S. 392

U. S. S. STERLET
S. S. 392

STERLET was built at Portsmouth Navy Yard
and commissioned on March 4, 1944.

★ ★ ★ ★ ★ ★
STERLET'S WARTIME PATROLS

NO.	CAPTAIN	DATE	DUR.	BASE	AREA	CLAIMED	CONFIRMED
1	OC ROBBINS	4407	53	PEARL	BONINS	4/14200	0
2	OC ROBBINS	4409	64	PEARL	EMPIRE	3.5/21900	1.3/13833
3	HH LEWIS	4501	66	PEARL	EMPIRE	2/15000	1/1148
4	HH LEWIS	4504	42	PEARL	POLAR CIRCLE	1/4000	2/4155
5	HH LEWIS	4507	48	PEARL	EMPIRE	0	0

STERLET'S VICTORIES

DATE	VESSEL	SIZE	TYPE	CAPTAIN	LOCATION
441025	JINEI MARU	10500	TANKER	OC ROBBINS	RYUKUS
441030	TAKANE MARU	10021	TANKER	OC ROBBINS	RYUKUS
	(Shared credit with *TRIGGER* and *SALMON*)				
450301	TATEYAMA MARU #3	01148	FREIGHTER	HH LEWIS	SHIKOKU
450429	KURITAKE MARU	01924	FREIGHTER	HH LEWIS	KIRULES
450429	TENRYO MARU	02231	FREIGHTER	HH LEWIS	KIRULES

STERLET helped serve as escort for *SALMON* after the latter was damaged in a running surface gun battle with three enemy anti-submarine vessels. She was in "Burt's Brooms" during Operation Hotfoot and cleared the way for Mitcher's carriers to strike the enemy homeland.

Commissioning ceremonies aboard *STERLET* at Portsmouth Navy Yard, Portsmouth, New Hampshire, March 6, 1944.

STERLET was decommissioned on September 18, 1948, and was sunk as a target in 1969.

Robert Fulton, inventor of the steamboat, also built a submarine which he described as a "Diving Boat." He demonstrated it to the French in 1801 in the Seine River and succeeded in destroying an old schooner hulk with his 'torpedo' which contained twenty pounds of gunpowder. This was the first instance of a vessel being destroyed by a torpedo.

U. S. S. TANG
S. S. 306

U. S. S. TANG
S. S. 306

TANG was built at Mare Island Navy Yard
and commissioned on October 10, 1943.

★ ★ ★ ★
TANG'S WARTIME PATROLS

NO.	CAPTAIN	DATE	DUR.	BASE	AREA	CLAIMED	CONFIRMED
1	RH O'KANE	4401	41	PEARL	MARIANAS	5/42000	5/21400
2	RH O'KANE	4403	61	PEARL	PALAU	0	0
3	RH O'KANE	4406	36	PEARL	E CHINA SEA	8/56000	10/39100
4	RH O'KANE	4408	34	PEARL	EMPIRE	5/22500	2/11500
5	RH O'KANE	4409	00	PEARL	FORMOSA	13/107324	7/21772

TANG'S VICTORIES

DATE	VESSEL	SIZE	TYPE	CAPTAIN	LOCATION
440217	GYOTEN MARU	06854	FREIGHTER	RH O'KANE	CAROLINES
440222	FUKUYANA MARU	03581	PASS-CARGO	RH O'KANE	MARIANAS
440223	YAMASHIMO MARU	06776	FREIGHTER	RH O'KANE	MARIANAS
440224	ECHIZEN MARU	02424	FREIGHTER	RH O'KANE	MARIANAS
440225	CHOKO MARU II	01794	FREIGHTER	RH O'KANE	MARIANAS
440624	TAMAHOKA MARU	06780	PASS-CARGO	RH O'KANE	KYUSHU
440624	TAINAN MARU #4	03175	FREIGHTER	RH O'KANE	KYUS14U
440624	NASUSAN MARU	04399	PASS-CARGO	RH O'KANE	KYUSHU
440624	KENNICHI MARU	01938	FREIGHTER	RH O'KANE	KYUSHU
440630	NIKKIN MARU	05705	FREIGHTER	RH C'KANE	YELLOW SEA
440701	TAIUN MARU #2	00998	FREIGHTER	RH O'KANE	YELLOW SEA
440701	TAKATORE MARU	00878	TANKER	RH O'KANE	YELLOW SEA
440704	ASUKAZAN MARU	06886	FREIGHTER	RH O'KANE	YELLOW SEA
440404	YAMAOKA MARU	06932	FREIGHTER	RH O'KANE	YELLOW SEA
440706	DORI MARU	01469	FREIGHTER	RH O'KANE	YELLOW SEA
440711	ROKO MARU	03328	FREIGHTER	RH O'KANE	SHIKOKU
440723	TSUKUSHI MARU	08135	TRANSPORT	RH O'KANE	SHIKOKU
441010	JOSHU GO	01658	FREIGHTER	RH O'KANE	FORMOSA STR
441011	OITA MARU	00711	FREIGHTER	RH O'KANE	FORMOSA STR
441023	TOUN MARU	01915	FREIGHTER	RH O'KANE	FORMOSA STR
441023	WAKATAKE MARU	01920	FREIGHTER	RH O'KANE	FORMOSA STR
441023	TATSUJU MARU	01944	FREIGHTER	RH O'KANE	FORMOSA STR
441025	KOGEN MARU	06600	FREIGHTER	RH O'KANE	FORMOSA STR
441025	MATSUMOTO MARU	07024	FREIGHTER	RH O'KANE	FORMOSA STR

TANG received Presidential Unit Citations for all five of her patrols. She is 2nd in number of vessels sunk and 4th in enemy tonnage destroyed. She is also 2nd in number of U.S. airmen rescued (23). On the fifth patrol in the Formosa Strait, she was struck by her own errant torpedo (her 24th and last) and went down by the stern. Only nine men survived to be picked up by the enemy and they spent the remainder of the war in a prisoner of war camp. Commander O'Kane received the Medal of Honor.

TANG during trials at Mare Island Navy Yard, San Francisco, California, December 2, 1943.

U. S. S. THREADFIN
S. S. 410

THREADFIN was built at Portsmouth Navy Yard and commissioned on August 30, 1944.

★ ★ ★

THREADFIN'S WARTIME PATROLS

NO.	CAPTAIN	DATE	DUR.	BASE	AREA	CLAIMED	CONFIRMED
1	JJ FOOTE	4412	54	PEARL	EMPIRE	1/2000	1/1800
2	JJ FOOTE	4503	51	PEARL	EMPIRE	0	1/900
3	JJ FOOTE	4506	53	PEARL	E CHINA SEA	1/5200	1/630

THREADFIN'S VICTORIES

DATE	VESSEL	SIZE	TYPE	CAPTAIN	LOCATION
450130	ISSEI MARU	00861	FREIGHTER	JJ FOOTE	SHIKOKU
450328	MIKURA	00900	FRIGATE	JJ FOOTE	RYUKUS
450720	MINESWEEPER #39	00630	MINESWEEPER	JJ FOOTE	YELLOW SEA

THREADFIN was part of Operation Iceburg off Honshu and Kyushu and reported the sortie of Japanese warships through the Bungo Suido. This advance notice enabled Mitcher's airmen to obliterate what proved to be the last remnants of the Imperial Navy.

A twin launching at Portsmouth Navy Yard, Portsmouth, New Hampshire, June 26, 1944. *THREADFIN* is on the right.

THREADFIN was decommissioned on December 10, 1962, and transferred to the Turkish Navy in 1973 as the ***BIRINA INONU***.

U. S. S. TILEFISH
S. S. 307

TILEFISH was built at Mare Island Navy Yard
and commissioned on December 15, 1943.

★ ★ ★ ★ ★
TILEFISH'S WARTIME PATROLS

NO.	CAPTAIN	DATE	DUR.	BASE	AREA	CLAIMED	CONFIRMED
1	RM KEITHLY	4404	54	PEARL	EMPIRE	0	0
2	RM KEITHLY	4406	55	PEARL	LUZON STRT	1/1700	0
3	RM KEITHLY	4409	44	PEARL	POLAR CIRCLE	4/8100	0
4	RM KEITHLY	4412	48	PEARL	POLAR CIRCLE	1/9000	1/527
5	WF SCHLECH	4501	56	PEARL	EMPIRE	1/700	1/492
6	WF SCHLECH	4508	33	PEARL	EMPIRE	0	0

TILEFISH'S VICTORIES

DATE	VESSEL	SIZE	TYPE	CAPTAIN	LOCATION
441222	CHIDORI	00527	PT BOAT	RM KEITHLY	SHIKOKU
450305	MINESWEEPER #15	00492	MINESWEEPER	WF SCHLECH	RYUKUS

TILEFISH suffered severe target shortages during her last patrols, as did most boats. At this stage of the war, many were cruising on the surface like destroyers and targets became scarcer and smaller with each passing week.

TILEFISH at Mare Island Navy Yard, March 2, 1944.

TILEFISH was decommissioned on October 12, 1959, and transferred to the Venezuelan Navy in 1960 as the *CARITE*.

U. S. S. TREPANG
S. S. 412

U. S. S. TREPANG
S. S. 412

TREPANG was built at the Mare Island Navy Yard
and commissioned on April 22, 1944.

★ ★ ★ ★ ★
TREPANG'S WARTIME PATROLS

NO.	CAPTAIN	DATE	DUR.	BASE	AREA	CLAIMED	CONFIRMED
1	RM DAVENPORT	4409	36	PEARL	EMPIRE	3/22300	2/1750
2	RM DAVENPORT	4412	35	PEARL	LUZON STRT	4/35000	3/13048
3	AR FAUST	4501	57	PEARL	EMPIRE	1/6100	2/2261
4	AR FAUST	4504	32	PEARL	E CHINA SEA	3/11600	3/6159
5	AR FAUST	4506	47	PEARL	EMPIRE	3/3700	1/606

TREPANG'S VICTORIES

DATE	VESSEL	SIZE	TYPE	CAPTAIN	LOCATION
441001	TAKUNAN MARU	00751	FREIGHTER	RM DAVENPORT	SHIKOKU
441011	TRANSPORT #105	01000	LANDING CRAFT	RM DAVENPORT	SHIKOKU
441206	BANSHU MARU #31	00748	FREIGHTER	RM DAVENPORT	S CHINA SEA
441206	JINYO MARU	06862	FREIGHTER	RM DAVENPORT	S CHINA SEA
441206	FUKUYO MARU	05463	FREIGHTER	RM DAVENPORT	S CHINA SEA
450224	USUKI MARU	00875	FREIGHTER	AR FAUST	HONSHU
450303	NISSHO MARU #2	01386	GUNBOAT	AR FAUST	TSUSHIMA
450428	TRANSPORT #146	01000	LANDING CRAFT	AR FAUST	TSUSHIMA
450430	MIHO MARU #3	0466	FREIGHTER	AR FAUST	YELLOW SEA
450504	MINESWEEPER #20	00492	MINESWEEPER	AR FAUST	YELLOW SEA
450707	KOUN MARU #2	00606	PASS-CARGO	AR FAUST	SEA OF JAPAN

TREPANG received a Navy Unit Commendation for Patrol #1 under R.M. Davenport. During Operation Detachment (Iwo Jima), *TREPANG* operated with the "Mac's Mops" wolf pack where a new high speed torpedo was used with some success. During the last months of the war targets became very scarce with vessels worthy of a torpedo almost non-existant.

TREPANG at Mare Island Naval Shipyard, San Francisco, California, July 12, 1944.

TREPANG was decommissioned on June 27, 1946, and sunk as a target in 1969.

Seven United States submarine commanders received the Medal of Honor. Three were awarded posthumously.

TENCH CLASS

TENCH Class boats were the last design freeze of the war. Built during 1944-1945, they were close copies of *GATO/BALAO* boats, but with better internal layout and increased strength. About 40 tons larger in displacement, they were about a half knot faster and had a range of 12,000 miles. They were armed with a 5-inch deck gun and some carried 40mm anti-aircraft weapons. The crew compliment was 85. A total of thirty-one *TENCH* Class boats were completed, but not all were finished in time to conduct war patrols. The *TENCH* Class boats were built at Portsmouth Navy Yard, Portsmouth, New Hampshire. A *TENCH* Class boat, *U.S.S. TORSK*, has the distinction of sinking the last Japanese vessel to fall victim to a U.S. submarine in World War II.

U. S. S. TENCH
S. S. 417

U. S. S. TENCH
S. S. 417

TENCH was the first of her class and built at the Portsmouth Navy Yard.
She was commissioned on October 6, 1944.

★ ★ ★

TENCH"S WARTIME PATROLS

NO.	CAPTAIN	DATE	DUR.	BASE	AREA	CLAIMED	CONFIRMED
1	WB SIEGLAFF	4502	55	PEARL	EMPIRE	1/4300	0
2	TS BASKETT	4505	37	PEARL	EMPIRE	4/15800	4/5069
3	TS BASKETT	4507	53	PEARL	EMPIRE	0	0

TENCH'S VICTORIES

DATE	VESSEL	SIZE	TYPE	CAPTAIN	LOCATION
450602	MIKAMISAN MARU	00861	FREIGHTER	TS BASKETT	SEA OF JAPAN
450604	RYUJIN MARU #3	00517	FREIGHTER	TS BASKETT	SEA OF JAPAN
450609	KAMISHIKA MARU	02857	FREIGHTER	TS BASKETT	SEA OF JAPAN
450610	SHOEI MARU #6	00834	TANKER	TS BASKETT	SEA OF JAPAN

TENCH came late to the scene of action and was plagued by target shortages. The last of the Japanese Merchant Marine was confined mostly to the Inland Sea, and this was where *TENCH* scored her kills, some of the last of the war.

TENCH going down the ways at the Portsmouth Navy Yard, Portsmouth, New Hampshire, August 1944.

TENCH was decommissioned on June 15, 1946, and scrapped in 1973.

Three appendectomies, all in 1942, were performed aboard United States submarines. The attendant publicity surrounding the success of these operations and the excellent PR gained by the Navy prompted Admiral King to order that no more be done. The Navy had been lucky so far and he did not want to risk the possibility of a failed operation. As of early 1943, whenever appendicitis was diagnosed, a PBY was dispatched to rendezvous with the boat, remove the patient and transport him to the nearest Naval Hospital.

U. S. S. ARGONAUT II
S. S. 475

ARGONAUT II was built at Portsmouth Navy Yard
and commissioned on January 15, 1945.

★

ARGONAUT II'S WARTIME PATROL

NO.	CAPTAIN	DATE	DUR.	BASE	AREA	CLAIMED	CONFRMED
1	JS SCHMIDT	4506	52	PEARL	E CHINA SEA	0	0

ARGONAUT II did not claim any victories, nor were any credited to her.

ARGONAUT II at Panama Bay, May 14, 1945.

ARGONAUT II was decommissioned on December 2, 1968, and transferred to the Canadian Navy as the *RAINBOW*.

During the Battle of Mobile Bay Admiral David Farragut, warned by his Flag Captain that torpedoes were ahead, ordered, "Damn the torpedoes. Captain Drayton, go ahead." Legend has replaced the last part of the order with "Full speed ahead." That is not the only inaccuracy in this statement. The torpedoes mentioned were actually contact mines, which were known as torpedoes for many years. In fact, a contact mine had sunk the lead ship in Farragut's squadron as he ascended the river.

U. S. S. CUTLASS
S. S. 478

CUTLASS was built at Portsmouth Navy Yard
and commissioned on March 17, 1945.

CUTLASS'S WARTIME PATROL

NO.	CAPTAIN	DATE	DUR.	BASE	AREA	CLAIMED	CONFRMED
1	HL JUKES	4508	22	PEARL	POLAR CIRCLE	0	0

CUTLASS did not claim any victories, nor were credited to her.

A post-war photograph of *CUTLASS*.

CUTLASS was decommissioned on April 12, 1971, and transferred to the Taiwanese Navy that same year.

Great Britain entered World War II with seventy submarines scattered from home and channel waters through the Mediterranean Sea and the far east. The most ever in service at any one time was eighty-eight boats in 1945. She lost seventy-four boats during the war. Most of these were lost in the Mediterranean during the German invasion and the later evacuation of North Africa. The British sank 550 enemy vessels of all types, including 35 submarines.

U. S. S. QUILLBACK
S. S. 424

QUILLBACK was built at Portsmouth Navy Yard
and commissioned on December 29, 1944.

★

QUILLBACK'S WARTIME PATROL

NO.	CAPTAIN	DATE	DUR.	BASE	AREA	CLAIMED	CONFIRMED
1	RP NICHOLSON	4505	53	PEARL	EMPIRE	0	0

QUILLBACK claimed no victories, nor were any credited to her.

QUILLBACK after her "Guppy" conversion, October 25, 1955.

QUILLBACK was decommissioned on May 8, 1952, stricken from the lists and sold for scrap in 1974.

When the Commander-in-Chief of the German U-Boat Service, Admiral Karl Doenitz, received reports of the failures of the magnetic exploders on German torpedoes, he ordered them discontinued. He also ordered research on the GNAT (German Naval Acoustic Torpedo) to be stepped up. This torpedo homed in on the sound of a ship's propellers. The unit was only partially successful and U-Boat skippers depended on the old reliable contact exploder-type torpedo.

S. S. RUNNER II
S. S. 476

RUNNER II was built at the Portsmouth Navy Yard
and commissioned on February 6, 1945.

★

RUNNER II'S WARTIME PATROLS

NO.	CAPTAIN	DATE	DUR.	BASE	AREA	CLAIMED	CONFIRMED
1	RH BASS	4506	30	PEARL	EMPIRE	1/600	1/630
2	RH BASS	4508	29	PEARL	EMPIRE	0	0

RUNNER II'S VICTORY

DATE	VESSEL	SIZE	TYPE	CAPTAIN	LOCATION
450710	MINESWEEPER #27	00630	MINESWPEEPER	RH BASS	SEA OF JAPAN

RUNNER II was among those boats assigned to sweep the waters off Kyushu in preparation for Halsey's third fleet strike against the Japanese homeland. She was also privileged to be among the twelve boats present at the surrender in Tokyo Bay

RUNNER II off Portsmouth Navy Yard, Portsmouth, New Hampshire, March 15, 1945.

RUNNER II was decommissioned on January 25, 1969, stricken from the lists and sold for scrap in 1971.

U. S. S. THORNBACK
S. S. 418

THORNBACK was built at Portsmouth Navy Yard
and commissioned on October 13, 1944.

★

THORNBACK'S WARTIME PATROL

NO.	CAPTAIN	DATE	DUR.	BASE	AREA	CLAIMED	CONFIRMED
1	EP ABRAHAMSON	4506	52	PEARL	EMPIRE	0	0

THORNBACK claimed no victories, nor was she credited with any.

THORNBACK in Panama Bay, March 31, 1945.

THORNBACK was decommissioned on April 6, 1946, and transferred to the Turkish Navy in 1971.

———————————

The first known self-propelled torpedo was invented by Robert Whitehead, an Austrian Naval Engineer. A miniature submarine, it had a forty horsepower engine operated by compressed air which drove twin screws. It was first employed by fast torpedo boats, not submarines. The destroyer was designed to counter these early torpedo boats and was originally designated "Torpedo Boat Destroyer."

U. S. S. TIGRONE
S. S. 419

TIGRONE was built at Portsmouth Navy Yard
and commissioned on October 25, 1944.

★ ★

TIGRONE'S WARTIME PATROLS

NO.	CAPTAIN	DATE	DUR.	BASE	AREA	CLAIMED	CONFIRMED
1	H CASSEDY	4503	43	PEARL	E CHINA SEA	0	0
2	H CASSEDY	4505	44	PEARL	EMPIRE	0	0
3	VE SCHUMACKER	4507	41	PEARL	EMPIRE	0	0

TIGRONE claimed no victories, nor was she credited with any.

Rescued airmen pose on deck of the *TIGRONE* while she was on lifeguard duty..

TIGRONE was decommissioned on March 30, 1946, stricken from the lists and sold for scrap in 1975.

U.S.S. TIRANTE
S.S. 420

TIRANTE was built at the Portsmouth Navy Yard and commissioned on November 6, 1944.

★ ★

TIRANTE'S WATRIME PATROLS

NO.	CAPTAIN	DATE	DUR.	BASE	AREA	CLAIMED	CONFIRMED
1	GL STREET	4503	52	PEARL	E CHINA SEA	8/28300	6/12621
2	GL STREET	4505	57	PEARL	E CHINA SEA	3/7400	2/3265

TIRANTE'S VICTORIES

DATE	VESSEL	SIZE	TYPE	CAPTAIN	LOCATION
450325	FUJI MARU #3	00703	TANKER	GL STREET	SW KYUSHU
450328	NASE MARU	01218	FREIGHTER	GL STREET	SW KYUSHU
450409	NIKKO MARU II	05507	TRANSPORT	GL STREET	YELLOW SEA
450414	JUZAN MARU	03943	PASS-CARGO	GL STREET	YELLOW SEA
450414	COAST DEF #31	00800	FRIGATE	GL STREET	YELLOW SEA
450414	NOMI	00900	FRIGATE	GL STREET	YELLOW SEA
450611	HAKUJU MARU	02220	FREIGHTER	GL STREET	SW KYUSHU
450708	SAITSU MARU	01045	PASS-CARGO	GL STREET	YELLOW SEA

TIRANTE received a Presidential Unit Citation for Patrol #1, one of the most remarkable made this late in the war. Commander Street was awarded the Medal of Honor for his record-breaking performance.

Going down the ways at Portsmouth Navy Yard, Portsmouth, New Hampshire, August 9, 1944.

TIRANTE was decommissioned on August 20, 1946, stricken from the lists and sold for scrap in 1962.

U. S. S. TORO
S. S. 422

TORO was built at Portsmouth Navy Yard
and commissioned on December 8, 1944.

★ ★

TORO'S WARTIME PATROLS

NO.	CAPTAIN	DATE	DUR.	BASE	AREA	CLAIMED	CONFIRMED
1	JD GRANT	4504	54	PEARL	EMPIRE	0	0
2	JD GRANT	4507	36	PEARL	EMPIRE	0	0

TORO came late to the scene of action and was plagued by target shortages.

TORO off Isles of Shoals near Portsmouth Navy Yard, Portsmouth, New Hampshire.

TORO was decommissioned on February 2, 1946, stricken from the lists and sold for scrap in 1965.

U. S. S. TORSK
S. S. 423

TORSK was built at the Portsmouth Navy Yard
and commissioned on December 8, 1944.

★ ★

TORSK'S WARTIME PATROLS

NO.	CAPTAIN	DATE	DUR.	BASE	AREA	CLAIMED	CONFIRMED
1	BE LEWELLEN	4504	63	PEARL	EMPIRE	0	0
2	BE LEWELLEN	4507	50	PEARL	SEA OF JAPAN	4/6000	3/2476

TORSK'S VICTORIES

DATE	VESSEL	SIZE	TYPE	CAPTAIN	LOCATION
450713	KAIHO MARU #3	00873	FREIGHTER	BE LEWELLEN	SW HONSHU
450714	COAST DEF #13	00800	FRIGATE	BE LEWELLEN	SW HONSHU
450714	COAST DEF #47	00800	FRIGATE	BE LEWELLEN	SW HONSHU

TORSK, like many of her class, suffered from a severe shortage of targets, as Marus and Japanese warships became more and more scarce. On the day before the war's end, she managed to sink a small freighter, and on the very last day of the war, sent two coast defense vessels to the bottom. *TORSK* has the singular honor of sinking the last Japanese ship to fall victim to a U.S. submarine in World War II.

TORSK underway at high speed, probably off the Jersey coast.

TORSK is now a National Historic Monument laying in the Inner Harbor at Baltimore, Maryland.

U. S. S. TRUTTA
S. S. 421

TRUTTA was built at Portsmouth Navy Yard
and commissioned on November 16, 1944.

★ ★
TRUTTA'S WARTIME PATROLS

NO.	CAPTAIN	DATE	DUR.	BASE	AREA	CLAIMED	CONFIRMED
1	AC SMITH	4503	42	PEARL	E CHINA SEA	0	0
2	FP HOSKINS	4506	46	PEARL	E CHINA SEA	0	0

TRUTTA came late to the scene of action and was plagued by target shortages.

Captain E.B. McKinney, USN (l.) and Lt. Commander Eugene McCaine on the deck of *TRUTTA*.

TRUTTA was decommissioned on June 15, 1946, stricken from the lists and sold for scrap in 1972.

APPENDICES

A   Pacific Submarines Ranked by Number of Sinkings (top 25)

B   Pacific Submarines Ranked by Tonnage Destroyed

C   Pacific Captains Ranked by Number of Victories

D   Pacific Captains Ranked by Tonnage Destroyed

E   Navy Unit Commendations

F   Presidential Unit Commendations

G   Submarine Losses in World War II, All Causes and Locales

H   Wolf Packs Operating in the Pacific Theater -
         SUBPAC Force (Hawaii)

I   Wolf Packs Operating in the Pacific Theater -
         SUBSOWESPAC Force (Australia)

J   U.S. Submarines Present at the Surrender Ceremonies in Tokyo Bay,
         September 2, 1945

K   Medals of Honor Awarded

A - PACIFIC SUBMARINES RANKED BY NUMBER OF SINKINGS

Rank	Boat	Victories
1	TAUTOG	26
2	TANG	24
3	SILVERSIDES	23
4	FLASHER	21
5	SPADEFISH	21
6	SEAHORSE	20
7	WAHOO	20
8	GUARDFISH	19
9	RASHER	18
10	SEAWOLF	18
11	TRIGGER	18
12	BARB	17
13	SNOOK	17
14	THRESHER	17
15	BOWFIN	16
16	HARDER	16
17	POGY	16
18	SUNFISH	16
19	TINOSA	16
20	DRUM	15
21	FLYING FISH	15
22	GREENLING	15
23	JACK	15
24	GRAYBACK	14
25	KINGFISH	14

B - PACIFIC SUBMARINES RANKED BY TONNAGE DESTROYED

Boat	Tonnage	Victories	Boat	Tonnage	Victories
FLASHER	104564	21.5	RATON	044178	13
RASHER	099901	18	PINTADO	042956	08
BARB	097579	17.3	REDFISH	042615	05
TANG	093824	24	QUEENFISH	041718	08.3
SILVERSIDES	090080	23	STURGEON	041350	09
TRIGGER	089892	18.3	PUFFER	038960	08.5
SPADEFISH	088091	21	CABRILLA	038767	07
DRUM	080580	15	HAKE	037923	07
JACK	076687	15	SANDLANCE	037368	10
SNOOK	075473	17	TROUT	037144	12
SEAWOLF	074042	18.5	HAMMERHEAD	037062	11.5
TAUTOG	072606	26	PARCHE	036146	08.5
SEAHORSE	072529	20	STEELHEAD	0344609	04
GUARDFISH	072424	19	CAVALLA	034180	04
GUDGEON	071047	12	SCAMP	034108	05
BOWFIN	070132	16.5	HADDOCK	033585	08
TINOSA	068655	16.5	TAMBOR	033479	11
SEALION II	068297	11	ATULE	033379	06
THRESHER	066172	17	SARGO	032777	07
GRAYBACK	063835	14	GROWLER	032607	10
FINBACK	062941	13.3	BALAO	031920	06
POGY	062633	16	TRITON	031788	11
FLYING FISH	062485	15.5	TUNNY	030394	06.3
BONEFISH	061345	12	POLLACK	030278	11
WHALE	060149	09.5	NAUTILUS	029899	06.5
WAHOO	060038	20	SEA DEVIL	029519	07
SUNFISH	059815	16	GATO	029360	09.5
ARCHERFISH	059800	02	PETO	0029139	07
GREENLING	059234	15	DACE	028689	06
GURNARD	057866	10	GUAVINA	028567	07
CREVALLE	056114	09.5	SAURY	028542	05
HARDER	054002	16	ASPRO	028189	06
LAPON	053443	11	PARGO	027983	09
BLUEFISH	053407	12.5	SKATE	027924	10
PICUDA	052760	12.8	SKIPJACK	027924	06
RAY	051454	12.3	TARPON	027910	02
ALBACORE	049861	10	SEAL	027765	07
KINGFISH	048868	14	SALMON	027447	04.3
PLUNGER	048328	12	PAMPANITO	027332	05
SWORDFISH	047928	12	COD	026985	08
SEADRAGON	047008	10.3	GUITARRO	025401	08.3
BLUEGILL	046212	10	GUNNEL	024265	06
HALIBUT	045257	12	TREPANG	023850	11
SAILFISH	045029	07	REDFIN	023724	06

PACIFIC SUBMARINES RANKED BY TONNAGE DESTROYED, cont.

Boat	Tonnage	Victories	Boat	Tonnage	Victories
PADDLE	022755	06	BOARFISH	010413	01.5
SAWFISH	022504	06	FLIER	010380	01
SHARK II	021672	04	SCULPIN	009835	03
HADDO	021618	09	PORPOISE	009741	03
SEA DOG	021469	09	BARBERO	009126	03
POMPANO	021443	05	BREAM	008869	02.3
POMFRET	020936	04	POMPON	008772	03
GRAYLING	020575	05	JALLAO	008645	01.5
SEARAVEN	020492	03	GRAMPUS	008836	01
GAR	020392	08	ICEFISH	008404	02
BANG	020181	08	APOGON	007575	03
HARDHEAD	020146	09	MINGO	007163	02
HERRING	019959	06	MUSKALUNGE	007163	01
CROAKER	019710	06	KETE	006881	03
DARTER	019429	03	S-39	006500	01
BASHAW	019269	03	PICKEREL	006472	04
STERLET	019143	04.3	RUNNER	006274	02
STINGRAY	018558	04	BURRFISH	005894	01
SCORPION	018316	04	PERMIT	005741	03
CERO	018159	05	FLOUNDER	005530	01.5
BLENNY	018087	07	S-35	005430	01
GROUPER	017983	04	ANGLER	005401	03
SENNET	017726	07	S-30	005228	01
S-44	017070	03	AMBERJACK	005225	02
SPEARFISH	017065	04	TENCH	005069	04
COBIA	016835	06	S-37	004676	02
BECUNA	016656	04.5	SPOT	004592	01.5
TIRANTE	015886	08	S-42	004400	01
BARBEL	015263	06	BLACKFIN	004325	02
TUNA	014986	04	BILLFISH	004302	03
GRENADIER	014457	01	RAZORBACK	004287	01.5
HOE	013999	03	GABILAN	004204	03.5
NARWHAL	013829	07	SPRINGER	003940	04
SEA ROBIN	013172	06	THREADFIN	003394	03
BAYA	013059	04.5	CAPELIN	003127	01
HAWKBILL	013031	06	PLAICE	002943	04
BESUGO	012450	04	S-31	002864	01
SNAPPER	012324	04.5	CHARR	002850	00.5
PIRANHA	012277	02	CABEZON	002631	01
S-38	011073	02	TORSK	002473	03
SEGUNDO	011029	03	SCABBARDFISH	002345	02
BATFISH	011020	06.5	BLACKFISH	002087	01
SHAD	010778	03.5	PIKE	002022	01
RONQUIL	010615	02	LAGARTO	001845	02
TULLIBEE	010579	03	PIPEFISH	001818	02

PACIFIC SUBMARINES RANKED BY TONNAGE DESTROYED, cont.

Boat	Tonnage	Victories	Boat	Tonnage	Victories
SEA OWL	001689	02	ROCK	000834	01
SPIKEFISH	001660	01	RUNNER II	000630	01
S-28	001368	01	GRUNION	000600	02
BUMPER	001189	01	CHUB	000492	01
S-41	001036	01	BLUEBACK	000300	01
TILEFISH	001019	02	LIZARDFISH	000100	01

C - PACIFIC CAPTAINS RANKED BY NUMBER OF VICTORIES

Captain	Victories	Tonnage	Captain	Victories	Tonnage
O'KANE, R.H.	24	93824	LOWRANCE, V.L.	08	34199
CUTTER, S.D.	19	72000	DAVENPORT, R.M.	08	29662
MORTON, D.W.	19	55000	KIRKPATRICK, C.	08	22749
FLUCKEY, E.B.	16.3	95360	GALLAHER, A.R.	08	20181
DEALEY, S.D.	16	54002	STREET, III, G.L.	08	15886
WHITAKER, R.T.	14.5	60846	TYREE, A.K.	07.5	42928
UNDERWOOD, G.W.	14	75386	SELBY, R.G.	07.5	38159
GROSS, R.L.	14	65735	RAMAGE, L.P.	07.5	06681
TRIEBEL, C.O.	14	58837	FOLEY, R.J.	07.5	26235
COYE, J.J.	14	39000	GRIDER, G.W.	07	43718
SIEGLAFF, W.B.	13	32886	BROACH, J.C.	07	37923
BASKETT, T.S.	12	27273	HOGAN, Jr., T.W.	07	34329
BRUTON, H.C.	11	54564	DEMPSEY, J.C.	07	30794
LEWELLEN, B.E.	11	23685	GALANTIN, I.J.	07	22031
MOORE, J.A.	10.5	45689	SHEA, M.W.	07	17139
ANDREWS, C.H.	10	57234	HAZZARD, W.H.	07	18087
DORNIN, R.E.	10	54595	GREENUP, F.A.	07	14246
BARR, Jr., E.L.	10	46212	HYDEMAN, E.T.	07	14036
METCALF, R.M.	10	40040	SCOTT, J.A.	06.5	30394
BASS, R.H.	10	37977	ASHLEY, J.H.	06.3	24930
GARRISON, M.E.	10	37368	WOGAN, T.L.	06	46730
KLAKRING, T.B.	10	33122	McGREGOR, L.D.	06	44637
DONAHO, G.R.	09.5	29870	THOMPSON, W.C.	06	36062
REICH, E.T.	09	59839	MAURER, J.H.	06	33379
GRIFFITH, W.T.	09	45874	STYLES, R.E.	06	27308
SHELBY, R.G.	09	45613	FERRALL, W.E.	06	26841
RISSER, E.E.	09	40931	DAVIS, J.W.	06	26039
WARD, N.G.	09	39302	WILLINGHAM, Jr., J.H.	06	25636
LAUGHON, W.R.	09	38340	AUSTIN, M.H.	06	23724
PORTER, G.E.	09	30940	GILMORE, H.W.	06	22681
KEFAUVER, R.	09	23081	McMILLAN, D.	06	22277
LEE, J.E.	09	23081	CLARK, A.H.	06	21534
GERMERS-HAUSEN, W.J.	09	16277	WARDER, F.B.	06	18719
POST, Jr., W.S.	08.5	54213	BECKER, A.L.	06	16835
KINSELLA, W.T.	08.5	34101	KEATING, Jr., R.A.	06	15263
LOUGHLIN, C.E.	08.3	41718	SCANLAND, Jr., F.W.	06	13180
HASKINS, E.D.	08.3	25400	STIMSON, P.C.	06	13172
MUNSON, H.G.	08	67630	SMITH, F.M.	06	10457
BURLINGAME, C.C.	08	46865	FAUST, A.F.	06	09026
CLAREY, B.A.	08	42956	STEVENSON, W.A.	05.5	27120
DYKERS, T.M.	08	42417	MARTIN, J.C.	05.5	26578
STONE, L.T.	08	39266	BROCKMAN, W.H.	05.5	23829
RICE, R.H.	08	39100	FYFE, J.K.	05.5	05534
WEISS, D.F.	08	09047	CHAPPLE, W.G.	05.3	19159
			BLANCHARD, J.W.	05	36629

PACIFIC CAPTAINS RANKED BY NUMBER OF VICTORIES, Cont.

Captain	Victories	Tonnage	Captain	Victories	Tonnage
EBERT, W.G.	05	34108	GRUNER, W.P.	04	11407
EDGE, L.T.	05	27016	AMBRUSTER, S.H.	04	10766
COE, J.W.	05	26130	HARTMAN, I.S.	04	10162
MOORE, J R	05	23978	ZABRISKIE, D.	04	09939
ROSS, P.H.	05	23226	FENNO, Jr., F.W.	04	09144
GARNETT, P.W.	05	23079	ADKINS, J.A.	04	09086
KRAPF, A.E.	05	22015	QUIRK, P.D.	04	08922
MILLICAN, W.J.	05	21525	JARVIS, B.C.	04	08855
TAYLOR, A.H.	05	18747	LYNCH, F.C.	04	06982
MURPHY, C.L.	05	18278	LATHAM, R.C.	04	05901
BENSON, R.S.	05	17652	REED, J.W.	04	05461
HUTCHINSON, E.S.	05	17530	McCRORY, W.W.	04	05268
NOWELL, B.H.	05	17507	STEVENS, C.B.	04	02943
PETERSON, G.E.	05	17145	HULL, J.L.	03	21841
NIMITZ, Jr., C.W.	05	14636	LENT, W.A.	03	20439
BELL, D.B.	05	14179	AZER, J.B.	03	18989
LYNCH, R.B.	05	10088	McCAIN, J.S.	03	17452
WILKINS, C.W.	05	09024	BROWNE, G.H.	03	16636
HARPER, T.E.	05	07529	MONROE, H.S.	03	16045
LATTA, F.D.	05	07450	BANISTER, A.B.	03	15596
WALKER, F.D.	04.5	40169	COLE, C.C.	03	15383
BURROWS, A.C.	04.5	25517	JUKES, H.L.	03	14571
HENDERSON, C.M.	04.5	21770	STEPHAN, E.C.	03	14451
DASPIT, L.R.	04.5	19907	BAER, D.G.	03	14177
RAYBORN, A.	04.5	12835	HESS, J.B.	03	13974
TIEDEMAN, C.	04.5	11651	SCHADE, A.F.	03	12973
SHEPARD, E.T.	04.3	28105	THOMAS, W.M.	03	12558
KOSSLER, H.J.	04	34180	CALDWELL, R.H.	03	12516
WHELCHEL, D.L.	04	30659	NELSON, W.T.	03	12255
WILLIAMSON,	04	30118	HENSEL, K.G.	03	12243
McKINNEY, E.B.	04	28125	TURNER, J.H.	03	12132
CLAGGETT, B.D.	04	26298	FULP, J.D.	03	11029
SUMMERS, P.E.	04	26132	BRINDUPKE, C.F.	03	10579
DROPP, A.H.	04	22280	CHAPPELL, L.H.	03	09835
BLAKELY, E.N.	04	21672	GRENFELL, E.W.	03	09785
SMITH, C.C.	04	19270	MIDDLETON, J.R.	03	09195
WYLIE, W.N.	04	18316	MOSLEY, S.P.	03	09086
WALES, G.H.	04	17925	WRIGHT, W.L.	03	08859
HARRAL, B.J.	04	17352	BERTHRONG, R.	03	08834
McMAHON, B.F.	04	16610	HURD, K.C.	03	08279
HYDE, J.M.	04	15684	WILLIAMS, J.W.	03	07259
WHITE, D.C.	04	13807	SANDS, E.T.	03	06908
EDDY, I.C.	04	13804	ACKERMAN, E.	03	06881
CLARK, C.R.	04	12925	O'NEIL, Jr., G.E.	03	06813
LAUTRUP, G.W.	04	12581	STEINMETZ, E.H.	03	06643

Captain	Victories	Tonnage	Captain	Victories	Tonnage
LAKE, R.C.	03	05900	WHELAND, K.R.	02	00592
CLEMENTSON, M.K.	03	05735	CORBUS, J.	01.5	09004
LEWIS, H.H.	03	05303	ICENHOWER, J.B.	01.5	08645
FARLEY, L.C.	03	04302	STEVENS, J.E.	01.5	05531
ALSTON, A.H.	03	03543	BROWN, C.D.	01.5	04287
WILLIAMS, R.R.	03	03507	STURR, H.D.	01.5	02917
FOOTE, J.J.	03	03394	HARLFINGER, F.J.	01.3	16192
GERWICK, J.	03	02734	ROBBINS, O.C.	01.3	13841
RAMIREZ-DEARLLAND, M.	02	15657	ENRIGHT, J.F.	01	59000
GRADY, J.B.	02	15642	McCLINTOCK, D.H.	01	12000
LOCKWOOD, R.	02	05565	CROWLEY, J.D.	01	10380
DRY, M.H.	02	14799	SIMPSON, H.S.	01	10016
McCREA, W.B.	02	13099	EARLE, P.J.	01	08156
RUBLE, H.E.	02	12277	MEWHINNEY, L.S.	01	08066
FUHRMAN, A.S.	02	12255	PIECZENT-KOWSKI, H.A.	01	08033
STOVALL, W.S.	02	11641	DODGE, H.B.	01	07354
STALEY, J.J.	02	11586	RUSSILLO, M.P.	01	07163
HULL, H.	02	10136	ACKER, F.C.	01	06962
JOHNSON, R.W.	02	10020	GAGE, N.D.	01	06923
NICHOLS, R.E.	02	09253	DISSETTE, E.F.	01	06500
PARKS, L.S.	02	08885	VOGE, R.G.	01	06440
PUTNAM, C.F.	02	08458	OLSEN, E.	01	06243
MOLUMPHY, G.G.	02	08246	IRVIN, W.D.	01	06070
HAGBERG, O.E.	02	07332	PERKINS, W.B.	01	05894
BOURLAND, J.H.	02	06274	HAWK, E.C.	01	05871
PARKER, F.M.	02	06219	McMASTER, CASSEDY, H.	01	05700
MONTROSS, K.E.	02	06074	CASSEDY, H.	01	05693
MEHLHOP, D.L.	02	05309	MERRILL, W.R.	01	05486
BOLE, J.A.	02	05225	HARDIN, J.T.	01	05484
DeTAR, J.L.	02	04805	BRINKER, R.M.	01	05480
BENNETT, C.L.	02	04742	KENNEDY, M.G.	01	05309
BOWERS, J.M.	02	04668	CARMICK, E.S.	01	05226
HOUSE, A.C.	02	04613	McKNIGHT, J.R.	01	04999
FARRELL, R.M.	02	03125	HOLTZ, A.H.	01	04697
OLSEN, R.I.	02	02994	NICHOLS, J.C.	01	04556
GIMBER, S.H.	02	02901	GREGORY, R.V.	01	04472
OAKLEY, Jr., T.B.	02	02810	KIRK, O.G.	01	04400
FORBES, G.W.	02	02750	VAN LEUNEN, P.	01	04368
WALKER, W.W.	02	02710	LEWIS, J.H.	01	04122
CONNOLE, D.R.	02	02576	LOOMIS, S.C.	01	03943
COLE, O.R.	02	02391	SAUNDERS, W.A.	01	03291
GUNN, F.A.	02	02345	MARSHALL, E.E.	01	03127
DERAGON, W.N.	02	01818	McKENZIE, G.	01	03057
ABELE, M.L.	02	00600	ANDERSON, W.L.	01	03039

PACIFIC CAPTAINS RANKED BY NUMBER OF VICTORIES, Cont.

Captain	Victories	Tonnage	Captain	Victories	Tonnage
SCHOENI, W.P.	01	02962	SISLER, V.A.	01	01018
BACON, B.E.	01	02929	JULIHN, L.V.	01	00900
SELLARS, R.F.	01	02864	REFO, M.P.	01	00900
WAHLIG, F.H.	01	02857	WORTHINGTON, R.K.	01	00800
WATKINS, F.T.	01	02830	FLACHSENHAR, J.J.	01	00834
REYNOLDS, J.R.	01	02776	DWYER, C.R.	01	00800
LAIRD, Jr., G.H.	01	02734	WRIGHT, W.H.	01	00800
HAMMOND, D.T.	01	02705	PARHAM, W.B.	01	00762
HESS, F.G.	01	02411	MILLER, H.E.	01	00630
NICHOLAS, N.J.	01	02411	KEITHLY, R.M.	01	00527
WATERMAN, J.	01	02219	RHYMES, C.D.	01	00492
STEVENSON, H.C.	01	02212	SCHLECH, W.F.	01	00492
McGIVERN, C.F.	01	02211	HAINES, J.L.	01	00200
DAVIDSON, J.F.	01	02087	BUTLER, O.M.	01	00100
GRANT, J.D.	01	01936	ST. ANGELO, A.R.	00.5	04175
MANAGHAN, R.R.	01	01660	FITZ-PATRICK, J.P.	00.5	01400
KITCH, W.L.	01	01580	NAUMAN, H.K.	00.3	03340
McCALLUM, J.L.	01	01230			

D - PACIFIC SUBMARINE CAPTAINS RANKED
BY TONNAGE DESTROYED

Name	Tonnage	Name	Tonnage
FLUCKEY, E.B.	95360	BLANCHARD, J.W.	36629
O'KANE, R.H.	93824	THOMPSON, W.C.	36062
UNDERWOOD, G.W.	75386	HOGAN, Jr., T.W.	34329
CUTTER, S.D.	72000	LOWRANCE, V.L.	34199
MUNSON, H.G.	67630	KOSSLER, H.J.	34180
GROSS, R.L.	65735	EBERT, W.G.	34108
WHITAKER, R.T.	60846	KINSELLA, W.T.	34101
REICH, E.T.	59839	MAURER, J.H.	33379
ENRIGHT, J.F.	59000	KLAKRING, T.B.	33122
TRIEBEL, C.O.	58837	SIEGLAFF, W.B.	32886
ANDREWS, C.H.	57234	PORTER, G.E.	30940
MORTON, D.W.	55000	DEMPSEY, J.C.	30794
DORNIN, R.E.	54595	WHELCHEL, D.L.	30659
BRUTON, H.C.	54564	SCOTT, J.A.	30394
POST, Jr., W.S.	54213	WILLIAMSON,	30118
DEALEY, S.D.	54002	DONAHO, G.R.	29870
BURLINGAME, C.C.	46865	DAVENPORT, R.M.	29662
WOGAN, T.L.	46830	McKINNEY, E.B.	28125
BARR, Jr., E.L.	46212	SHEPARD, E.T.	28105
GRIFFITH, W.T.	45874	STYLES, R.E.	27308
MOORE, J.A.	45689	BASKETT, T.S.	27273
SHELBY, E.E.	45613	STEVENSON, W.A.	27120
McGREGOR, L.D.	44637	EDGE, L.T.	27016
GRIDER, G.W.	43718	FERRALL, W.E.	26841
CLAREY, B.A.	42956	MARTIN, J.C.	26578
TYREE, A.K.	42928	CLAGGETT, E.B.	26298
DYKERS, T.M.	42417	FOLEY, R.J.	26235
LOUGHLIN, C.E.	41718	SUMMERS, P.E.	26132
RISSER, R.D.	40931	COE, J.W.	26130
WALKER, F.D.	40139	DAVIS, J.W.	26039
METCALF, R.M.	40040	WILLINGHAM, Jr., J.H.	25636
WARD, N.G.	39302	BURROWS, A.C.	25517
STONE, L.T.	39266	HASKINS, E.D.	25400
RICE, R.H.	39100	ASHLEY, J.H.	24930
WEISS, D.F.	39047	MOORE, J.R.	23978
COYE, J.J.	39000	BROCKMAN, W.H.	23829
LAUGHON, W.R.	38340	AUSTIN, M.H.	23724
SELBY, F.G.	38159	LEWELLEN, B.E.	23685
BASS, R.H.	37977	ROSS, P.H.	23226
BROACH, J.C.	37923	KEFAUVER, R.	23081
GARRISON, M.E.	37368	LEE, J.E.	23081
RAMAGE, L.P.	36681	GARNETT, P.W.	23079

PACIFIC SUBMARINE CAPTAINS RANKED BY TONNAGE DESTROYED
Cont.

Name	Tonnage	Name	Tonnage
KIRKPATRICK, C.	22749	COLE, C.C.	15383
GILMORE, H.W.	22681	KEATING, Jr., R.A.	15263
DROPP, A.H.	22280	DRY, M.H.	14799
McMILLEN, D.	22277	NIMITZ, Jr., C.W.	14636
GALANTIN, I..J.	22031	JUKES, H.L.	14571
KRAPF, A.E.	22015	STEPHEN, E.C.	14451
HULL, J.L.	21841	GREENUP, F.A.	14246
HENDERSON, C.M.	21770	BELL, D.B.	14179
BLAKELY, E.N.	21672	BAER, D.C.	14177
CLARK, A.H.	21534	HYDEMAN, E.T.	14036
MILLICAN, W.J.	21525	HESS, J.B.	13974
LENT, W.A.	20439	ROBBINS, O.C.	13841
GALLAHER, A.R.	20181	WHITE, D.C.	13807
DASPIT, L.R.	19907	EDDY, I.C.	13804
SMITH, C.C.	19270	SCANLAND, Jr., F.W.	13180
CHAPPLE, W.G.	19159	STIMSON, P.C.	13172
AZER, J.B.	18989	McCREA, V.B.	13099
TAYLOR, A.H.	18747	SCHADE, A.F.	12973
WARDER, F.B.	18719	CLARK, C.R.	12925
WYLIE, W.N.	18316	RABORN, A.	12835
MURPHY, C.L.	18278	LAUTHRUP, G.W.	12581
SHEA, M.W.	18139	THOMAS, W.M.	12558
HAZZARD, W.H.	18087	CALDWELL, R.H.	12516
WALES, G.H.	17925	RUBLE, H.E.	12277
BENSON, R.S.	17652	NELSON, W.T.	12255
HUTCHINSON, E.S.	17530	FUHRMAN, A.S.	12255
NOWELL, B.H.	17507	HENSEL, K.G.	12243
McCAIN, J.S.	17452	TURNER, J.H.	12132
HARREL,	17352	McCLINTOCK, D.H.	12000
PETERSON, G.E.	17145	TIEDEMAN, E.	11651
BECKER, A.L.	16835	STOVALL, W.S.	11541
BROWNE, G.H.	16636	STALEY, J.J.	11586
McMAHON, B.F.	16610	GRUNER, W.P.	11407
GERMERSHAUSEN, W. J.	16277	FULP, J.D.	11029
HARLFINGER, F.J.	16192	AMBRUSTER, S.H.	10766
MONROE, H.S.	16045	BRINDUPKE, C.F.	10579
STREET, III, F.L.	15886	SMITH, F.T.	10457
HYDE, J.M.	15684	CROWLEY, J.D.	10380
RAMIREZ DE AREL-		HARTMAN, I.S.	10162
LANO, M.	15657	HULL, H.	10136
GRADY, J.B.	15642	LYNCH, R.B.	10088
BANISTER, A.B.	15596	JOHNSON, R.W.	10020
LOCKWOOD, R.	15565	SIMPSON, H.S.	10016
		ZABRISKIE, D.	09939

PACIFIC SUBMARINE CAPTAINS RANKED BY TONNAGE DESTROYED
Cont.

Name	Tonnage	Name	Tonnage
CHAPPELL, L.H.	09835	PERKINS, W.B.	05894
GRENFELL, E.W.	09253	HAWK, E.C.	05871
NICHOLS, R.E.	09253	CLEMENTSON, M.K.	05735
MIDDLETON, J.R.	09195	McMASTER, F.	05700
FENNO, Jr., F.W.	09144	CASSEDY, H.	05693
ADKINS, J.A.	09086	FYFE, J.K.	05534
MOSLEY, S.P.	09086	STEVENS, J.E	05531
FAUST, A.F.	09026	MERRILL, W.R.	05486
WILKINS, C.W.	09024	HARDIN, J.T.	05484
CORBUS, J.	09004	BRINKER, R.M.	05480
QUIRK, P.D.	08922	REED, J.W.	05461
PARKS, L.S.	08885	MEHLHOP, D.L.	05309
WRIGHT, W.L.	08859	KENNEDY, M.G.	05309
JARVIS, B.C.	08855	LEWIS, H.H.	05303
BERTHRONG, R.	08834	McCRORY, W.W.	05268
ICENHOWER, J.B.	08645	CARMICK, E.S.	05226
PUTNAM, C.F.	08458	BOLE, J.A.	05225
HURD, K.C.	08279	McKNIGHT, J.R.	04999
MOLUMPHY, G.G.	08246	DeTAR, J.L.	04805
EARLE, O.J.	08156	BENNETT, C.L	04742
MEWHINNEY, L.S.	08066	HOLTZ, A.H.	04697
PIECZENTKOWSKI, H.A.	08033	BOWERS, J.M.	04668
HARPER, T.E.	07529	HOUSE, A.C.	04613
LATTA, F.D.	07450	NICHOLS, J.C.	04556
DODGE, H.B.	07354	GREGORY, R.V.	04472
HAGBERG, O.E.	07332	KIRK, O.G.	04400
WILLIAMS, J.W.	07259	VAN LEUNEN, P.	04368
RUSSILLO, M.P.	07163	FARLEY, L.C.	04302
LYNCH, F.C.	06982	BROWN, D.C.	04287
ACKER, F.C.	06962	ST. ANGELO, A.R.	04175
GAGE, N.D.	06923	LEWIS, J.H.	04122
SANDS, E.T.	06908	LOOMIS, S.C.	03943
ACKERMAN, E.	06881	ALSTON, A.H.	03543
O'NEIL, Jr., G.E.	06813	WILLIAMS, R.R.	03507
STEINMETZ, E.H.	06643	FOOTE, J.J.	03394
DISSETTE, E.F.	06500	NAUMAN, H.K.	03340
VOGE, R.G.	06440	SAUNDERS, W.A.	03291
BOURLAND, J.H.	06274	MARSHALL, E.E.	03127
OLSEN, E.	06243	FARRELL, R.M.	03125
PARKER, F.M.	06219	McKENZIE, G.	03057
MONTROSS, K.E.	06074	ANDERSON, W.L.	03039
IRVIN, W.D.	06070	OLSON,	02994
LATHAM, R.C.	05901	SCHOENI, W.P.	02962
LAKE, R.C.	05900	STEVENS, C.B.	02943

PACIFIC SUBMARINE CAPTAINS RANKED BY TONNAGE DESTROYED
Cont.

Name	Tonnage	Name	Tonnage
BACON, B.E.	02929	GRANT, J.D.	01936
STURR, H.D.	02917	DERAGON, W.N.	01818
GIMBER, S.H.	02901	MANAGHAN, R.R.	01660
SELLARS, R.F.	02864	KITCH, W.L.	01580
WAHLIG, F.H.	02857	FITZ-PATRICK,	01400
WATKINS, F.T.	02830	McCALLUM, J.L.	01230
OAKLEY, Jr., T.B.	02810	SISLER, V.A.	01018
REYNOLDS, J.R.	02776	JULIHN, L.V.	00900
FORBES, G.W.	02750	REFO, M.P.	00900
GERWICK, J.	02734	WORTHINGTON, R.K.	00880
LAIRD, Jr. G.H.	02734	FLACHSENHAR, J.J.	00834
WALKER, W.W.	02710	WRIGHT, W.H.	00800
HAMMOND, D.T.	02705	DWYER, C.R.	00800
CONNOLE, D.R.	02576	PARHAM, W.B.	00762
NICHOLAS, N.J.	02411	MILLER, H.E.	00630
HESS. F.G.	02411	ABELE, M.L.	00600
COLE, O.R.	02391	WHELAND, K.R.	00592
GUNN, F.A.	02345	KEITHLY, R.M.	00527
WATERMAN, J.	02219	RHYMES, C.D.	00492
STEVENSON, H.C.	02212	SCHLECH, W.F.	00492
McGIVERN, C.F.	02211	HAINES, J.L.	00200
DAVIDSON, J.F.	02087	BUTLER, O.M.	00100

E - NAVY UNIT COMMENDATIONS

Boat	For Patrol Numbers	Commanding Officer
ASPRO	1	H. C. STEVENSON
ASPRO	2	W. A. STEVENSON
ATULE	1	J. H. MAURER
BARB	12	E. B. FLUCKEY
BERGALL	2	J. M. HYDE
BLUEGILL	1 & 3	E. L. BARR, Jr
BONEFISH	1,3 & 4	T. W. HOGAN, Jr
BONEFISH	5 & 6	L. T. EDGE
BOWFIN	6	J. CORBUS
CREVALLE	1 & 2	H. G. MUNSON
CREVALLE	3 & 4	F. D. WALKER, Jr
CROAKER	1	J. E. LEE
DACE	5	E. B. CLAGGETT
DARTER	4	D. H. McCLINTOCK
GRAYBACK	7	E. C. STEPHAN
GRAYBACK	8,9 & 10	J. A. MOORE
GROWLER	1,2 & 3	H. W. GILMORE
GROWLER	10	T. B. OAKLEY, Jr
GUITARRO	1,2, & 3	E. D. HASKINS
GURNARD	2,3,4 & 5	C. H. ANDREWS
HADDO	7	C. W. NIMITZ, Jr
HALIBUT	10	I. J. GALANTIN
HAMMERHEAD	2	J. C. MARTIN
HAWKBILL	1,3 & 4	F. W. SCANLAND, Jr
LAPON	3,4 & 5	L. T. STONE
LAPON	6	D. G. BAER
PARGO	7	D. B. BELL
PERMIT	10	C. L. BENNETT
PICUDA	1 & 2	A. RABORN
PICUDA	3	G. R. DONAHO
PICUDA	4 & 5	E. T. SHEPARD
PLUNGER	2,3 & 4	D. C. WHITE
PLUNGER	6 & 10	R. H. BASS
POGY	5 & 6	R. M. METCALF
PUFFER	4	R. G. SELBY
RATON	4	J. W. DAVIS
RATON	6	M. W. SHEA
RAY	5 & 6	W. T. KINSELLA
SEA DEVIL	3	R. E. STYLES
SEAWOLF	4 & 7	F. B. WARDER
SEAWOLF	10 & 12	R. L. GROSS
SKATE	1 & 2	E. B. McKINNEY
SKATE	3	W. P. GRUNER
SKATE	7	R. B. LYNCH
SUNFISH	9	E. E. SHELBY

NAVY UNIT COMMENDATIONS, Cont.

Boat	For Patrol Numbers	Commanding Officer
SUNFISH	11	J. W. REED
SWORDFISH	1,2 & 4	C. C. SMITH
TAUTOG	2	J. H. WILLINGHAM, Jr
TAUTOG	5,6,8,9 & 10	W. B. SIEGLAFF
TAUTOG	11	T. S. BASKETT
THRESHER	13	D. C. MacMILLAN
TREPANG	1	R. M. DAVENPORT
TRIGGER	9	F. J. HARLFINGER

F - PRESIDENTIAL UNIT CITATIONS

Boat	For Patrol Numbers	Commanding Officer
ALBACORE	2 & 3	R.C. LAKE
ALBACORE	7 & 8	J. W. BLANCHARD
ARCHERFISH	5	J.E. ENRIGHT
BARB	8,9,10 & 11	E.B. FLUCKEY
BATFISH	6	J. K. FYFE
BOWFIN	2	W. T. GRIFFITH
CAVALLA	1	H. J. KOSSLER
FLASHER	3 & 4	R. T. WHITAKER
FLASHER	5	G. W. GRIDER
GATO	4,5,6,7 & 8	R. J. FOLEY
GREENLING	1,2. & 3	H. C. BRUTON
GUARDFISH	1 & 2	T. B. KLAKRING
GUARDFISH	8	N. G. WARD
GUDGEON	1 & 2	E. W. GRENFELL
GUDGEON	3	H. B. LYON
GUDGEON	4,5,6,7 & 8	W. S. POST, Jr
HADDOCK	2	A. H. TAYLOR
HADDOCK	5,6 & 7	R. M. DAVENPORT
HARDER	1,2,3,4 & 5	S. D. DEALEY
JACK	1 & 3	T. M. DYKERS
JACK	5	A. E. KRAPF
NAUTILUS	1,2 & 3	W. H. BROCKMAN
PARCHE	1 & 2	L. P. RAMAGE
PINTADO	1,2 & 3	B. A. CLAREY
QUEENFISH	1 & 2	C. E. LAUGHLIN
RASHER	1	E. S. HUTCHINSON
RASHER	3 & 4	W. R. LAUGHON
RASHER	5	H. G. MUNSON
REDFISH	1	R. D. KING
REDFISH	2	M. H. AUSTIN
SAILFISH	10	R. E. WARD
SALMON	11	H. K. NAUMAN
SANDLANCE	5	M. E. GARRISON
SEAHORSE	2,3 & 4	S. D. CUTTER
SEALION II	2 & 3	E. T. REICH
SILVERSIDES	4 & 5	C. C. BURLINGAME
SILVERSIDES	7 & 10	J. J. COYE
SPADEFISH	1 & 2	G. W. UNDERWOOD
TANG	1,2 & 3	R. H. O'KANE
TANG (SECOND AWARD)	4 & 5	R. H. O'KANE
TINOSA	4	L.R. DASPIT
TINOSA	5 & 6	D. F. WEISS
TIRANTE	1	G. L. STREET, III
TRIGGER	5	R. S. BENSON

PRESIDENTIAL UNIT CITATIONS, cont.

Boat	For Patrol Numbers	Commanding Officer
TRIGGER	6 & 7	R. E. DORNIN
TROUT	2 & 3	F. W. FENNO, Jr
TROUT	5	L. P. RAMAGE
TUNNY	2 & 5	J. A. SCOTT
WAHOO	3	D. W. MORTON

G - SUBMMARINE LOSSES IN WORLD WAR TWO
All Causes and Locales

Boat	Date	Location	Cause	Survivors
Sealion	411210	Cavite	Air Raid	All
S-28	420120	Makassar	Ran Aground	All
S-26	420124	Off Panama	Accident	All
Shark	420211	Menado	Depth Charges	None
Perch	420303	Java Sea	Depth Charges	53
S-27	420619	Amchitka Island	Ran Aground	All
Grunion	4207??	Sirius Point	Depth Charges	None
S-39	420814	Rossel Island	Ran Aground	All
Argonaut	430110	Rabaul	Surface Fire	None
Amberjack	430216	Rabaul	Depth Charges	None
Grampus	430315	Blackett Strait	Surface Fire	None
Triton	430315	Admiralties	Depth Charges	None
Pickerel	430403	Northern Honshu	Depth Charges	None
Grenadier	430422	Penang	Damage/Scuttled	All
Runner	4305??	Kirules	Unknown	None
R-12	430612	Off Key West	Accident	All
Cisco	430928	Sulu Sea	Depth Charges	None
Pompano	4309??	Honshu	Unknown	None
Grayling	4309??	Tablas Strait	Unknown	None
S-44	431007	Paramishuru	Surface Fire	Two
Wahoo	431011	La Peruse Strait	Aircraft	None
Dorado	431012	Carribean Sea	Friendly Fire	None
Corvina	431116	Off Truk	Submarine Torpedo	None
Sculpin	431119	Off Truk	Surface Fire	41
Capelin	4311??	Celebes	Unknown	None
Scorpion	4401??	Yellow Sea	Unknown	None
Grayback	440226	East China Sea	Aircraft	None
Trout	440229	Ryukus	Depth Charges	None
Tullibee	440327	Pelews	Own Torpedo	One
Gudgeon	4404??	Marianas	Unknown	None
Herring	440601	Kirules	Shore Batteries	None
Golet	440614	Honshu	Depth Charges	None
S-28	440614	Hawaii	Accident	None
Robalo	440726	Palawan	Unknown	Four
Flier	440813	Balabac Strait	Mine	13
Harder	440824	Caiman Point	Depth Charges	None
Seawolf	441003	Moratai	Friendly Fire	None
Tang	441024	Formosa Strait	Own Torpedo	9
Darter	441024	Bombay Shoal	Ran Aground	All
Shark II	441024	Hainan	Depth Charges	None
Escolar	4410??	Yellow Sea	Unknown	None
Albacore	441107	Hokkaido	Mine	None

SUBMMARINE LOSSES IN WORLD WAR TWO, Cont.
All Causes and Locales

Boat	Date	Location	Cause	Survivors
Growler	441108	South China Sea	Unknown	None
Scamp	4411??	Tokyo Bay	Unknown	None
Swordfish	450112	Nansei Shoto	Unknown	None
Barbel	450204	Palawan	Aircraft	None
Kete	4503??	Nansei Shoto	Unknown	None
Trigger	4503??	Nansei Shoto	Unknown	None
Snook	4504??	East China Sea	Unknown	None
Lagarto	450503	Gulf of Siam	Depth Charges	None
Bonefish	450618	Toyama Wan	Depth Charges	None
Bullhead	450806	Lombok Strait	Aircraft	None

H - WOLF PACKS OPERATING IN THE PACIFIC THEATER

SUBPAC FORCE   (HAWAII)

Capt C.B Momsen
CERO
SHAD
GRAYBACK

Cdr F.B. Warder
SNOOK
HARDER
PARGO

Lt Cdr. C.F Brindupke
TULLIBEE
HADDOCK
HALIBUT

Capt. G.E. Peterson
PARCHE
BANG
TINOSA

Cdr. F.W. Fenno
  "Fenno's Ferrets"
PICUDA
PERCH
PETO

Cdr. D.F. Weiss
TINOSA
SEALION
TANG

Capt. L.N. Blair
  "Blair's Blasters"
SHARK
TUNNY
PINTADO

Capt. W.V. O'Regan
  "Mickey Finns"
APOGON
THRESHER
GUARDFISH
PIRANHA

Lt. Cdr. A.R. Gallaher
BANG
SEAHORSE
GROWLER

Capt. W.D. Wilkin
  "Wilkin's Wildcats"
ROCK
SAWFISH
TILEFISH

Cdr. L.S. Parks
PARCHE
HAMMERHEAD
STEELHEAD

Cdr. S.P. Moseley
  "Moseley's Marauders"
BILLFISH
SAILFISH
GREENLING

Cdr. G.R. Donaho
  "Donk's Devils"
SPADEFISH
REDFISH
PICUDA

Cdr. T.B. Oakley
  "Ben's Busters"
GROWLER
PAMPANITO
SEALION

Cdr. E.R. Swinburne
  "Ed's Eradicators"
TUNNY
QUEENFISH
DARTER

Capt. C.W. Wilkins
  "Wilkins' Bears"
SEAHORSE
WHALE
SEGUNDO

Cdr. A.H. Holtz
  "Holtz's Cats"
BAYA
BECUNA
HAWKBILL

Cdr. R.S. Benson
  "Benson's Dogs"
RAZORBACK
CAVALLA
PIRANHA

Cdr. F.C. Acker
POMFRET
SNOOK
COBIA

Lt. Cdr. G.H. Browne
SNOOK
COBIA

Cdr. A.B. Banister
  "Banister's Beagles"
SAWFISH
ICEFISH
DRUM

Cdr. E.N. Blakely
  "Blakely's Behemoths"
SHARK
BLACKFISH
SEADRAGON

Cdr. W.J. Millican
  "Millican's Marauders"
ESCOLAR
PERCH
CROAKER

Cdr. J.S. Coye, Jr.
  "Coye's Coyotes"
SILVERSIDES
SALMON
TRIGGER

WOLF PACKS OPERATING IN THE PACIFIC THEATER, Cont.

SUBPAC FORCE   (HAWAII)

Cdr. W.J. Millican
   "Millican's Marauders"
ESCOLAR
PERCH
CROAKER

Lt. Cdr. T.L. Wogan
   "Wogan's Wolves"
BESUGO
GABILAN
RONQUIL

Cdr. J.P. Roach
   "Roach's Raiders"
HADDOCK
HALIBUT
TUNA

Cdr. B.A. Clarey
   "Clarey's Crushers"
PINTADO
JALLAO
ATULE

Cdr. T.B. Klakring
   "Burt's Brooms"
SILVERSIDES
SAURY
TAMBOR
TRIGGER
STERLET
BURRFISH
RONQUIL

Cdr. G.W. Underwood
   "Underwood's Urchins"
SPADEFISH
SUNFISH
PETO

Cdr. L.D. McGregor
   "Sandy's Sluggers"
REDFISH
SHAD
BANG

Cdr. C.E. Loughlin
   "Loughlin's Loopers"
QUEENFISH
BARB
PICUDA

Cdr. L.P. Ramage
   "Red's Rowdies"
PARCHE
POMFRET
SAILFISH

Cdr. F.W. Fenno
   "Fennomints"
PAMPANITO
SEACAT
PIPEFISH
SEARAVEN

Cdr. R.M. Davenport
   "Roy's Rangers"
TREPANG
SEGUNDO
RAZORBACK

Cdr. C.L. Bennett
   "Bennett's Blazers"
SEAOWL
PIRANHA
SEA POACHER

Cdr. V.L. Lowrance
   "Rebel's Rippers"
SEA DOG
SEA ROBBIN
GUARDFISH

Cdr. W.S. Post
   "Post's Panzers"
SPOT
ICEFISH
BALAO

Cdr. W.A. Stevenson
   "Steve's Stingers"
ASPRO
CROAKER
SAWFISH

Cdr. M.K. Clementson
   "Clementson's Clippers"
BLUEBACK
SEA FOX
PUFFER

Cdr. J.C. Nichols
SILVERSIDES
TAUTOG

Cdr. C.E. Louglin
   "Loughlin's Loopers II "
QUEENFISH
BARB
PICUDA

Cdr. W.B. Perkins
BURRFISH
POGY
RONQUIL

Cdr. J.F. Enright
   "Joe's Jugheads"
ARCHERFISH
BATFISH
BLACKFISH

Cdr. G.W. Underwood
   "Underwood's Urchins II "
SPADEFISH
POMPON
ATULE
BANG

Cdr. A.G. Schnable
   "Al's Sharks"
PILOTFISH
FINBACK
RASHER

SUBPAC FORCE   (HAWAII)

Cdr. C.B. Stevens
    "Clyde's Cannibals"
PLAICE
SCABBARDFISH
SEA POACHER

Cdr. Frank Latta
    "Latta's Lancers"
LAGARTO
HADDOCK
SENNET

Cdr. E. E. Shelby
    "Shelby's Shellackers"
GATO
SUNFISH
JALLAO

Cdr. B.F. McMahon
    "Mac's Mops"
PIPER
STERLET
TREPANG
POMFRET
BOWFIN

Cdr. J.D. Fulp
    "Fulp's Fiddlers"
SEGUNDO
SEA CAT
RAZORBACK

Cdr. C.L. Bennett
    "Bennett's Blazers"
SEA OWL
PIRANHA
PUFFER

Cdr. J.R. Middleton
    "Middleton's Mobsters"
THRESHER
PETO
SHAD

Cdr. W.B. Sieglaff
    "Barney's Boxers"
TENCH
SEA DEVIL
BALAO
GROUPER

Cdr. W.S. Post
    "Post's Panzers"
SPOT
SEA FOX
QUEENFISH

Cdr. R.W. Peterson
    "Pete's Panthers"
ICEFISH
KINGFISH

Cdr. R.G. Latham
    "Latham's Locators"
TINOSA
SPADEFISH
TIRANTE

Cdr. Hiram Cassedy
    "Hiram's Hecklers"
TIGRONE
BULLHEAD
BLACKFISH

Cdr. J.F. Walling
    "Walling's Whalers"
SNOOK
BURRFISH
BANG

Cdr. E.T. Hydeman
    "Earl's Eliminators"
SEA DOG
THREADFIN
TRIGGER

Cdr. N.J. Nicholas
    "Nick's Nippers"
SILVERSIDES
HACKLEBACK
THREADFIN

Cdr. A.C. Smith
TRUTTA
LIONFISH
PARCHE
SUNFISH

Cdr. J.A. Adkins
    "Caddy's Caddies"
COD
POMPON

Cdr. R. Kefauver
    "Russ's Rustlers"
SPRINGER
TREPANG
RATON

Cdr. B.F. McMahon
    "Mac's Mops"
PIPER
POMFRET
PLAICE
SEA POACHER

I - WOLF PACKS OPERATING IN THE PACIFIC THEATER

SUBSOWESPAC FORCE (AUSTRALIA)

Cdr. R.T. Whitaker
FLASHER
CREVALLE
ANGLER

Cdr. F.D. Walker, Jr
CREVALLE
ANGLER

Cdr. E.D. Haskins
GUITARRO
RATON
GUNNEL

Cdr. H.G. Munson
RASHER
BLUEFISH

Cdr S.D. Dealey
HARDER
HADDO
HAKE
RAY

Cdr. C.W. Nimitz, Jr
HADDO
HAKE

Cdr. R.T. Whitaker
FLASHER
LAPON
BONEFISH

Cdr. D.H. McClintock
DARTER
DACE

Cdr. V.B.McCrea
HOE
ASPRO
CABRILLA

Cdr. K.A. Adkins
COD
RAY

Cdr. E.L. Barr
BLUEGILL
ANGLER

Cdr. W.G. Chapple
BREAM
GUITARRO
RATON

Cdr. I.S. Hartman
BARBERO
REDFIN
HADDO

Cdr. T.B. Oakley, Jr
GROWLER
HAKE
HARDHEAD

Cdr. W.T. Kinsella
RAY
RATON
BATFISH

Cdr. F.A. Greenup
HARDHEAD
HAKE

Cdr. G.E. O'Neil, Jr
GUNNEL
MUSKALUNGE

Cdr. J.G. Martin
HAMMERHEAD
LAPON
PADDLE
MINGO

Cdr. J.E. Stevens
FLOUNDER
BASHAW
GUAVINA

Capt. E.H. Bryant
HAWKBILL
FLASHER
BECUNA

Cdr. Earl Tiedman
GUAVINA
BASHAW

Cdr. A.H. Holtz
BAYA
HOE
CAVALLA

Cdr. H.D. Sturr
BECUNA
FLASHER
HOE
PADDLE
DACE

Capt. E.H. Bryant
HAWKBILL
BAYA
CAVALLA

Cdr. F.C. Lucas, Jr
CAIMAN
BLENNY
LAPON

Cdr. N.D. Cage
GURNARD
GUITARRO

Cdr. T.L. Wogan
BESUGO
HARDHEAD
COBIA
BLACKFIN
GURNARD

WOLF PACKS OPERATING IN THE PACIFIC THEATER, Cont.

SUBSOWESPAC FORCE (AUSTRALIA)

Cdr. A.H. Holtz
BAYA
CAVALLA

Cdr. F.C. Lucas, Jr.
CAIMAN
SEALION

Cdr. B.C. Hills
PERCH
GABILAN
SEALION
BARBEL

Cdr. E.L. Barr, Jr
BLUEGILL
BREAM
BARBEL

Cdr. R.L. Gross
BOARFISH
CHARR

Cdr. T.H Henry
KRAKEN
PARGO

Cdr. J.E. Stevens
FLOUNDER
HAKE
PARGO

Cdr P.E. Summers
PAMPANITO
GUAVINA

Cdr. E.F. Steffanides
TUNA
BARBEL
BLACKFIN

Cdr. F.D. Boyle
CHARR
TUNA
BLACKFIN

Cdr. G.W. Grider
FLASHER
BASHAW

Cdr. J.M. Hyde
BERGALL
BLOWER
GUITARRO

Cdr. H.D. Sturr
BECUNA
BLENNY
GUAVINA
BAYA

Cdr. G.H. Laird, Jr
HAMMERHEAD
BAYA

Cdr. H.J. Kossler
CAVALLA
HOE
HAMMERHEAD

Cdr. B.A. Clarey
PINTADO
HAWKBILL

Cdr. J.H. Campbell
BLOWER
BASHAW

Cdr. P.E. Summers
PAMPANITO
MINGO
SEALION
CAIMAN

Cdr. B.A. Clarey
PINTADO
CAIMAN

Cdr. H.B. Dodge
BRILL
CHUB

Cdr. M.K. Clementson
BLUEBACK
BERGALL
HAWKBILL
BLACKFIN
FLASHER
BLUEGILL
BASHAW

Cdr. R.A. Keating, Jr
ROCK
GUAVINA
COBIA
BLENNY
BAYA

Cdr. J.R. Stevens
FLOUNDER
SEA ROBIN
CHUB

Lt. Cdr. W.L. Fey, Jr.
CAIMAN
SEALION
MINGO

Cdr. F.D. Boyle
CHARR
BESUGO
GABILAN

Cdr E.L. Barr, Jr
BLUEGILL
BASHAW
CROAKER

J - U.S. SUBMARINES PRESENT AT THE SURRENDER CEREMONIES IN TOKYO BAY SEPTEMBER 2, 1945

ARCHERFISH	PILOTFISH
CAVALLA	RAZORBACK
GATO	RUNNER II
HADDO	SEGUNDO
HAKE	SEA CAT
MUSKALUNGE	TIGERONE

K. MEDALS OF HONOR AWARDED

John P. Cromwell (Posthumously)

Samuel D. Dealey (Posthumously)

Eugene B. Fluckey

Howard W. Gilmore (Posthumously)

Richard H. O'Kane

Lawson P. Ramage

George L. Street

BIBLIOGRAPHY

Bagnasco, Emilio, *Submarines of World War Two*. Annapolis, MD: Naval Institute Press, n.d. (Translation from original Italian.)

Blair, Clay, *Silent Victory*. New York: J.B. Lippincott, 1975.

Dictionary of American Naval Fighting Ships, 7 Volumes. Washington, DC: U.S. Government Printing Office.

Enright, Joseph F., *Shinano*. New York: St. Martin's Press, 1987.

Fitzsimons, Bernard, General Editor, *The Illustrated Encyclopedia of the 20th Century - Weapons and Warfare*, 28 Volumes. New York: Columbia House, 1967.

Lowder, Hughston E., *Batfish*. Englewood Cliffs, NJ: Prentice-Hall, 1980.

Mendenhall, Corwin, *Submarine Diary*. Chapel Hill, NC: Algonquin Books, 1991.

Morrison, Samuel Eliot, *Naval Operations in World War II,* Vol. XIV. Boston, MA: Little, Brown and Co., 1961.

Navy History Division, "Ships' Histories." Washington, DC: Washington Navy Yard

Rohwer, Jurgen, *Axis Submarine Successes, 1939-1945*. Annapolis, MD: Naval Institute Press, 1983.

Roscoe, Theodore, *United States Submarine Operations in World War II*. Annapolis, MD: Naval Institute Press, 1949.

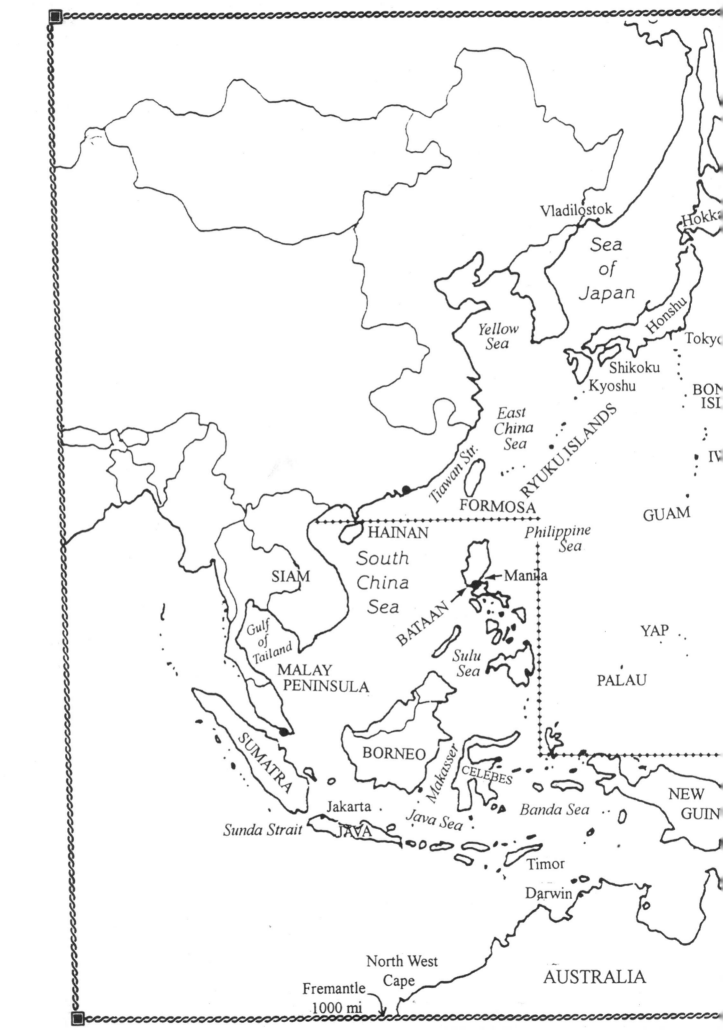